PROJECT MANAGER

How to pass the PMP® Exam without dying in the attempt

Aligned to the PMBOK® GUIDE 4th Edition

pablolledó
projectManagement

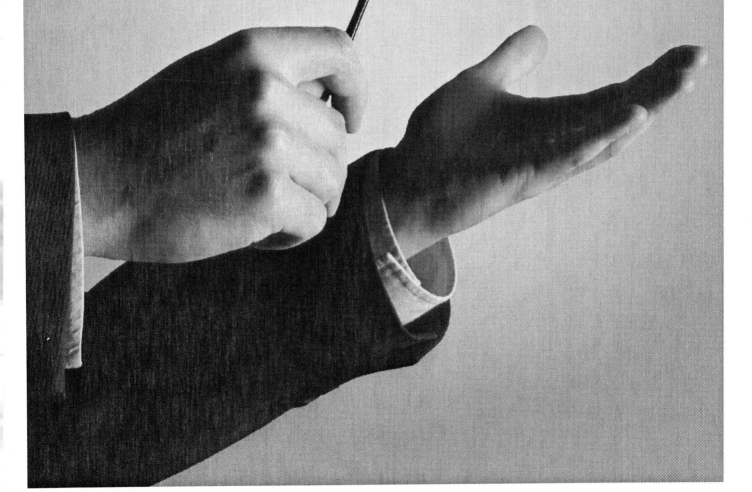

Order this book online at www.trafford.com
or email orders@trafford.com

Most Trafford titles are also available at major online book retailers.

Printed in the United States of America.

ISBN: 978-1-4269-7158-7 (sc)
ISBN: 978-1-4269-7159-4 (e)

Library of Congress Control Number: 2011909110

Trafford rev. 06/02/2011

 www.trafford.com

North America & international
toll-free: 1 888 232 4444 (USA & Canada)
phone: 250 383 6864 ✦ fax: 812 355 4082

Paul Leido

Project Manager:
How to pass the PMP® Exam without dying in the attempt

2nd ed., 2011, USA.
433 p. ; 21x28 cm.

1. Administration. 2. Management.

ISBN: 978-1-4269-4422-2

Author: Pablo Lledó (PMP®)

Editors: Jessica González Solís (PMP®)
         Luis M. Santana Ortiz, (PMP®)

Graphic Design: Samanta Gallego

Edition published by:

"PMI", "PMBOK", "PMP" and "OPM3" are registered marks of the Project Management Institute, Inc.

The quotations shown with * were taken from: Project Management Institute [A Guide to the Project Management Body of Knowledge (PMBOK® Guide) - Fourth Edition], Project Management Institute, Inc., (2008). Copyright and all rights reserved. Material from this publication has been reproduced with the permission of PMI®.

pablolledo is a Trademark owned by Pablo Lledó

V 2.2

To: Marcela, Máximo, Martín and Salvador

Do you want to become a PMP®?

It does not make any sense to read multiple books to prepare for your international PMP® certification when you already have in your hands one of the most complete books, which will help you save many study hours.

With this book, that includes 50 exercises and 470 questions, you will realize how much you know and how much you have left to study in order to become a PMP®. If you would like to practice with more simulation questions you may acquire simulators at www.pablolledo.com.

Pablo Lledó is a Project Management Professional (PMP®, Project Management Institute), Master of Science in Project Analysis (University of York, England), has an MBA in Project Management, an MBA in International Business and has a Bachelors degree in Economics.

Within his professional experience he stands out by his performance in project analysis for Towers Perrin (England). Currently he is the President of MasConsulting, a company specialized in Project Management. (www.masconsulting.com.ar)

Pablo, in addition to being professor at prestigious Universities, has published two other Project Management textbooks with one of the most prestigious publishers around the world, Pearson Prentice Hall. In the last years he has been selected to be a speaker at international Project Management Institute congresses.

Advantages of studying from this book:
  ✓ To have a complete guide to study the PMP® Exam
  ✓ To learn what is it that you don't know
  ✓ To get information and tips for the exam
  ✓ To save time and money
  ✓ To be very close to approving the PMP® Exam
  ✓ To become a better Project Manager

Why buy this book if I can get it for free?

Due to information piracy and the lack of professional ethics, it is possible that this book may have reached you even though you did not buy it. I remind you that this is against the code of professional ethics you are going to sign with PMI®; therefore, I invite you to invest only $9.90 to purchase this book at www.pablolledo.com and continue to develop your good professional behavior.

In return of your small investment, I will be at your service to personally answer any type of question about this book or other subject related to project management. You may reach me at pl@pablolledo.com entering your purchasing # reference in the subject line.

PROJECT MANAGER

How to pass the PMP® Exam without dying in the attempt

Table of Content

..

Prologue

More and more leaders of organizations realize that excellent Project Managers make things happen, and transform a strategic plan into tangible results. The knowledge and skills of these professionals are invaluable to any industry and to any type of organization: profit or non-profit. We congratulate you for your interest in becoming a Project Management Professional (PMP®) and on selecting this book to help you achieve it.

As avid executors and instructors of these practices, we have read many books on the subject, including the PMBOK® Guide on many occasions. The difference with this one is that it won't only help you pass the exam because it is correct and complete; it will help you understand how to apply these practices on a daily basis; it will make it practical instead of conceptual. Pablo does this in an informal, colloquial, fun kind of way; and that makes it easy to follow and understand. He offers different perspectives to a same concept and many, many exercises that help you think and achieve those very important "Aha! moments".

We feel honored on having had the opportunity of working with Pablo editing this book. We met Pablo while working for PMI® on the validation of the PMBOK® Guide. We believe that great teams are made of great people, and not necessarily of shining leaders. Therefore, as the Project Leader, Jessica selected Pablo and all the other members of the team because their curriculum vitae intimidated her. Pablo's direct communication style caught our attention and professional interest, and so when he called to ask us to work with him on this project, we did not think it even once... we said yes. We hope you enjoy the final product and that you believe, as we do, that our level of professionalism, sense of commitment and responsibility, and attention to detail contributed to a quality delivery.

This book is not the silver bullet to passing the PMP® Exam. But with this book, the right attitude, and dedication, we have no doubt you will achieve your goal, and better yet, be able to put the knowledge into practice and help your organization materialize their plans.

Jessica González Solís, PMP®, ITILf

Jessica is a PMP® with a B.S. in Chemical Engineer, and a Masters in Project Management (Keller Graduate School of Management). She is the founder of Business Essentials, Inc. and has over 12 years of experience in Project Management. She volunteered as the VP of Programs of the PR PMI Chapter and as the Project Leader of the PMBOK® Guide validation. She stands out as a contributor to the creation of BABOK 1.6 for the International Institute of Business Analysis.

Luis Santana Ortiz, PMP®, CBCP, CISA

Luis is a PMP®, Certified Business Continuity Professional (CBCP), and a Certified Information Systems Auditor (CISA). He has a Bachelors degree in Management of Information Systems. Luis is the co-founder and current President of Business Essentials, Inc. He has more than 10 years of experience as a PM and has practiced the profession in both private and public sectors in the USA. Luis stands out as one of the best CBCPs in PR and is considered an expert on the field.

CHAPTER #1

INTRODUCTION

Chapter 1 - INTRODUCTION

It should be noted that this book is based on the current version of A Guide to the Project Management Body of Knowledge (PMBOK® Guide fourth edition). Also, the author recognizes that some content of the book is based on adaptations of PMP® Exam preparation textbooks from recognized authors such as Rita Mulcahy, Michael Newell, Joseph Phillips and Kim Heldman. These authors were the main mentors, not only to help the author of this book to pass his PMP® Exam, but also to develop one of the most complete books in this field.

"PMI®", "PMBOK®", "PMP®" and "OPM3®" are registered marks of the Project Management Institute, Inc. The PMI® has not participated in the publication of this book. Any conceptual error is of the sole responsibility of the author.

Scope of the book

There is a growing trend for companies to require their Project Managers the PMP® certification.

This international certification is administered by the Project Management Institute, the most recognized organization worldwide on this subject: www.pmi.org.

Although this book is focused on preparing you for the PMP® Exam, all of its content is geared towards those who want to become better project managers and achieve successful projects.

Symbols

☺ **Joke**. Just to relax the reading.

✍ **Remember**

☝ **Important**!

? **Question**

📖 **Exercise**

✋ **Stop the Reading** to solve a question or exercise.

⬇ **Input** for a process.

✂ **Tool** or technique for a process.

↗ **Output** of a process.

🦎 **Insect**. Just to fill up a blank space.

Abbreviations

PMI®: Project Management Institute
PMP®: Project Manager Professional
PM: Project Manager
WBS: Work Breakdown Structure

Simulation Questions

This book is complemented with **simulation questions** specially designed for those professionals who want to become a PMP®.

At the end of each chapter you will find questions to reinforce or complement what you have learned. A summary of these questions grouped by knowledge area is presented in the following table.

#	EXAM	Subject	Quantity of Questions
0	DIAGNOSTIC	All	50
1	Framework	General concepts	15
2	Processes	5 Process Groups	15
3	Integration	Integration Management	15
4	Scope	Scope Management	15
5	Time	Time Management	15
6	Cost	Cost Management	15
7	Quality	Quality Management	15
8	Human Resources	Human Resource Management	15
9	Communication	Communication Management	15
10	Risk	Risk Management	15
11	Procurement	Procurement Management	15
12	FINAL 1	All	200
		TOTAL	**415**

To practice with more simulation questions visit www.pablolledo.com. There you will find a simulator test bank including more questions organized by process groups and other exams.

PMP® Exam characteristics

The exam consists of 200 multiple choice questions to answer in a maximum of 4 hours.

Incorrect answers do not subtract points from the total score.

> ☝ *Incorrect answers do not have negative marks; therefore you should always answer ALL the questions even if you do not know the correct answer.*

There are 25 hidden questions that are not graded, but you do not know which of them are. Therefore, you need to answer the whole exam. These hidden questions are sample questions to be evaluated for future exams.

The passing score varies, but you will obtain your PMP® certification if you answer correctly approximately 70% of the questions.

The PMP® Exam is exclusively administered by the PMI®, but you may take it at any institute that has computers able to provide international exams. The exam date is set by the candidate. For more information visit: www.prometric.com/pmi.

You may find all the information about the exam costs and how to become a member of PMI® at www.pmi.org.

> ✎ The *PMI®* usually changes the exam characteristics, the requisites for application, the costs, and the passing scores.

> ☺ *Taking the exam for the second time is cheaper! Therefore, don't get discouraged if you think you will not pass it the first time.*

Why should I become a PMP®?

The main reasons for taking the exam are:
- ✓ **International certification** to demonstrate knowledge in project management
- ✓ **Requisite** for many multinational companies
- ✓ An investment to obtain an **economic return ($$$)**
- ✓ **To become a better** project manager

This last reason should be your main objective. Even if you decide not to take the exam, this book will help you learn the best tools and processes that will allow you to become a better project manager and achieve successful projects.

Remember that achieving successful projects means:
- ✓ Having a **satisfied client**
- ✓ Completing the **scope** agreed upon all parties
- ✓ Complying with the **schedule, budget, and quality**
- ✓ Working with **human resources** committed to the project
- ✓ Not having misunderstandings due to bad **communication**
- ✓ Preventing instead of reacting, with good **risk** management
- ✓ Have a good **procurement** process with our vendors

Characteristics of the exam questions

The 200 questions of the PMP® Exam are distributed within five process groups. The following table shows the approximate amount of questions by area.

Process Group	% of questions
Initiation	13%
Planning	24%
Execution	30%
Monitoring and Controlling	25%
Closing	8%

Within the questions' main characteristics, we can say that:
- ✓ 5% require **memorization**
- ✓ 5% require **formulas**
- ✓ 5% mention Earned Value Management

> ✎ *Most of the students only had doubts with 20% of the questions*

The following are a few examples of the type of questions that you will find in the exam.

? Situational

1. You have been the project manager of a construction project for 150 days. During the execution phase, a contractor tells you that the bricks ordered will be delayed one day. What you should do?
    A. Ignore it, because it is not a significant delay
    B. Inform to your sponsor as soon as possible
    C. Call your client to explain him the problem
    D. Meet with the project team to evaluate alternatives

> ✎ *Most of the exam questions are situational in order to train you to become a good PM in practice.*

? Multiple correct answers

2. You are starting a project for the planning of a sub-fluvial tunnel, for which you do not have enough experience. What should you do?
    A. Contact other project managers with experience in sub-fluvial tunnels
    B. Apply all the processes explained on the PMBOK® Guide
    C. Analyze the company's historical records on similar projects
    D. Identify all of the stakeholders

There are multiple correct answers for this question. Which one should I choose? Always concentrate on the most correct answer.

> ☞ *Many questions have multiple correct answers. This is why you should always read UNDERLINE answer before choosing the one you think is correct.*

? Irrelevant Information

3. After traveling 950 kilometers on your vehicle to Springfield, 90 liters of gasoline was consumed at a cost of $1.50 per liter. Based on this data, you estimate the mobility costs in a transportation project with the following tool:
    A. Earned value technique
    B. Parametric Estimating
    C. Bottom-up Estimating
    D. Analogous Estimating

You will find many questions with complementary information that is not needed in order to answer correctly.

☝ *Do not be fooled by questions with irrelevant information*

？ The ones I do not know

4. There are 34 stakeholders identified on your project for the re-forestation of deserted zones. Choose the CORRECT answer:

    A. There are 561 communication channels

    B. The number of stakeholders is too big to have good communication

    C. There are 578 communication channels

    D. There is not enough information to answer

✎ *It doesn't matter how much you study, there will always be questions that you cannot answer! The day of the exam you will get some questions whose contents were not on this book nor in the PMBOK® Guide.*

？ Integration

5. When is the process of Estimate Activity Durations finalized?

    A. The time estimates can be done in each work package

    B. Each work package is defined in the WBS dictionary

    C. CPM technique have been implemented

    D. Risk Management processes within the Planning process group have been finalized

It is not enough to know a particular area to be able to answer some questions. Instead you will need to integrate multiple knowledge areas.

You already want to know the correct answers? But you have not even started to study yet!

☝ *If you want to become a PMP®, it is not enough to practice questions and learn their answers. A word of advice:*

  1st - Read and study the processes on the PMBOK® Guide

  2nd - Study this book as a complement to the PMBOK® Guide

  3rd - Practice with simulation questions

✎ *To pass the exam, not only you have to study, but also you must have working experience in project management.*

However, since we know you are still anxious about the answers, here are the correct answers to the previous 5 questions.

Q #	Correct Answer	Explanation
1	D	A: 1 day is not enough information B: inform the Sponsor ASAP is usually a bad practice C: inform the client should be performed after evaluating alternatives with the team D: this is the best practice, before informing the Sponsor and/or Client.
2	C	A: true, but you should contact other PM after analyzing the historical records B: false, you should not apply every process in every project C: the first thing to do is analyze the historical records D: true, but you should identify stakeholders after analyzing the historical records
3	B	A: the earned value technique is not used in this case B: the parametric estimating used historical data to estimate values C: the bottom-up estimating is not used in this case D: the analogous estimating is not used in this case
4	A	B, C, and D are incorrect. Study chapter on Communications Management. [34 x 33] / 2 = 561
5	D	A: false, it is necessary to done a risk analysis before finishing B: false, this is not necessary to estimate durations C: false, CPM technique does not include risk analysis D: To understand this question you need to study not only time management, but also integrate it with risk management.

Are you ready to start?

The following 50 questions are part of the diagnostic exam. These will help you to set up your own baseline.

> ✐ When you finish this diagnostic exam, do not look for the correct answers. Finish studying the whole book, then come back and do it again to see how much you have improved.

Recommendations on answering the simulation exams:

✓ Think about big projects. For example: 5,000 employees, a budget of $1 billion, estimated target date in 5 years, etc. This way, all processes in the PMBOK® Guide and the exam questions will make sense.

✓ Quickly identify the question within long narratives. It is usually by the end of the paragraph.

✓ ALWAYS READ EVERY OPTIONS before answering. Remember, there could be multiple correct answers. If you do not read all the options, the probability of failing the exam is higher.

✓ Quickly eliminate incorrect answers.

✓ Respond based on the PMBOK® Guide, not your experience. Often, what we do in practice is not what we should do in our projects.

✓ If you do not know the answer, choose one and mark the question for revision. During the exam, you can come back to change an answer to a question at any time.

✓ The answer to choose is not always grammatically correct.

✓ Control your distress feelings with questions that you do not know the answer. Choose an answer randomly and continue the exam as if nothing happened.

✎ The real time average to respond each question is 1 minute and 12 seconds. However, if you practice with a target of 1 minute, once you are finished with all the questions you will be able to use that extra time to review the more difficult ones.

Exam 1 - Diagnostic

Number of questions: 50
Time to respond: 1 hour
Points to pass: 80% (40 correct answers)

1. The project manager is in a meeting explaining to the team what are the next milestones that need to be completed within the Project Plan. What are the characteristics of a milestone?
   A. Duration equals zero
   B. Indicates the completion of a main event within the project
   C. Establishes the completion of the main deliverables
   D. Changes network logic to overlap phases

2. All of the following statements are part of the Project Plan, except:
   A. Work Breakdown Structure
   B. Budget Management Plan
   C. Responsibility Matrix
   D. Quality Management Plan

3. Which of the following is the most recommended alternative for a conflict resolution?
   A. Collaborate
   B. Force
   C. Confront
   D. Withdraw

4. Once the Project Scope Statement is completed, the client and the sponsor shortened the schedule by four weeks and decided that the process to create the Work Breakdown Structure (WBS) will stay out of the project. The project manager informs them that the WBS should not be eliminated. Why is the project manager suggesting this? Because the WBS _____

    A. Provides the basis to reuse in other projects
    B. Helps achieve project commitment from the team
    C. Provides a hierarchical diagram of the project
    D. Is used to estimate activities, costs, and resources

5. In a commercial project, the project manager has identified the project risks, has performed the risk probability and impact assessment, and has assigned risks to different risk owners. The next step will be to put this information in the:

    A. Risk Registry
    B. Risk Triggers
    C. Risk List
    D. Risk Response Plan

6. The duration of a project changes if:

    A. The contingency reserve is spent
    B. The critical path changes
    C. Three people leave the project
    D. There is no slack on the critical path

7. Which of the following elements is created as a result of initiating a hotel expansion project?

    A. Project Plan
    B. A signed contract
    C. The assignment of the Project Manager
    D. Corrective actions

8. A multinational company is implementing project management processes within the organization and has decided to implement a Project Management Office (PMO). There is strong executive management support for the creation of this office and a solid methodology that includes policies, certified project managers, and an advanced schedule management system. What is needed first to ensure the most probability of success with this organizational change?

    A. Clearly defined goals and objectives for the Project Management Office
    B. Competent project managers
    C. A solid time reporting system for all team members
    D. A detailed set of rules and procedures

9. You must choose one of the four projects presented on the following table. The projects are mutually exclusive and cannot be repeated in time. Which project will you choose?

Project	Net present value	Duration (# of years)
1	$1,200	3
2	$500	1
3	$2,000	6
4	$1,500	2

    A. Project 1
    B. Project 2
    C. Project 3
    D. Project 4

10. Your company's executive management is evaluating two projects. Project "North" has 35% probability of losing $800 and 65% probability of winning $2,400. Project "South" has 40% probability of losing $1,400 and 60% probability of winning $3,000. Which of the projects do they select based on the greatest expected monetary value?
    A. The expected monetary value is not significant on either to make a selection
    B. Project North
    C. Project South
    D. Both projects have the same expected monetary value

11. During the monitor and control phase you detect that your project has a significant delay. You received approval to compress your project by incorporating 5 engineers to the project team. The negotiated cost is $150/hr per person. The additional engineers contracted will work on the project until it comes back to normal, based on the Project Plan. What type of contract is this?
    A. Time and materials
    B. Fixed Price or Lump Sum
    C. Cost plus percentage of cost
    D. Reimbursable costs

12. During the Scope Control process the project manager should worry about:
    A. Having team members participating in this process
    B. The changes being beneficial to the project
    C. The project sponsor being responsible for this process
    D. Not changing the original project schedule

13. As a good project manager, you have completed the work breakdown structure, the scope management plan, and the stakeholder requirements. If the client requests a change, what is necessary to determine its impact on the project?
    A. Resource Histogram
    B. Responsibility Matrix
    C. Performance Reports
    D. A Monte Carlo simulation

14. What is the base of Maslow's Hierarchy of Needs?
   A. Safety
   B. Physiological Needs
   C. Esteem
   D. Self-actualization

15. A project has a planned value (PV) of $1,000, an earned value (EV) of $800, and an actual cost (AC) of $1,200. What is the cost performance index (CPI) for this project?
   A. 1.25
   B. 0.83
   C. 0.80
   D. 0.67

16. You planned 8 months for the project duration. However, the project was completed in 6 months. The following characteristics will happen on the closing process, EXCEPT:
   A. Formal acceptance of the project results from the client
   B. A cost-benefit analysis
   C. An update of the project records
   D. A decrease of resource distribution

17. The following propositions are true, EXCEPT:
   A. Stakeholders should not be involved in the development of the Project Management Plan, unless they are part of the project team.
   B. The project manager should identify the stakeholder's needs and expectations.
   C. The Communications Management Plan is part of the Project Management Plan
   D. Every change to the project needs to be evaluated

18. What is the most important aspect of project closure?
   A. All of the physical activities are completed and the task list is closed
   B. The client formally accepts that the project is completed
   C. The project's budget and all the project accounts are closed
   D. All resources assigned to the project have been released and reassigned

19. Who is responsible for developing the final project management plan?
   A. Project Sponsor
   B. Project Team
   C. Client
   D. Project Manager

20. Utilizing the following table and diagram, what is the activity sequence that makes the critical path?

Task	Duration	Task	Duration
A	2 weeks	F	4 weeks
B	3 weeks	G	7 weeks
C	2 weeks	H	5 weeks
D	5 weeks	K	4 weeks
E	0 weeks	L	3 weeks

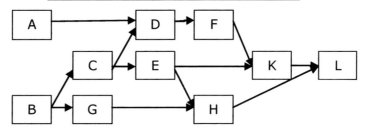

    A. B G H L
    B. A D F K L
    C. B C E K L
    D. B C D F K L

21. Using the previous question, if task D is completed 4 weeks before schedule, what is the impact on the project's duration?
    A. Duration is reduced by one week
    B. Duration is reduced by three weeks
    C. Duration is reduced by four weeks
    D. There is no change in the project's duration

22. How many communication channels are required in a project with 30 persons?
    A. 150
    B. 270
    C. 444
    D. 435

23. You work in an organization with no rules regarding special gifts. One of the company's most important vendors gives you and your family air tickets to Disney World. What would be the best course of action?
    A. Accept the gift and influence the company into buying the vendor's products
    B. Ask the vendor for an additional set of tickets for the General Manager
    C. Refuse the offer and advise the vendor on the company's standard procurement process
    D. Look for legal counseling before accepting the offer

24. Your project has a total slack of -45. What should you do?
    A. Get more resources for the activities on the critical path
    B. Release resources to avoid unnecessary costs
    C. Hire more people for the project
    D. Extend the project's duration

25. Which of the following risk response strategies are used for positive and negative risks?
    A. Share
    B. Transfer
    C. Accept
    D. Mitigate

26. Quality assurance in a project means:
    A. Define the organizational quality practices
    B. Ensure compliance with six sigma
    C. Utilize a Pareto Diagram to show sample points
    D. Utilize organizational quality measures for the project

27. The project manager has evaluated different alternatives of schedule compression through fast tracking. In addition, he has done a Monte Carlo simulation to evaluate the impact of the different alternatives. What is the result of the process of schedule development?
    A. Update each activity's resource needs
    B. The work breakdown structure
    C. Recommend preventive actions
    D. Estimate activity duration

28. What is the leadership style usually used with a non-collaborative team member who needs to be controlled in every task?
    A. McGregor's Theory of Y
    B. McGregor's Theory of X
    C. McClelland's Theory of Needs
    D. Tuckman's Theory of Team Development

29. You have just replaced the project manager of a software development project that started 16 months ago. You found on the project management plan that the total estimated cost is $675,000, the project should be completed in 24 months, the actual cost is $300,000, and is 25% completed. What is the budget at completion?
    A. 1,200,000
    B. 675,000
    C. 3,000,000
    D. 1,050,000

30. Based on the previous question, what is the schedule variance?
    A. -157,351
    B. -289,750
    C. -281,250
    D. Not enough information to respond

31. After many months of complaints, your company has not reached consensus with the contractor on the closing of the contract for the mining project. The contractor affirms that it complied with the scope comprised within the contract. However, the company affirms that the contractor has not completed all the work agreed upon. Who should resolve this conflict between both parties?
   A. A lawyer
   B. A PMP® with expertise in conflict resolution
   C. An arbitrator
   D. The functional managers of both companies

32. A good project manager tends to _____ above anything else when performing active communications.
   A. Write reports
   B. Call people
   C. Listen
   D. Help

33. What is the tool and technique LEAST used during the process of gathering project requirements?
   A. Delphi Technique
   B. Prototypes
   C. Focus groups
   D. Requirements traceability matrix

34. During what process of Project Procurement Management, expert judgment is LEAST important?
   A. Close Procurements
   B. Plan Procurements
   C. Administer Procurements
   D. Conduct Procurements

35. You are the project manager for a project that consists of closing an atomic plant. During the project execution, the five most important members of your team get sick with cholera, which causes them to be out of the project for six months. You request help to the Project Management Office and within two weeks five new persons are sent to replace your sick team members. You know that some of these people have been conflictive in the past. What is the first thing you should do during the kickoff meeting with the new team?
   A. Put emphasis on the fact that you have the authority in this project
   B. Review the agenda to evaluate alternatives of recuperating the lost time
   C. Discuss the project impact on the budget
   D. Define the team's roles and responsibilities

36. You have just been hired with a new company and you believe that one of the company's certified PMP® is violating PMI's Code of Professional Conduct. What should you do?
   A. Quit the company
   B. Confront the PMP® and loudly discuss with him so the rest of the company hears it
   C. Allow time to pass to see if the violation to the code of conduct is repeated. If this is the case, inform the situation on the next shareholders meeting.
   D. Put the infractions in writing, discuss them with other PMPs, and evaluate the next steps to take.

37. In which project phase do the stakeholders have more influence?
   A. Initial phase
   B. Intermediate phases
   C. Final phase
   D. All of the above

38. You and your project team are evaluating alternatives about the project management plan. What is the principal advantage of applying crashing techniques?
   A. Improve productivity
   B. Shorten the duration of the project
   C. Intensify the work breakdown structure
   D. Intensify change controls

39. During the execution of a property development project, you discovered an error during the design phase that will not allow the installation of fiber optic cables separate from phone cables. What is the best course of action?
   A. Contract designers with more expertise
   B. Evaluate alternatives to solve the problem
   C. Reduce the technological complexity of the project
   D. Add additional functionality to the project that will cover the technical deficiency until the client is satisfied

40. Which of the following matrix structures gives more control to the project manager?
   A. Strong Matrix
   B. Weak Matrix
   C. Balanced Matrix
   D. Functional

41. The following INPUTS are necessary to manage project stakeholder expectations, EXCEPT:
   A. Stakeholder Registry
   B. Issues Log
   C. Stakeholder management strategy
   D. Change requests

42. What are the most important factors to take into account when developing a communications plan?
   A. Project sponsors and their needs
   B. Risk management plan and process improvements
   C. Work breakdown structure and project schedule
   D. Conduct and administer procurements

43. You are the project manager for a very important project. You do not believe in the subjective templates with progress percentages submitted by your team members as a project tracking mechanism. What would be the best method to control a work package that consists in developing the terms and conditions of a contract?
    A. Fixed formula
    B. Pareto Diagram
    C. Weighted milestones
    D. Percentage completed

44. During the project execution, one person is added to the project team. The project manager should inform the project sponsor that the impact to the project will be:
    A. There is not enough information to determine the effect
    B. The project duration will be reduced
    C. A scope change will be required
    D. The quality of the project will increase

45. You are an experienced project manager in the company. Today you received an email from a project manager on a competing company, with whom you play tennis every weekend, asking for your help on a new project. What should you do?
    A. Tell him that the answers to his problem will probably be found on the PMBOK® Guide
    B. Do not take risks and delete the email
    C. Tell him that you will help him next weekend when you play tennis
    D. Go to your superior and discuss the situation before making any contact

46. The lessons learned during a project's administrative closure are BETTER utilized on a new project during the following process group:
    A. Monitoring and Control
    B. Execution
    C. Closing
    D. Planning

47. Your office renovation project has a budget at completion of $68,000. According to the schedule, today the project should be 65% completed, but it is only 50% completed. What is the earned value of the project?
    A. $ 44,200
    B. $ 34,000
    C. $ 10,200
    D. -$ 10,200

48. Whose responsibility is to have a clear message?
    A. The project sponsor
    B. The project coordinator
    C. The sender
    D. All

49. In a project, you measure the finish results against the design specifications. This is an example of quality _____
   A. Benchmarking
   B. Assurance
   C. Control test
   D. Audit

50. The planning is in an advanced stage for a project that deals with a market study about a new product's potential demand. The project manager and his team are ready to start the cost estimation stage. The client asked for the costs to be estimated as soon as possible. What estimating method should the Project team use?
   A. Parametric
   B. Bottom-up
   C. Analogous
   D. Reserve analysis

☞ *Do not look for the explanations for each question until you finish studying the whole book and do this exam for a second time.*

Answers and explanations are at the end of the book

☞ *Do not be fooled by questions with irrelevant information*

CHAPTER #2
FRAMEWORK

Chapter 2 – FRAMEWORK

> *Protagonists have projects; victims, excuses.*
> Pablo Lledó (1971-?) Argentinean economist and project manager

In this chapter we will develop basic project management concepts that you will apply for the rest of the book.

When you finish this chapter, you should have learned the following concepts:
- ✓ PMI generalizations
- ✓ Difference between project and operation
- ✓ Project management context
- ✓ Project Management Office (PMO)
- ✓ Organizational systems
- ✓ Stakeholders
- ✓ The triple constraint
- ✓ Project life cycle
- ✓ OPM3: Organizational Project Management Maturity Model
- ✓ Project management knowledge areas

PMI Generalizations

There are some implicit generalizations within the PMBOK® Guide that you should be aware of in order to be a good project manager (PM). Some of these assumptions may seem unrealistic, but good and experienced PMs take them into consideration in order to achieve successful projects.

The following is a summary of 10 more important PMI's generalizations:

1. The company has defined and uses project management policies and procedures.

2. There is always historical information of similar projects available to be used for planning future projects.

3. The PM is assigned during project initiation, it has power and authority, and its main role is to prevent problems, not to fix them.

4. All the work and stakeholders are identified prior to the start of the project.

5. The work breakdown structure is the base for all the planning.

6. The time and cost estimates are not finished without a risk analysis.

7. The PM defines metrics to measure quality prior to the start of the project.

8. Each knowledge area has its plan: scope, time, cost, quality, human resources, communications, risk, and procurement.

9. The Project Plan is approved by the main stakeholders, is realistic, and everyone is convinced that it can be done.

10. Every project is closed with lessons learned.

> ✎ Remember these generalizations when preparing to take the PMP® Exam. You should take them as project management assumptions.

Project vs. Operation

Is building a house a project or an operation? How about making a pizza?

As usual, the answer to this question is: it depends!

> ☺ Every time you are asked something, you can answer: "it depends". Surely you may be right. It is a shame that on the PMP® Exam there is no option to select "it depends" as an answer. Otherwise we would all be PMP®s by now!

In order to respond to these questions, we have to know the definition of project and operation. We will use PMBOK® Guide definitions *:

PROJECT: a <u>temporary</u> endeavor undertaken to create a unique product, service, or result.

OPERATIONS: an organizational function performing the <u>ongoing execution</u> of activities that produce the same product or provide a <u>repetitive</u> service.

Therefore, if building a house is something temporary and unique, there is no doubt that it is a project. But if a company sells houses through the

Internet and everyday builds and ships the same type of pre-fabricated houses to different clients, then surely that is an operation.

On the other hand, for the chef of a pizza restaurant, making pizzas is part of the restaurant operations. However, for some of us to make a pizza could fall in the category of a project.

We can conclude that the definition of a project does not depend on its complexity or magnitude, but on its characteristics of unique and temporary. A project could be as simple as planning your son's birthday party, or as complex as sending a rocket to the moon.

> ☝ *This book is focused on project management and planning; therefore, we should not look here for tools to solve day to day operational problems.*

Project management context

Projects are included within a bigger context. The following figure summarizes the hierarchical level where projects are framed.

Project management context

First, every project should be aligned within the organization's strategic plan. The second hierarchical level could be a portfolio that may include different programs and/or projects.

A program is a group of related projects that are managed together. An example of a program could be the creation of a new city as a result of multiple projects such as Roads, Services and Buildings.

> ☝ *Every project should be framed within the organization's strategic plan.*

✎ This book focuses on project management. PMI has a certification in portfolio and program management, PgMP, which is not part of the scope of this book.

Project Management Office (PMO)

The project management office (PMO) is an entity within the organization that facilitates a centralized and coordinated management of projects.

Some of the main roles of the PMO are:
1. Provide project management methodologies
2. Provide support for project management (e.g. training)
3. Assign project managers and be accountable for project's successes or failures

Some of the functions usually performed by the PMO are:
1. Manage project interrelationships
2. Provide lessons learned for new projects
3. Collaborate on the assignment of shared resources
4. Get involved in the project initiation processes

✎ It is recommended that the members of a PMO should be PMP®s.

Not every company has a PMO, but there is a strong tendency to incorporate PMOs in organizations to improve the efficiency in project management.

Stakeholders

Project stakeholders are those people or organizations whose interests might be affected as a result of the project.

How do you feel about identifying stakeholders on a real project you may be working on?

✋ Take the next 3 minutes thinking about the answer before moving on.

✍ *Most of the projects usually have the following stakeholders: sponsor, client, user, project manager, workers, government and community.*

This list of stakeholders is only for illustration purposes, since it is usually much more extensive.

Let us look at an example to see the difference between Sponsor, Client, and User. An editorial requests the development of software for a new electronic book from an information systems company. The president of the information systems company assigns a project manager to the project. In this example, the Sponsor is the president of the information systems company, the Client is the editorial, and the User is the person buying the electronic book on the market.

Generally, there is conflict of interest between stakeholders. For example, in a project for the development of a new technology for cellular phones, the technical people are interested in achieving the maximum connection speed; the commercial manager is worried about finishing the project as early as possible to beat the competition; the financial manager does not want to invest more than $100,000 in research; and the stockholder wants a return on investment over 40%. Or in a house painting project, the architect wants to paint it black and the engineer wants to paint it white. How do we solve these opposite interests? Do we negotiate to develop a product that satisfies all parties? Should we paint the house gray?

It is usually very difficult, if not impossible, to satisfy all stakeholders with the same project. On the other hand, if you do a "grey" project you could end up with a product that did not satisfy anybody and it failed commercially.

> ✍ If you try to satisfy every stakeholder you will be signing your project's death certificate.

Although stakeholder management is a complex topic, there are certain basic steps that should be followed:

1. **Identify** all of them. If stakeholder appears once the project is in execution, they may request changes and this implies time and money.

2. Determine their **requirements** and **expectations**, and include these into project requirements.

3. **Communicate** with them.

4. Whenever possible, **manage their influence**, in relation to their requirements, in order to have a successful project.

Finally, remember that as a PM you will make decisions that will not make every stakeholder happy. Whenever this happens, do not lose sight of the Client, since this is the one you must satisfy in order to have a successful project.

> ☝ *Stakeholders are identified across the complete project life cycle, but especially on the initiation phases.*

📖 Exercise 2.1 – Stakeholder Management

The project manager must effectively manage all the stakeholders in order to achieve a successful project.

In the following table, mark which stakeholder management activities you do in your projects.

Assign project responsibilities to stakeholders	
Communicate what they need to know on time	
Determine their expectations and transform them into requirements	
Evaluate their expertise and capabilities	
Have them sign a formal project acceptance form at project closure	
Identify each stakeholder by first and last name	
Identify all of their requirements	
Influence the stakeholders	
Inform them about which requirements can be done, which ones cannot, and why	
Have them sign a commitment that those are all of their requirements	

Score:
Add up how many activities you do on your projects.
0-5: you probably have too many changes on your projects
6-8: you are doing well
9-10: your projects are in excellent hands

Organizational structure

There are three types of organizational structures:
1. Projectized
2. Functional
3. Matrix

In **projectized** organizations, team members usually work on the same physical location and project managers have great independence and authority. This type of structure is usually found in companies that obtain their main income from projects. For example, big consulting firms tend to adopt this type of structure.

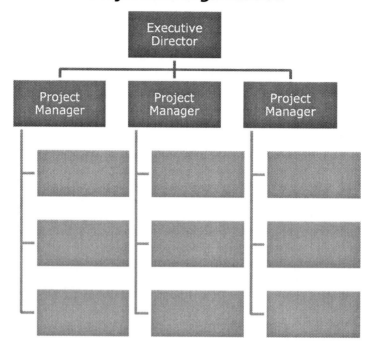

Projectized organization

On the other hand, the most traditional organizational structure is **functional**. In these types of hierarchical structures, each employee has a superior and people are grouped by specialty: engineering, marketing, production, etc.

Functional organization

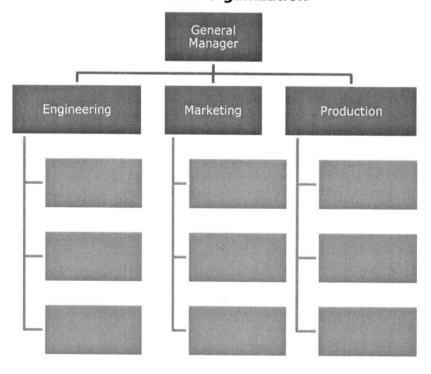

This type of organization dates to 1920, when Henry Ford, and then Frederick Taylor, imposed the division of labor and business administration theories. Although functional structures were very useful in the past to improve efficiency in mass production processes, currently they are not considered the standard for an efficient and effective project management.

Projects based on traditional functional structures tend to be biased toward the same focus and culture of the functional department that sponsors the project. On the other hand, each functional department acts independently from the rest.

It is not justifiable for every organization to have projectized structures, as it is not optimum for project management to keep working with functional structures that are non-flexible. The organizational structure recommended as it relates to project management is the matrix organization.

In a **matrix** organization the functional structure is kept, but a projectized structure is created which utilizes resources from the rest of the organization. For example, for a new product development project, the PMO could assign a project manager that will be part of a team with people from different functional departments.

It is not necessary to have a PMO in the organization to have a matrix structure. There could be a PM that reports directly to the executive management or any other functional management.

Matrix organization

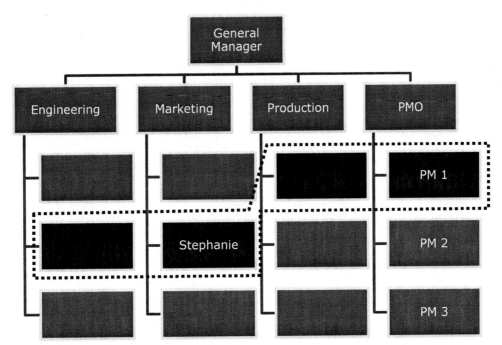

Not everything is that simple in matrix structures. For example: Stephanie, working at the Marketing department, has been assigned to Project 1. She is having issues with her Marketing functional manager and now will have more challenges due to the fact that she will also be reporting to the PM of Project 1.

Even though the inconvenience of having two "bosses" and other problems that we will see below, the matrix organization is a better structure for project management than functional structures dating back to 1920.

Matrix structures usually come in three types:
1. Strong Matrix: if the PM has more power than the functional manager
2. Weak Matrix: if the functional manager has more power than the PM
3. Balanced Matrix: when the PM and the functional manager share power and decision making

By definition, the PM has power and authority. A PM with no authority it is not a PM, he/she could be the following:
✓ **Project Coordinator**: little authority to make decisions
✓ **Project Expeditor**: no authority to make decisions

> ✍ A tight matrix organization means that every member of the team works on the same physical location. This has no relation with the matrix structures mentioned in this section.

📖 Exercise 2.2 – Organizational Structures

Based on your experience, document on the following table the advantages and disadvantages of the different organizational structures in relation to project management.

+ ADVANTAGE	- DISADVANTAGE
Functional Organization	
Projectized Organization	
Matrix Organization	

 Take 15 minutes to the answer before moving on with the reading.

Answers to Exercise 2.2

+ ADVANTAGE	- DISADVANTAGE
Functional Organization	
+ Only one "boss" + Organization grouped by specialties => specialization	- Biased projects toward functional areas - Project manager without authority
Projectized Organization	
+ Efficient organization + Loyalty to the project + Effective communications	- Nowhere to go when project is completed - Lack of specialists - Duplicate functions =>inefficient resource utilization
Matrix Organization	
+ Control over resources + Efficient resource utilization + Better project coordination + Better horizontal and vertical communication + At project completion I keep my functional position	- Additional administration - Harder to communicate and control - 2 "bosses" - More probability of conflict - Functional manager's priorities could differ from the PM's priorities

✎ On the exam you will compare advantages and disadvantages of a matrix organization versus a functional organization.

✎ *In summary:*
Functional = "Independent silos"
Projectized = "Nowhere to go when completed"
Matrix = "2 bosses"

Project Objectives and Constraints

The main characteristics of project objectives are the following:
- ✓ Established at Initiation (Scope)
- ✓ Perfected during Planning
- ✓ Are the Project Manager's responsibility
- ✓ Clear, <u>achievable</u>, and transferable

How do we know that the project is completed? We simply have to analyze if the objectives were achieved.

Did you notice that the word "achievable" was underlined? Many times, managers set unrealistic and unachievable objectives in projects, to make team members work harder. For example, *"I told her to sell 100 units so she sells at least 50, because if I said 50 she was really going to sell 25"*. This type of policy or bad practice reduces the project team's morale and goes against achieving successful projects.

On the other hand, sometimes we hear phrases like *"I want it done by yesterday with a $1 budget"*. This would be a clear example of not understanding that every project has a **constraints**.

Historically, the triple constraint variables were three: scope, time, and cost (resources). We will see later on that nowadays there are more than three variables.

The Triple Constraint (traditional)

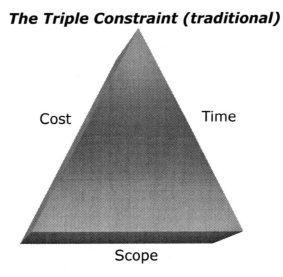

Let us see an example where the triple constraint is extended to four variables, taking into consideration "quality", which in the past was included with scope.

The project manager is confronted with the conflict of managing the opposing interests of these variables: scope, time, cost, and quality. Only three of these can be established at the same time.

If the client requests certain scope to be achieved with the project, under a predetermined quality standard, and a specific deadline, the adjustable variable will be the amount of resources needed to do the project. This includes not only monetary resources, but materials and human resources.

If the constraints are given in terms of time (a deadline), available resources (a limited budget), and quality standards, the project manager can only negotiate with the stakeholders the magnitude of the scope, in order to have a project on schedule, reaching quality standards, and on budget. For example, a project for the construction of a building whose original scope was 20 floors, could be reduced to 10 floors in order to comply with the triple constraint.

If a project team member received a fixed amount of working hours, the project scope and the due date, the variable that will be automatically adjusted is quality of work.

Finally, if the scope, quality, and available resources have been predetermined for the project, the adjustable variable will be the schedule.

Let us see another example like the construction of a canal with locks and a defined scope of 600 million tons of traffic per year. Suppose that the contractor did a good job with the calculations and submitted a very competitive offer that said: "*we will deliver it in 10 years for a total cost of $5,000 millions*".

If the Client says: "*How come you are delivering in 10 years! That is outrageous! If it is not delivered in 5 years, I do not want it*". In this situation, the triple constraint variable to be adjusted could be the price. For example, the contractor's response could be: "*What you are asking is only feasible if we add more personnel, machinery, and we work 24 hours a day. Therefore, the budget will now be $8,000 millions*".

However, if the Client answers: "*Are you crazy! I cannot even pay the original $5,000 million that you asked for! I need you to complete the project in 5 years with no more than $3,000 million. Just do it!*"

The variable that can be adjusted in this situation is the scope. The contractor could answer: "*Based on the short time and the restricted budget, the best that we can do is a project with a capacity of 300 million tons per year*".

If the Client insists on the original scope of 600 million tons per year, a 5 year deadline, and a budget of $3,000 millions, there is no doubt that the project will fail with the following consequences:

✓ The original scope will not be met
✓ Additional non-contracted costs will be added
✓ The project will not be on schedule
✓ The project will not meet the minimum quality standards
✓ The client will not be satisfied
✓ Etc., etc., etc.

> ✎ *It is impossible to arbitrarily establish all the triple constraint variables. Some of these variables will end up adjusting by themselves.*

> ☺ *At MasConsulting we work GOOD, FAST, and CHEAP...*
> *But you can only choose two of those attributes!*

Nowadays, the term "triple constraint" is still popular. However, in the constraint equation you will not find only three variables. Now you will find the following six variables: scope, time, cost, quality, resources and risk.

How does the risk affect the triple constraint? For example, a successful project met the established scope, time, cost, quality and resources. However, if you execute the same project ten times, you will only get a successful project one out of ten.

The Project Constraints

Today, the term "triple constraint" refers to these six variables. We should know that it is impossible to set all these variables in an arbitrary way. Furthermore, we have to understand the interrelation between these project constraints in order to develop a plan that is realistic and achievable.

> ☝ *If one project constraint changes, the PM must evaluate the impact on the rest of the variables.*

Project Life Cycle

Do not confuse *project* life cycle with *product* life cycle.

The **product life cycle** is the time between product developments until it is retired from the market. Generally, many projects are originated during a product life cycle, as shown in the next figure.

Product Life Cycle

The **project life cycle** refers to the different project **phases**, from initiation until completion. In the next figure we can see different examples of project phases.

Life cycle of different projects

Investment Projects				
Phase 1 Idea	**Phase 2** Profile	**Phase 3** Pre-feasibility	**Phase 4** Feasibility	**Phase 5** Investment
Construction Projects				
Phase 1 Feasibility	**Phase 2** Planning	**Phase 3** Design	**Phase 4** Production	**Phase 5** Launch
Information Systems Projects				
Phase 1 Analysis	**Phase 2** Design	**Phase 3** Build	**Phase 4** Tests	**Phase 5** Deployment
				Time

Generally, each project phase ends with a deliverable which entitles the next phase to either start or not. For example, if the feasibility study is not approved by the sponsor, the planning phase cannot start.

> ✎ The exam does not have detailed questions about project phases

The following figure represents a standard project life cycle.

Project Life Cycle *

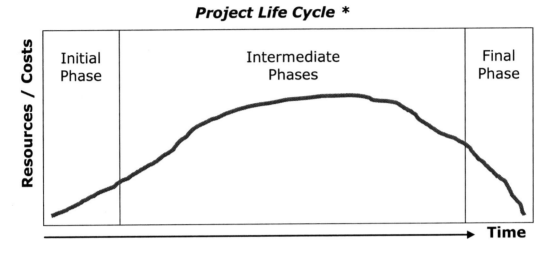

Generally, few resources are utilized in the initial phase of a project, which implies low costs. During the intermediate phases, most of the budget is consumed. In the final phase, the cost is relatively low.

Which project phase is the one with the most uncertainty? At the initial phase. The more advanced a project is, the more certainty of a successful project.

Which project phase is the one where stakeholders are more influential? Stakeholders can better influence over changes at project initiation. For example, is easier to bring down a second floor wall on the blueprint, than bring it down once the building has advanced up to the fifth floor.

> ✎ The cost of changes increases as the project advances.

Do not confuse the project life cycle with the five process groups that you will see later on: initiating, planning, executing, monitoring and controlling, and closing.

Process Groups

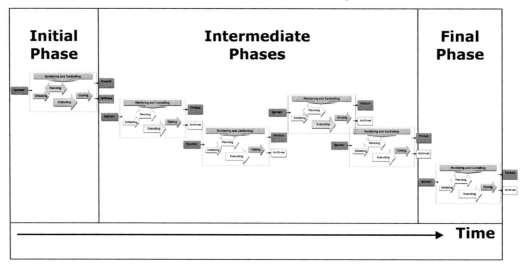

Each phase of the project life cycle can be considered a project on its own. Every project requires **processes**.

> ✎ In big projects, the five process groups are repeated for each project phase.

Phases and Process Groups

Knowledge Areas

To become a good PM you must know different project management areas of knowledge.

Based on the PMBOK® Guide, there are nine knowledge areas:
1. Project Integration Management
2. Project Scope Management
3. Project Time Management
4. Project Cost Management
5. Project Quality Management
6. Project Human Resource Management
7. Project Communication Management
8. Project Risk Management
9. Project Procurement Management

These areas are not independent of each other; they are interrelated.

Knowledge Areas

Scope

Time

Procurement

Cost

Quality

Risks

Communications

Human Resources

OPM3

PMI® has developed a tool based on surveys that allows a company to analyze its organizational maturity level in relation to project management.

This tool is called OPM3®: **O**rganizational **P**roject **M**anagement **M**aturity **M**odel.

There are more than 585 recognized best practices developed that are used to evaluate a company's organizational maturity level.

A company's organizational maturity level can be analyzed not only for projects, but for programs and portfolios as well.

Once a company has been diagnosed with its maturity level in project management, they can access multiple benchmarking reports to be able to compare themselves with the average industry. In addition, with the diagnosis and baseline, the OPM3 tool allows them to create action guides to improve its maturity level.

> ✍ For the exam you should only know that OPM3 exists. Usually, it only appears as a response option in a question.

The Role of a Project Manager

Do not confuse the role of a functional manager with the role of a project manager. While the functional manager is dedicated to the management of a specific area in the company and to resolve problems, the PM focuses on achieving the objectives of an assigned project. In addition, the PM is proactive in order to mitigate problems.

On the other hand, while the functional manager reports to the company's general manager or CEO, the project manager could report to the program manager or the portfolio manager. However, in a weak matrix organizational structure, the PM could report directly to the functional manager.

Successful project managers are those who have excellent general coordination and communication capabilities, combining their knowledge, management capacity, and their interpersonal skills.

Some of the most important interpersonal skills a PM should have are: leadership, teamwork, communication, decision making, knowledge, and negotiation.

> ✍ A good PM has the ability to make things happen.

Exam 2 – Framework

| Number of questions: 15 |
| Time to answer: 15 minutes |
| Passing Score: 80% (12 correct answers) |

1. After many months of negotiating with the Client, the company's General Manager tells you that you have been assigned as the project manager for the project called "IP Telecommunications". On the planning meeting with senior management, they make you aware of this project's importance, in order to gain a portion of the demand in the market that has not been covered and which they have been wanting to service for the past three years. Which type of planning does this project belongs to?
   A. Program planning
   B. Portfolio planning
   C. Strategic planning
   D. Product life cycle

2. In which project management process group stakeholders are identified?
   A. Controlling and Closing
   B. Initiating, Planning, Executing, Monitoring and Controlling
   C. Planning, Monitoring and Controlling
   D. Initiating and Planning

3. When defining the triple constraint, which of the following elements will be considered the most important by the project team?
   A. First quality, second cost, and then time
   B. Quality
   C. Scope
   D. All are of equal importance, unless otherwise specified

4. In a project dealing with the construction of a cell phone network with 1,800 workers and an estimated cost of $7,800,000, information management and the communication with the stakeholders have been out of control for the past 3 months. Therefore, a project manager has been contracted to collaborate with the solution of this inconvenience. What characteristic does a Project Expediter have?
   A. Project Expediter is another way to name the Project Manager
   B. The Project Expediter has limit or no authority to make decisions
   C. The Project Expediter is the same as the Project Coordinator
   D. The Project Expediter has authority to make decisions

5. You work as a project manager in a company with a traditional functional structure. Your authority level in projects will be:
   A. High
   B. Moderate
   C. Balanced
   D. Low

6. A company that sells products on the Internet has decided that each customer request will be considered a project. This company sells products that range from $10,000 to $2,000,000. Project managers will have a maximum of 3 days to respond to each customer request. If the request cannot be served within this deadline, their obligation is to inform the program manager. It is not required that the project managers do any additional planning or documentation, only that they inform their daily status of responses to customer requests. How would you define this situation?
   A. Each customer request is a project, since it has a beginning and an end
   B. Customer requests exceeding $1,000,000 should be treated as projects
   C. Since there are multiple requests, it should be referred to as portfolio management
   D. This is an operation

7. In which project stage stakeholders have more influence?
   A. At the beginning
   B. Minutes before finalizing the project
   C. After completing the project management plan
   D. In the middle of the execution stage

8. You are working with an Actuarial Consulting firm which has a projectized structure. In addition, there is a Project Management Office (PMO) in the firm. The main role of the PMO is:
   A. Support the project sponsor
   B. Identify stakeholders
   C. Support the project manager
   D. Support the project team

9. You are a project manager in a matrix organization and you are managing a database update project. What should be your main role in this project?
   A. Control project stakeholders
   B. Control unnecessary changes
   C. Exceed client expectations
   D. Develop the project management plan

10. During the project execution, two team members get in a fight and do not want to keep working together on the project. You, as the project manager, set up a meeting with the workers and the functional manager. After the meeting, you stay with the functional manager and both come up with a solution to this conflict. You are most likely working in what type of organization?
    A. Balanced Matrix
    B. Functional
    C. OPM3
    D. Strong Matrix

11. A project manager is an industrial engineer specialized in communications and personnel administration. One of the projects that he is in charge is being delayed by the large amount of changes being requested. The project is for the deployment of a customer claims software, which is being installed in 12 company departments distributed within 5 countries. This project is utilizing 25 project management processes and once completed, it should significantly improve company operations. What could be the main cause of the problems with this project?
    A. Some stakeholders have not been identified
    B. The project manager was not trained to understand the organizational structure
    C. The project should have used more project management processes
    D. The project manager should have been a software engineer

12. Which of the following items is FALSE?
    A. The product life cycle extends from the product conception until its market retirement
    B. The product life cycle can generate many projects
    C. Generally, resource utilization is greater during the intermediate phases of the project life cycle
    D. The project life cycle has three process groups

13. Which one of the following is not a project management process group?
    A. Initiating
    B. Planning
    C. Monitoring and Controlling
    D. Design

14. Which of the following statements best describes a project deliverable?
    A. The resources utilized by the project to complete the work
    B. The product or tangible service created by the project team
    C. The result of the planning phase
    D. A temporary effort to create a product or service

15. A project manager has been assigned to a new project in an area where he has little experience. This project is three times as big as any project he has ever managed. The project manager has a friend that has managed similar projects in the past. What should the project manager do?
    A. Talk to the prior project manager and ask for counseling
    B. Wait until project execution to see if he will need help
    C. Obtain historical records from the PMO
    D. Make sure that every stakeholder approves the scope of the project

Lessons Learned

✓ Project Management knowledge areas
✓ Product and project life cycle
✓ Project Coordinator
✓ Project phases and process groups
✓ Project Expeditor
✓ Stakeholders, Stakeholder Management
✓ OPM3
✓ Functional organization
✓ Matrix organization: strong, weak, balanced
✓ Projectized organization
✓ PMO: Project Management Office
✓ Project, Program, Portfolio
✓ Triple Constraint
✓ Role of the project manager
✓ Operations

CHAPTER #3
PROCESSES

Chapter 3 - PROCESSES

> *Knowledge is not something separated and self-sufficient, but is involved in the process by which life sustains and develops.*
>
> John Dewey (1859-1952) American Philosopher

In this chapter we will develop the project management process groups. Later in each chapter of this book we will present a specific analysis for each of them.

When you finish this chapter, you should have learned the following concepts:
- ✓ Initiating Process Group
- ✓ Planning Process Group
- ✓ Executing Process Group
- ✓ Monitoring and Controlling Process Group
- ✓ Closing Process Group

Process Groups

We will understand a **process** as diagrammed in the following figure:

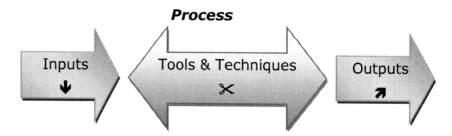

When processes are related, the outputs of one process usually are the inputs of the next process.

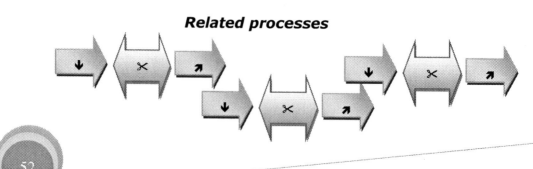

We could think of <u>inputs</u> in the following way: what do I need to start the process? <u>Tools</u> help us process those inputs to reach the <u>outputs</u>: what do I obtain as a result?

The PMBOK® Guide mentions 5 project management process groups:

1. **Initiating** process group: the project objectives are defined, key stakeholders are identified, the project manager is assigned, and the project is formally authorized to kick-off.

2. **Planning** process group: the project scope is defined, the project objectives are refined and the project management plan is developed to be the course of action for a successful project.

3. **Executing** process group: all of the resources are integrated to implement the project management plan.

4. **Monitoring and controlling** process group: the project's progress is tracked and corrective actions are applied as needed.

5. **Closing** process group: the acceptance of project deliverables is formalized with the client.

In each of these five process groups exist specific processes distributed among the different knowledge areas as summarized in the following table:

Processes per process group and knowledge area

	Initiating	Planning	Executing	Controlling	Closing
Integration	1	1	1	2	1
Scope		3		2	
Time		5		1	
Cost		2		1	
Quality		1	1	1	
Human Resources		1	3		
Communications	1	1	2	1	
Risks		5		1	
Procurement		1	1	1	1
TOTAL	**2**	**20**	**8**	**10**	**2**

For example, the two processes within the initiating process group are the following:
1. Develop project charter (Integration)
2. Identify stakeholders (Communications)

There are 42 project management processes that a good PM should know. Each of these processes, with its inputs, tools, and outputs, will be developed in the following chapters of this book. It is not necessary to apply all process in every project. The processes to be applied depend on the project context, project type, company resources, etc.

✎ *25% of the exam questions are related to processes. You should study well the inputs, tools and techniques, and the outputs of each of the processes within the PMBOK® Guide.*

It should be noted that the process groups are not independent of each other, and it is not necessary that one group finishes 100% for the next group to start. There is a strong relationship between all of the process groups, as it is diagrammed in the following figure.

Project management process groups

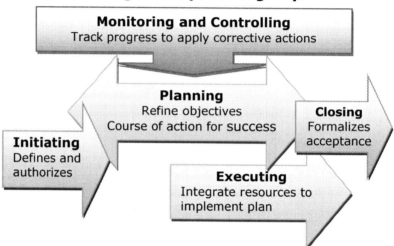

For example, it is not necessary that all of the initiating processes are 100% completed in order to start the planning processes. We should neither pretend to finish planning to start executing, given that the perfect plan does not exist. Captured lessons learned during executing, monitoring and controlling will continue to improve the project management plan as an iterative process.

The monitoring and controlling processes overlap with the rest of the processes since there should be monitoring and controlling from the beginning of the project. Lastly, the closing processes usually overlap with the planning, executing, and monitoring and controlling.

There is a strong relationship between the PMBOK® Guide process groups and the quality management processes developed by Walter A. Shewhart and W. Edwards Deming in their recognized **Plan – Do – Check – Act**. This relationship is summarized in the following figure:

Relationship between PMBOK® Guide processes and Quality

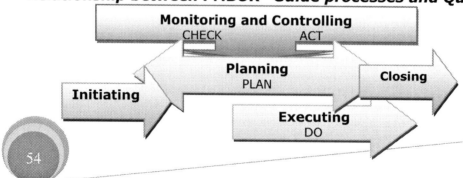

📖 **Exercise 3.1** ✂ To cut. Template in: www.pablolledo.com

INITIATING	PLANNING	EXECUTING	CLOSING
CONTROLLING	N/A		INTEGRATION
SCOPE	TIME	COST	QUALITY
HUMAN R.	COMMUNICAC.	RISKS	PROCUREMENT

Project Charter	Control Costs	Manage Project Team	Project Plan
Administer Procurements	Control Schedule	Manage Project	Plan Risk Responses
Acquire Project Team	Control Project Work	Distribute Information	Plan Procurements
Qualitative Risk Analysis	Control Risks	Conduct Procurements	Plan Quality
Quantitative Risk Analysis	Create WBS	Estimate Costs	Plan Communications
Perform Quality Assurance	Define Activities	Estimate Durations	Plan Risk Management
Close Procurements	Define Scope	Estimate Resources	Collect Requirements
Close Project	Develop Schedule	Manage Stakeholder	Sequence Activities
Control Scope	Develop Project Team	Identify Stakeholders	Verify Scope
Perform Quality Control	Develop Human Resource Plan	Identify Risks	
Change Control	Determine Budget	Report Performance	

This page is blank in case you cut the previous page

📖 <u>Exercise 3.1 – Processes Puzzle</u>

1. Find a big table or space where you can put the puzzle pieces.

2. Cut the pieces along with the process groups and put in 5 columns.

| INITIATING | PLANNING | EXECUTING | CONTROLLING | CLOSING |

3. Cut the pieces with the 9 knowledge areas and put them in 9 rows.

| INTEGRATION |

| SCOPE |

...

...

...

| PROCUREMENT |

4. Cut the 42 processes. Note: to simplify some processes may not be named exactly as in the PMBOK® Guide.

5. Put each process in its correct location using the following table aid.* The planning processes should be one below the other in chronological order.

	Initiating	Planning	Executing	Controlling	Closing
Integration	1	1	1	2	1
Scope		3		2	
Time		5		1	
Cost		2		1	
Quality		1	1	1	
Human Resources		1	3		
Communications	1	1	2	1	
Risks		5		1	
Procurement		1	1	1	1
TOTAL	**2**	**20**	**8**	**10**	**2**

6. ✋ Take 20 minutes to answer. After seeing the answer, repeat the game without the table aid as many time as necessary until you put all pieces in the right place.

<u>Note</u>: this game is an adaptation of Rita Mulcahy´s PMP® Exam Prep book.

Answer Exercise 3.1 *

	Initiating	Planning	Executing	Controlling	Closing
Integration	. Project Charter	. Project Management Plan	. Manage Project	. Control project work . Change Control	. Close Project
Scope		. Collect requirements . Define Scope . Create WBS		. Verify Scope . Control Scope	
Time		. Define Activities . Sequence Activities . Estimate Resources . Estimate Durations . Develop Schedule		. Control Schedule	
Cost		. Estimate Costs . Determine Budget		. Control Costs	
Quality		. Plan Quality	. Perform Quality Assurance	. Control Quality	
Human Resources		. Develop Human Resource Plan	. Acquire Project Team . Develop Project Team . Manage Project Team		
Communic.	. Identify Stakeholders	. Plan Communications	. Distribute Information . Manage stakeholder	. Report Performance	
Risks		. Plan Risk . Identify Risks . Qualitative Risk Analysis . Quantitative Risk Analysis . Plan Risk Responses		. Control Risks	
Procurement		. Plan Procurements	. Conduct Procurements	. Administer Procurements	. Close Procurements
TOTAL	2	20	8	10	2

* Project Management Institute, Ibidem.

At this point you might be asking yourself: What is the meaning of each of these 42 processes? To get this answer you must read carefully the rest of the chapters. In the meantime, we will continue with the general development of the 5 process groups.

Initiating Process Group

What things do you think you need before starting a project?

✋ Take5 minutes to think about this answer before moving on.

According to the PMBOK® Guide the <u>inputs</u> to these initiating processes are the following:

↓ **Enterprise environmental factors**: culture, systems, human resources, etc.

> ✎ *The enterprise environmental factors are a type of backpack that the PM should aware of in order to have a successful project.*

↓ **Organizational process assets**: policies, <u>processes</u>, norms, historical information and lessons learned

> ✎*The organizational process assets are very useful in not having to reinvent the wheel.*

↓ **Project statement of work** from the sponsor or client

↓ **A contract or business case**

The following are other <u>inputs</u> to consider before starting a project:

↓ **Strategic plan:** how does the project fit in the overall strategy

↓ **Industry standards**

↓ **Project triggers:** problem, market opportunity, business requirement, change in technology, legislation, etc.

↓ **Description of product or service**

↓ **Stakeholders**

After these inputs, different tools and techniques are applied, that we will see later on, that allow us to obtain the following <u>outputs</u>:

↗ **Project charter**

↗ **Stakeholder** register and stakeholder management strategy

Although these are the two outputs that the PMBOK® Guide mentions, we should also consider the following <u>outputs</u> from the initiating process group:

↗ Preliminary **objectives**

↗ **Project Manager**

↗ **Formal authorization** to proceed with the planning process group

> ✎ *Top management should participate in the initiating process group activities.*

📖 Exercise 3.2 – Initiating

Which of the following items do you perform during the initiation of a project? Assume that you are a top management position within an Enterprise.

Create a clear and easy to understand statement of work	
Define the project organizational structure	
Define the deliverables acceptance criteria	
Define the project and product objectives, explicitly stating what is in scope and out of scope	
Document the business need (or problem to solve)	
Document the preliminary risks identified	
Document assumptions and constraints	
Develop the project charter including the project manager and the level of authority assigned	
Identify stakeholders, their level of influence and associated risks	
Identify organization´s current processes and standards	

Score:

Add up how many of these activities you currently perform:
        0-5: bad start, you will most likely run into issues
        6-8: so, so... still have to improve the project start
        9-10: very good, as long as the project charter is included

Planning Process Group

Planning will determine if the project scope is feasible. If feasible, planning will detail how the project will be conducted in order to achieve its objectives. Planning is gradual, making this process group repetitive and iterative.

The planning process group covers the highest quantity of processes. The following figure summarizes the 20 planning processes and their relationship.

Planning Process Group

Develop the Project Management Plan

Collect Requirements → Define Scope → WBS → Activities → Sequence → Duration → Schedule

WBS → Resources

Resources, 1. Cost 2. Budget, Human Resources, Quality, Communications, Procurement

Risks:
1. Plan
2. Identify
3. Qualitative An.
4. Quantitative An.
5. Response Plan

Iteration

✎ *A good plan is the key of a successful project, and it requires the participation of various team members!*

📖 Exercise 3.3 – Planning

In the following table mark the things you do when you plan a project.

Approval of the "final" plan by the sponsor, team and functional managers	
Create the work breakdown structure (WBS) and define each work package in the WBS dictionary	
Define roles and responsibilities of each team member	
Detail each WBS work package in an activity list	
Develop the schedule and budget along with the project team	
Develop the baselines (scope, time, cost, quality) and confirm with the project team that the objectives can be achieved	
Determine which of the 42 project management processes will be used	
Determine the quality standards and establish quality metrics	
Manage risks: identification, qualitative and quantitative analysis, response plan	
Plan how the project performance will be evaluated	
Plan the stakeholder communication needs	
Prepare the purchasing and acquisition documents	
Meet with management to negotiate resources	
Collect project requirements before starting planning	

Score:

0-7: bad plan, you will hardly have a successful project
8-13: mediocre plan, good opportunity for improvement
14: very good, you are ready for the execution of the project

Executing Process Group

The majority of the budget is invested in the executing process group. In this stage the PM has a proactive role to perform, among others, the following activities:

✓ Implement the project management plan
✓ Coordinate all processes
✓ Ensure that the product complies with the expected quality
✓ Acquire, develop and manage the project team
✓ Distribute the project progress information
✓ Manage the stakeholder expectations
✓ Perform the procurements of any required goods and services for the project

In the following figure the 8 executing processes are summarized.

Executing Process Group

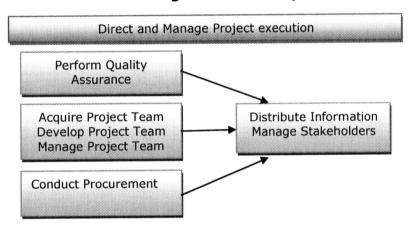

📖 Exercise 3.4 – Executing

In the following table mark the things you do when you direct and manage a project.

Ensure that all workers understand the work and have the necessary skills, information, and equipment to complete the tasks	
Focus your efforts in preventing problems and not in resolving them	
Concentrate on the exceptions and not in small details	
Distribute the information	
Document lessons learned	
Manage stakeholder expectations and communications channels	
Implement recognition and incentive programs	
Implement contingency plans	
Implement quality assurance processes	
Leadership, negotiation, facilitation, coaching, <u>COMUNICATION</u>	
Produce progress reports and recommend changes and corrective actions	
Hold coordination meetings	
Reconfirm resource availability with management	
Solicit vendor proposals and review them	
Use an integrated change control and authorization system	

Score:

0-10: you are probably not a PM
11-14: PM in development
15: a true PM

Monitoring and Controlling Process Group

In the monitoring and controlling process group the PM must ensure that only approved changes are implemented.

This is a continuous feedback process that allows to detect preventive actions and to recommend corrective actions.

> ✎ Except for the human resources knowledge area, all other knowledge areas are controlled.

The following figure summarizes the 10 monitoring and controlling processes.

Monitoring and controlling process group

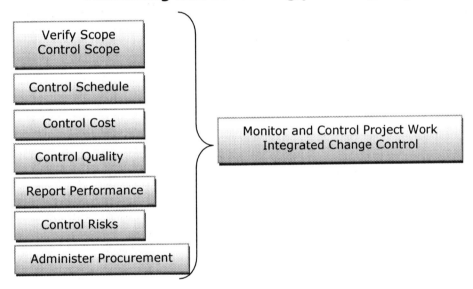

> ✎ *This is one of the worst scoring areas in the exam.*

📖 <u>Exercise 3.5 – Monitoring and controlling</u>

In the following table mark the things you do to monitor and control your projects.

Manage the cost and time contingency reserves	
Manage the contracts	
Ensure that only approved changes that passed through the integrated control change process are implemented	
Take time to improve quality and maintain periodic inspections	
Periodically elaborate schedule and cost estimate at completion	
Evaluate the effectiveness of the risk response plans	
Evaluate variations against the plan and recommend corrective actions	
Identify problem root causes	
Maintain progress meetings	
Recommend repairs, preventive actions, and corrective actions	
Inform all stakeholders of the project progress	
Use quality control tools	
Use conflict resolution tools	
Use earned value	
Verify project deliverables with the sponsor or client	

<u>Score</u>:

0-10: surely you will not have a successful project
11-14: need to continue to monitor and control
15: Excellent!

> ☺ *Control everything, given that the eye of the owner fattens the livestock!*

Closing Process Group

The two closing processes are: close procurements and close project or phase.

✎ *Every project that starts needs to be closed.*

In the closing of the procurements or external closing, you seek the formal acceptance from the client of the deliverables.

In the project closing, you perform activities for the administrative closing activities or internal closing, such as:
- ✓ Reintegrate the resources that no longer will be used
- ✓ Archive all of the information with indexes that facilitate their future utilization
- ✓ Document the lessons learned
- ✓ Celebrate!

✎ *During the exam the project closing questions are relatively easy*

📖 <u>Exercise 3.6 – Closing</u>

In the following table mark the things you do in the closing stage of your projects.

Update the process and procedures of the enterprise based on lessons learned	
Add the acquired skills to the team members registers	
Archive project registers with index to find information effectively in the future	
Close the contract obtaining final acceptance (sign-off) from the client	
Confirm that all the project requirements were met	
Create and distribute the final report	
Document lessons learned	
Celebrate the end of the project	
Measure client satisfaction	
Reintegrate resources	

<u>Score:</u>

0-5: in your next project you will make the same mistakes
6-9: you should improve closing your projects
10: Excellent! Your next similar project will be much better!

Principal Processes

If you want to pass your PMP® Exam it is very important that you study the inputs, tools and techniques, and the outputs for each of the 42 processes. In the following exercise we selected the processes that are repeated more often in the exam to force you to think in the principal inputs and outputs.

📖 Exercise 3.7 – Principal Processes

Complete the inputs and outputs in the following table for each process.

Process	Inputs	Outputs
Develop the plan		
Collect requirements		
Define Scope		
Define Activities		
Sequence Activities		
Estimate Resources		
Develop Schedule		
Plan Procurements		
Direct and Manage Project Execution		
Conduct Procurements		
Verify Scope		

✋ Take 20 minutes to complete the inputs and outputs of each process.

Answer Exercise 3.7

Process	Inputs	Outputs
Develop the plan	Project Charter	Project Management Plan
Collect requirements	Stakeholders	Requirements Requirements Traceability
Define Scope	Requirements	Statement of Work
Define Activities	Scope Statement	Activity list and milestones
Sequence Activities	Activity List	Network Diagrams
Estimate Resources	Activity List Resource Availability	Resource Requirements Resource Breakdown Structure
Develop Schedule	Activity List Network Diagrams Resource Requirements Resource Availability Activity Durations	Schedule
Plan Procurements	WBS Requirements Teaming agreements Risk Register Schedule Budget	Procurements Plan Statement of Work Make vs. Buy decision Procurement documents Selection criteria Change requests
Direct and Manage Project Execution	Project Management Plan Approved Change Requests	Deliverables Progress Reports Change Requests Updates
Conduct Procurements	Procurements Plan Procurement documents Selection criteria Qualified vendors Vendor proposals Make vs. Buy decision Change Requests	Selected vendors Contract adjudication Resource Availability Change Requests Updates
Verify Scope	WBS Requirements Traceability Validated Deliverables	Accepted Deliverables Change Requests Updates

☞ *Some inputs and outputs have not been included for these processes. Study from the PMBOK® Guide what's missing from each process.*

Exam 3 – Processes

> **Number of questions**: 15
> **Time to answer**: 15 minutes
> **Passing Score**: 80% (12 correct answers)

1. The Project Manager is explaining to the project team members the processes that will be used in the project life cycle of the next project. An engineer, expert on quality matters, refuses to apply these processes and in their place recommends the Shewart-Deming (Plan-Do-Check-Act). What could be the response of the project manager to this person?
   A. Those processes are similar to the ones I am proposing
   B. With those quality processes the project will not be effective
   C. It is mostly recommended to always use PMBOK® Guide processes
   D. I recommend that you get your PMP® certification to get a more general vision of the subject

2. There are only a few days left for the project to start. You don't have much time to continue to improve the planning process. What is the minimum that you must ensure before you start executing?
   A. That the project charter is completed
   B. Document all known risks before documenting the general assumptions
   C. Finalize the quality assurance before determining the quality metrics
   D. Create a list of activities before the creation of a network diagram

3. A multinational company is evaluating the alternative of constructing a new 85 floor building in the next few years. While elaborating the project management plan, the project team, usually, will be LESS involved in the creation of the following:
   A. Budget
   B. Plan to distribute the information
   C. Risk management plan
   D. Schedule

4. The sponsor is about to start the initiating process for an agricultural project. All of the following items are necessary before starting this project, EXCEPT for:
   A. Statement of Work
   B. Industry standards
   C. The Project Manager
   D. Business Requirement

5. During the planning stage the project manager requests to the project team to report on the percent complete of the tasks they are performing. One team member replies that he is not able to provide what is requested. What could be the root cause of this problem?
    A. The project manager did not obtain the formal authorization from the functional manager to use that resource
    B. The project does not have a proper recognition program to motivate the employees and facilitate their cooperation
    C. The project manager did not define the work packages
    D. The team member is not skilled to be in this team

6. The project manager is working with his team in the planning stage for a construction project of an industrial park. They are about to start the network diagram. Which of the following items is not necessary for this process?
    A. Activity durations
    B. Project scope statement
    C. Activity list
    D. List of milestones

7. The project manager and his project team were involved in the initiating process for a construction project of a hydroelectric power station for three months. After carefully identifying the stakeholders, the initiating process has been completed. Identify what just finished and what is about to start:
    A. Project management plan / Project execution
    B. Project charter / Project planning
    C. Project execution / Monitor and control the project
    D. Project charter / Project execution

8. You are executing a vehicle replacement project with a significant delay. What is needed to start?
    A. Approved changes
    B. Deliverables
    C. Progress Reports
    D. Update the project management plan

9. The client delivered the project scope statement. What is the next step?
    A. Complete the work packages
    B. Execute the project management plan
    C. Complete the scope verification
    D. Integrated change control

10. All of the following items are part of the monitoring and controlling process group EXCEPT:
    A. Verify scope
    B. Report performance
    C. Perform quality assurance
    D. Administer procurements

11. What are the project management process groups?
    A. Requirements, Development, Tests, Control
    B. Initiating, Planning, Executing, Monitoring and Controlling, Closing
    C. Initiating, Planning, Executing, Tests, Closing
    D. Initiating, Planning, Directing, Closing

12. Which of the following process requires the most iteration?
    A. Planning process group
    B. Administer procurements
    C. Closing process group
    D. Communications plan

13. Why is it so important that the stakeholders participate in the different project processes?
    A. Avoid scope changes
    B. Improve the probability of a satisfied client
    C. Determine the scope
    D. Serves for an effective communication

14. You are working in an oil well digging project. Along with your project team, you have just completed the initial project schedule and budget. The next thing to do is:
    A. Identify and quantify risks
    B. Determine the communication requirements
    C. Plan purchases and acquisitions
    D. Create the Gantt chart

15. The project team is executing a network installation project. Since the project started the team has been diligent in doing a periodic monitoring and controlling of the work. What will be the result of this process?
    A. Change requests
    B. Project management plan
    C. Information about the project performance
    D. Organizational process assets

Lessons Learned

- ✓ Organizational process assets
- ✓ Inputs and outputs
- ✓ Enterprise environmental factors
- ✓ Process interaction level
- ✓ Plan-do-check-act
- ✓ Closing process group
- ✓ Executing process group
- ✓ Initiating process group
- ✓ Planning process group
- ✓ Monitoring and Controlling process group

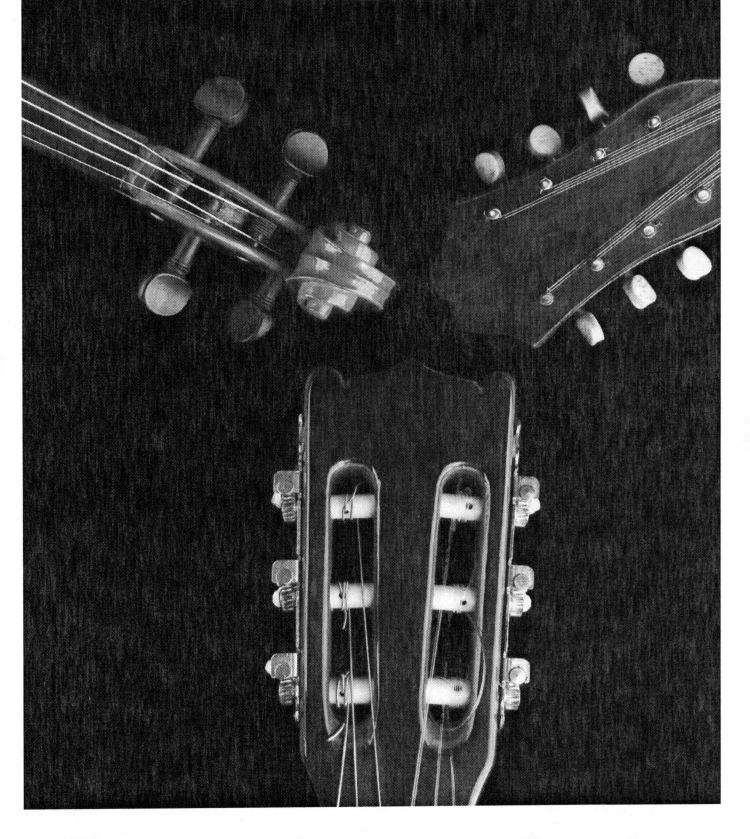

CHAPTER #4
INTEGRATION

Chapter 4 - INTEGRATION

> *No man is an island, entire of itself; every man is a piece of the continent, a part of the <u>main</u>.*
> John Donne (1572-1631) English poet.

Starting with this chapter we will develop the different knowledge areas of project management. In each of these areas we will see different processes. In this chapter we will study Project Integration Management.

At the end of the chapter you should have learned the following concepts:
- ✓ Project selection methods
- ✓ Project charter
- ✓ Project management plan
- ✓ Direct and manage project execution
- ✓ Monitor and control project work
- ✓ Integrated change control
- ✓ Close project

Project Initiation

In many organizations, the project manager does not participate on the selection of the projects that will be undertaken. Senior management or the Program/Portfolio Manager could be the ones applying some selection criteria to choose within different available projects.

The following are some tools that may be used for the selection of projects:

✂ **Benefit Measurement Methods**: scoring models, benefit contribution, economic model (Net Present Value, Internal Rate of Return), etc.

📖 <u>Exercise 4.1 – Project selection by benefit measurement</u>

You have to choose between three project alternatives (A, B, C) to diversify your company's products. You will apply a benefit measurement model including different criteria to be used for the selection.

The criteria to evaluate for the selection of the project are the following:
- 1st – Profitability using the Internal Rate of Return (the most important)
- 2nd – Market share increment (very important)
- 3rd – Improvements in company image (important)
- 4th – Gain new knowledge (low importance)

The Finance team has determined that the internal rate of return (IRR) is excellent in alternatives B and C, and very good in A.

The Marketing department estimates that the increment in market share is excellent in alternatives A and C, and very good in B.

General Management informed that the overall improvement in the image of the company is very good in alternatives C and D, and good in A.

The Human Resources management team said that the acquisition of new knowledge is excellent in alternatives A and B, and good in C.

Which project would you select as the best alternative? Why?

🖐 Take 10 minutes to solve this exercise.

Answer to Exercise 4.1

First, company directors should assign a relative weight to each criterion that they want to measure, based on their priorities. For example:

1st – Profitability = 40%
2nd – Market Share = 30%
3rd – Image = 20%
4th – New Knowledge = 10%

The sum of all these weights must be 100% and in our example, the relative weight of "profitability" must be greater than "market share", "market share" greater than "image", and "image" greater than "new knowledge".

In addition, a numeric scale should be assigned to each score. For example:

Excellent = 5
Very Good = 4
Good = 3
Not so good = 2
Bad = 1

Finally, a table like the following can be utilized to calculate the weighted average for each project by multiplying the relative weight for each criterion by its score.

CRITERIA	Weight	Project A		Project B		Project C	
		Score	Points	Score	Points	Score	Points
1st Profitability	40%	4	1.6	5	2.0	5	2.0
2nd Market Share	30%	5	1.5	4	1.2	5	1.5
3rd Company Image	20%	3	0.6	4	0.8	4	0.8
4th New Knowledge	10%	5	0.5	5	0.5	3	0.3
TOTAL	100%		4.2		4.5		**4.6**

In this example, we should select Project C because it has the greatest weighted average (4.6 points).

Note: The company could create a policy where a project with a criterion of "not so good" or "bad" cannot be selected, independently of its weighted average.

✂ **Mathematical models**: linear programming, integer programming, dynamic programming, multi-objective programming, etc.

📖 **Exercise 4.2 – Project selection with linear programming**

Your company is analyzing 7 investment projects that are mutually exclusive. Each project has an IRR that is greater than the company's opportunity cost, making each one a good project to implement. However, the company does not have enough funds to invest in all of them.

What would be the optimum project portfolio if you only have $4,700 to invest?

Project	Investment ($)	NPV
A	1,000	307
B	300	155
C	1,500	367
D	800	76

Project	Investment ($)	NPV
E	1,600	360
F	2,200	152
G	400	133

Note: Do not waste your time working with this response. Proceed directly to the answer below.

Answer to Exercise 4.2

To search for the optimum project combination we will construct an argument of linear programming with an objective subject to restrictions. For this, we will utilize a tool called "Solver", which is an add-in in the Excel software.

Objective: Maximize the summation of the project's NPVs

Restrictions:
- The total investment must be less or equal to $4,700
- You cannot have a partial project
- You cannot repeat the same project

Later, hundreds of iterations are performed on the Solver tool and the following optimum project portfolio is obtained: A, B, C, and E.

Project	Investment ($)	NPV	Variable	Investment ($)	NPV*
A	1,000	307	1	1,000	307
B	300	155	1	300	155
C	1,500	367	1	1,500	367
D	800	76	-	-	-
E	1,600	360	1	1,600	360
F	2,200	152	-	-	-
G	400	133	-	-	-
TOTAL	**7,800**	**1,550**		**4,400**	**1,189**

With the optimum project portfolio, the total investment is $4,400 with an aggregated NPV of $1,189.

It is not the objective of this book to go into details about the utilization of the Solver tool, but you could verify that with any other combination of projects and with the same restrictions, the sum of the NPV will be lower.

> ✍ The PM may not have to deal with the project selection processes; this is something that is usually done by top management.

Integration Processes

No matter what the company's motive to embark in a new project, to be successful, it is important to have a PM with a holistic vision of all parts of the project.

A project's integrated vision

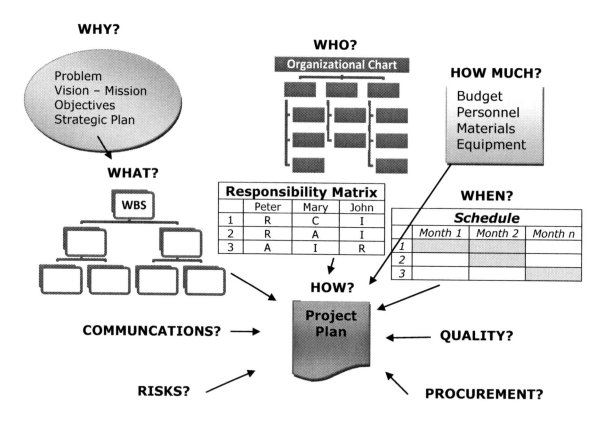

What is the main role of the **PM**?

... the **sponsor role**? and ... the **project team role**?

- PM's Role: Manage the project's integration and communicate to the stakeholders.

- Sponsor's Role: Avoid unnecessary changes and protect the project's resources.

- Project Team's Role: Complete the work per the project management plan.

We will develop the six processes of the PMBOK® Guide´s Project Integration Management that are distributed within the different process groups, as is shown on the following table.

Integration Processes *

Integration	Initiating	Planning	Executing	Controlling	Closing
	Develop Project Charter	Develop Project Management Plan	Direct and Manage Project Execution	. Monitor and Control Project Work . Perform Integrated Change Control	Close Project or Phase
Scope		3		2	
Time		5		1	
Cost		2		1	
Quality		1	1	1	
Human Resources		1	3		
Communications	1	1	2	1	
Risks		5		1	
Procurement		1	1	1	1
TOTAL	2	20	8	10	2

The six processes for the Project Integration Management are:
1. Develop Project Charter (Initiation)
2. Develop Project Management Plan (Planning)
3. Direct and Manage Project Execution (Executing)
4. Monitor and Control Project Work (Monitoring and Controlling)
5. Perform Integrated Change Control (Monitoring and Controlling)
6. Close Project or Phase (Closing)

Project Integration Management

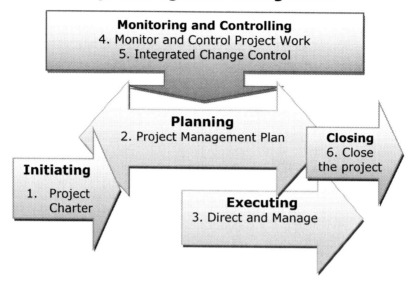

> ✍ A good PM has a holistic vision and it does not allow a tree to hide the forest.

Project Charter

What do we need to start developing the project charter?

- ↓ Enterprise environmental factors
- ↓ Organizational process assets
- ↓ Project statement of work (SOW)
- ↓ Business case: commercial need, unsatisfied demand, technology change, legal requirements, etc.
- ↓ Contract (if one exists)

The enterprise environmental factors (culture, systems, human resources, etc.) and the organizational process assets (policies, processes, rules, historical information, and lessons learned), are inputs needed for all the processes in the Planning process group. From this point forward, we will simply call them "environment" and "assets".

> ✍ The "environment" is the weight that the PM receives before planning and the "assets" are necessary to not re-invent the wheel.

> 👆 *The majority of the processes in the PMBOK® Guide requires "environment" and "assets" as inputs; therefore, we will not repeat these concepts for the rest of this book.*

With these inputs, we will apply the following <u>tool or technique</u>:

✂ **Expert judgment**: Experience given by people with specialized knowledge.

> 👆 *The majority of the processes in the PMBOK® Guide includes expert judgment as a tool; therefore this tool will not be mentioned again in all the processes of this book.*

As a result of the inputs and tool mentioned up to this point, the following output is obtained:

↗ **Project Charter:** document that formalizes the existence of the project and authorizes the PM to utilize organizational resources in the project activities.

This written document, in general, includes the following:
- ✓ Project justification: problem, opportunity, business requirement, etc.
- ✓ Measureable objectives and criteria for success
- ✓ General requirements
- ✓ General description of the project
- ✓ Preliminary risks
- ✓ Summary of schedule of milestones
- ✓ Summarized preliminary budget
- ✓ Acceptance criteria: What criteria must be met for the project to be successful? Who approves and signs if these criteria are met?
- ✓ Project Manager, responsibility, and level of authority
- ✓ Stakeholders
- ✓ Name of the sponsor and the level of authority that will sign the project charter

> ✎ *If there is no Project Charter, the project does not exist. The Project Charter should be generic, so it does not have to be modified anytime there are changes in the project.*

The following are two examples of a Project Charter.

Project Charter 1

MEMORANDUM
Date: 09-15-2010
Re: GSoft Implementation

To: General Managers
From: Vice-Presidents

After many months of negotiation, it is a pleasure to announce that our important client COLALESS Corp. has finally decided to hire our professional services for the Project.

As you can imagine, this is an excellent opportunity for our company and as usual, we are obligated to provide our best service to our client.

To be able to execute this important project, I have assigned John Lucky as Project Manager, reporting the project status directly to me.

I have given Mr. Lucky enough authority to administer all the necessary activities to comply with our contractual obligations. He will be responsible for managing the project deliverables on time and within budget.

The other key managers in the project team will be Marcel Pyme (Marketing), Giuseppe Franceschini (Commercialization), and Ane Giubetich (Finance).

The planning revision will be done within 60 days and its main objective will be the Project Plan's final approval. On that date I will approve the necessary budget, under the supervision of Mr. Lucky, in order to proceed to the next project phase.

Congratulations to all of you who made this possible. I request your unconditional support to Mr. Lucky and his project team in this great commercial opportunity.

Our client is confident about our products and professionals, just as I am confident that all of you will make it possible to complete this project on time and within budget. Let's get to work!

Mark Lang
President

> ✎ The most important thing about the Project Charter is mentioning who the PM is and its level of authority.

Project Charter 2

DATE: June 3rd, 2012

PROJECT NAME: PMI Tour Cono Sur 2012 - Mendoza

PROJECT JUSTIFICATION:
Promulgate the project management profession in Mendoza
Develop a new value added activity in the region

STRATEGIC OBJECTIVES:
Service: provide a value added service to PMI members
Recognition: the Chapter will be recognized as the organizational leader in Project Management in the region.

SUCCESS CRITERIA:
Minimum number of participants = 500
Minimum global score on satisfaction survey = 80%

HIGH LEVEL REQUIREMENTS
PMI Director to perform as the opening speaker and leadership meeting
Logistics support by company specialized in accreditations

PROJECT'S HIGH LEVEL DESCRIPTION
Networking opportunity with PMI's greatest authorities
30 international speakers covering current topics
Outdoor team work to maximize business relations

HIGH LEVEL RISKS

Identified Risk	*Preliminary Response Plan*
Speakers do not arrive	Have backup speakers in place
Poor volunteer dedication	Hire staff for the event
Not enough working capital	Cut setting and dining expenses

SUMMARY OF MILESTONE SCHEDULE
05-15-12: Signed contract with event location
07-15-12: Project management plan
11-10-12: Event execution
11-30-12: Finalize lessons learned document

BUDGET SUMMARY
Estimated income = $75,000; Estimated expenses = $60,000

REQUIREMENTS FOR PROJECT APPROVAL
Deliver lessons learned document to the Program Manager within 15 days after the event. The document must explain the achievement or non-achievement of success criteria.

PROJECT MANAGER AND LEVEL OF AUTHORITY
Project Manager: Paul Leido
Selects team members.
Approves: schedule, budget and communication plans.
Responsible for: agenda, logistics, sponsors, and project management.

Greg Bales (Program Manager)

Project Management Plan

Developing the project management plan is a planning process that requires many iterations and interrelations with the different knowledge areas in order to be completed.

What do I need to start?

↓ Project Charter

↓ Outputs from the other planning processes: requirements management plan, project scope statement, WBS, schedule, budget, quality management plan, human resource plan, communications plan, risk management plan, and procurement management plan.

What tools can I use?

✂ Expert judgment:

- Define the management methodology, **process** and tools necessary for a successful project. All the tools found in this book!

- Determine resources and project documents

- Establish the **PMIS** (Project Management Information System): automated system that includes all the tools that are utilized to gather and process information, report project status, and integrate project processes along its life cycle. For example: hardware, software, processes, dashboards, etc.

Project Management Information Systems

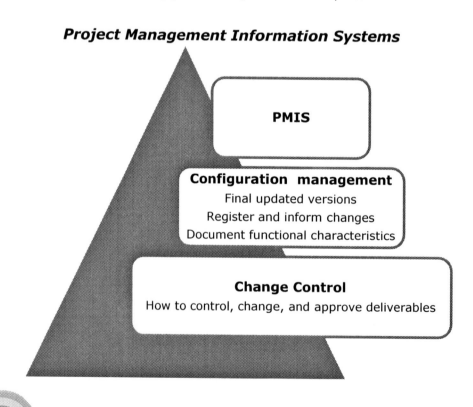

PMIS

Configuration management
Final updated versions
Register and inform changes
Document functional characteristics

Change Control
How to control, change, and approve deliverables

A sub-system of the PMIS is the **configuration management system**, where is explicitly specified how a product or service's functional and physical characteristics will be identified and documented; how changes will be controlled and informed; and how to verify that the product or service meets the requirements.

A sub-system of the configuration management system is the **change control system**, where is formally specified how project deliverables will be controlled, changed, and approved.

Another PMIS sub-system is the **work authorization system**. This system specifies the procedures for notifying the team or contractors when they should start the work. The objective is to perform the work in the right sequence and with the assigned time.

What do I get at the end of the process?

↗ **Project Management Plan**

This project plan integrates all plans from the rest of the knowledge areas and usually includes the following:
- ✓ Project life cycle
- ✓ Processes to utilize in each project phase
- ✓ Tools and techniques to utilize
- ✓ How the work will be executed and controlled
- ✓ Change management plan
- ✓ How will the configuration management be performed
- ✓ Baselines: scope, time, cost, quality.
- ✓ Risk registry
- ✓ THE 8 PLANS: scope, time, cost, quality, human resources, communications, risks, and procurement.
- ✓ Assumptions and restrictions

> ☝ *The project management plan is the reason for the existence of PMs.*

📖 Exercise 4.3 – Project Management Plan

Which of the following items do you do during the development of the project management plan?

Present plan options to the Sponsor	
Negotiate the best resources with management	
Analyze the project's impact to other projects	
Analyze stakeholders' abilities	
Meet with the stakeholders to define their roles	
Inform the stakeholders which objectives cannot be met	
Make sure management approve the schedule	
Give workers the possibility to approve the final schedule	
Define report formats and communications plan	
Add contingency reserves: time and costs	

Score:

0-5: bad plan, surely you will have problems during execution
6-8: not too bad, you can improve planning
9-10: very good!

> ☝ *Every plan requires many ITERATIONS and the active participation of the project team.*

The following scheme summarizes what we have seen until now.

Integrating from initiating until the project plan

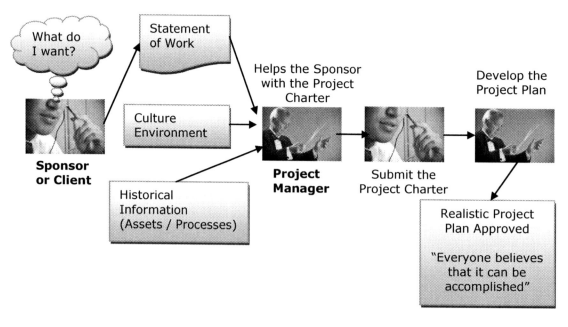

Direct and Manage Project Execution

During the process of direct and manage project execution, the PM and the work team will perform whatever is on the project management plan.

What do I need to start?

⬇ Project management plan

⬇ Approved change requests

What tools can I use?

✂ Project Management Information System (PMIS)

What do I get at the end of the process?

↗ Deliverables

↗ Work performance information: status report, schedule, costs, etc.

↗ Change requests sent to the Change Committee

↗ Updates to the Project Management Plan and Project Documentation

☝ *The PM should not approve changes; instead he can only request them to the Change Committee.*

Monitor and Control Project Work

The PM and other members of the project management team are responsible for monitoring and controlling project activities during all process groups.

> ☝ *Monitoring is observing what is happening in the project and Controlling is implementing corrective actions when something is not normal.*

What do I need to start?

⬇ Project management plan

⬇ Performance reports

What tools can I use?

✂ Expert judgment

What do I get at the end of the process?

↗ Updates

↗ Change requests sent to the Change Committee

> ☝ *The majority of the processes on the PMBOK® Guide have change requests as outputs, therefore these concepts will not be mentioned again in this book.*

Some of the suggested changes usually are **corrective actions** recommendations. The objectives of these actions are:
   ✓ Look for problems, instead of waiting for them to show up
   ✓ Have a realistic plan with updated baselines
   ✓ Find the root cause of a problem
   ✓ Return the project to its original plan (if necessary)

Other changes requested usually are **preventive actions** or requests to **repair defects** detected.

Corrective Actions Flowchart

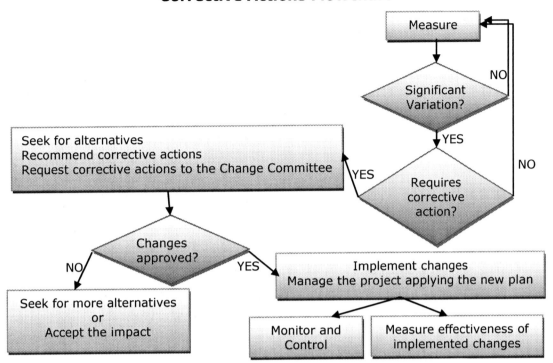

Integrated Change Control

The supervision and control of the project is the responsibility of the PM and its project management team. On the other hand, the process of integrated change control goes beyond the PM and it requires an integrated change committee.

This Change Committee can be composed of the following:
  - ✓ Sponsor (has vote)
  - ✓ Client (has vote)
  - ✓ Project Manager (no vote, only opinion)

This committee is the only one who can approve changes. The only exception to the rule would be in extreme cases where the PM could make emergency changes.

> ✎ *The process of Monitoring and Controlling is an "internal control", whereas the integrated change control is a type of "external control".*

It is practically impossible for a project to be executed exactly the same way as it was originally planned. Therefore, we should be flexible when managing changes in the project.

☺ *There are two main truths in life: all of us will die someday, and no project will be completed according to the original plan.*

What do I need to start?
- ↓ Project management plan
- ↓ Work performance information
- ↓ Change requests

What tools can I use?
- ✂ Change control meetings

What do I get at the end of the process?
- ↗ Approved/Rejected change requests
- ↗ Updates to the Project Management Plan and Project Documentation

Although changes are approved or rejected by the Change Committee, the PM must have a proactive role during the integrated change control. Some of the actions that the PM should perform during this process are:
- ✓ Inform stakeholders about the impact of the change to the triple constraint variables.
- ✓ Review all change recommendations and preventive actions.
- ✓ Reject any corresponding change request: those that are not aligned with the initial project objectives.
- ✓ Validate the repair of defects.
- ✓ Update the baselines and the project management plan.

🖎 *If a project is going through too many changes, you should ask yourself if a new project is preferable.*

? A stakeholder wants to increase the scope of the project. You estimate that this change will delay the project by 20 days. What is the next thing you should do?

    A. Look for alternatives to compress the agenda and include the change

    B. Ask the sponsor to approve the change

    C. Negotiate a time extension to include the change

    D. None of the above

Answer: D. Evaluate the impact of the change on the rest of the variables of the triple constraint: cost, quality, resources and risk.

    ✎ Approximately 5 questions on the exam deal with this type of question.

? A functional manager wants to make a change to the project. What are the next steps to follow?

Answer:

1st Evaluate the impact (Is it necessary? What is the effect on other variables?)

2nd Look for alternatives (compression, fast tracking, re-estimation)

3rd Get the approval from the Change Committee

4th Update the baseline and the plan

5th Notify the stakeholders

6th Manage the project according to the new plan

    ✎ The more advanced is the project, the more expensive will be the change.

Close Project or Phase

During this process, a project or phase is formally completed. The PM reviews the project information to make sure that nothing is pending and that the objectives defined in the scope are being met.

> ✏ *It does not matter why a project finishes... A project that finishes must be closed!*

What do I need to start?

- ⬇ Project management plan
- ⬇ Accepted deliverables

What tools can I use?

- ✂ Expert judgment

What do I get at the end of the process?

- ↗ Final product, service, or result transition
- ↗ Update project archives and historical information

The project closing phase is also called **administrative closure** or internal closure. Some of the typical activities of the project closure are:

- **Final project report**
  - ✓ Final budget
  - ✓ Final schedule
  - ✓ Archives index
  - ✓ Participant directory (vendors, consultants, executing and management team, etc.)
  - ✓ ARCHIVE all the documentation indexed, so it can be easily found in the future

- **Release project team**
  - ✓ Final evaluation of team members and the team as a whole
  - ✓ Update team member qualifications

- **Lessons learned**
  - ✓ What can we improve on our future projects?

Administrative Closure Survey

Client: Eli J Corp. Project Manager: Paul Leido		Start Date: 6-15-11 End Date: 12-20-13	
Project Scope	☐ Exceeded objectives	☐ Met objectives	☐ Not meet objectives
Due Dates	☐ Before schedule	☐ On time	☐ Delayed
Budget	☐ Less than estimated	☐ Within budget	☐ Greater than estimated
In general, the project was successful? Yes ☐ No ☐			

What was done well?

What could be improved?

What was done wrong?

What would you do different if you had to work on the same project?

What recommendations would you make for future projects?

⁺C
MasConsulting

Summarizing Integration

In the following figure we summarize the main outputs, inputs, and interrelations of the Integration Management processes.

Project Integration

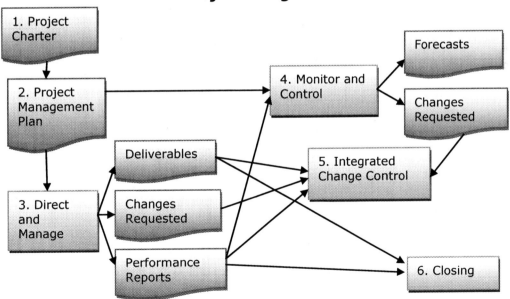

Exam 4 – Integration

Number of questions: 15
Time to respond: 15 minutes
Pass score: 80% (12 correct answers)

1. The project charter for the development of a premium wine has just been signed by a prestigious wine producer. This document has been formally accepted by the project manager and his project team, which have signed the document. In the project charter there is a description of the location where the project will be developed, as well as cost and time limitations. These descriptions of the project charter are:
   A. Assumptions
   B. Strategic plan
   C. Formal compromise of the stakeholders
   D. Restrictions

2. The main role for a sponsor committed with an aerospace project should:
   A. Prevent unnecessary changes and protect resources
   B. Integrate and communicate
   C. Identify unnecessary restrictions
   D. Collaborate with the project manager to develop the project management plan

3. Which of the following statements is a project restriction?
   A. Scope statement
   B. Contract
   C. Sponsor
   D. Project charter

4. The project manager and its team have defined the server, hardware, and software that will be utilized to document the functional characteristics of the product. This is part of what system?
   A. Change control
   B. Configuration management
   C. Work authorization
   D. Scope management

5. A software development company for commercial organizations is operating in a dynamic market. Which of the following changes should be the most important for the integrated change control committee? A change originated in _____:
   A. The contracting company that is developing the software
   B. The work team
   C. The scope of the project
   D. The market

6. There is an acquisition and merger project between two metallurgic companies. As the project manager, you need to establish the infrastructure needed to manage the communications. Which of the following systems or processes should be used in this case?
   A. Communications system
   B. Project management information system
   C. Work authorization system
   D. Communications planning

7. A project to build an industrial waste treatment plant is suffering too many changes to the project charter. Who is the main responsible to decide if those changes are necessary?
   A. The sponsor
   B. The project manager
   C. The main project stakeholder
   D. The stakeholders

8. The most important thing about the project charter is:
   A. Stakeholders are identified
   B. The project and its relation with the company's strategic plan is justified
   C. The return on investment is specified in detail
   D. The project manager is formally authorized to start with the planning processes

9. You have just finalized the planning processes in an engineering project. What are the tools that you will mostly use in the next phase?
   A. General management abilities, revision meetings, work authorization system
   B. Project management information system (PMIS), work breakdown structure (WBS), earned value management (EVM)
   C. General management abilities, revision meetings, earned value management (EVM)
   D. Work breakdown structure (WBS) and change control system

10. The sponsor is pressuring the project manager to deliver the project two weeks before the date agreed on the project management plan. What does the project manager have to do first?
    A. Look for alternatives to shorten the project's duration
    B. Get the approval from the change management committee
    C. Notify the sponsor about the new schedule and its impact on the cost
    D. Evaluate the impact

11. The following statements are part of the change control system in a small project, EXCEPT for:
    A. Procedures
    B. Lessons learned
    C. Rules
    D. Meetings

12. You have just arrived to the end of the project. Which of the following items is NOT part of the administrative closure process?
    A.   Reviewing deliverables with the Client
    B.   Update directory of qualified providers
    C.   Final evaluation of work team
    D.   Action item log to use for future projects

13. Which of the following items is NOT included in the configuration management for an organic coffee plantation project?
    A.   Identification of functional characteristics of a deliverable
    B.   Control changes on project deliverables
    C.   Validate the scope
    D.   Approve changes automatically

14. A work authorization system in the first phase of an investment project is utilized to manage:
    A.   When and in what sequence work will be performed
    B.   Who performs each activity
    C.   When each activity is finalized
    D.   Who performs each activity and when are finalized

15. During the execution of an image digitalization project, an integrated change control process is utilized. One of the outputs of this process is:
    A.   Work performance information
    B.   Update change request status
    C.   Change request
    D.   Project management methodologies

Lessons Learned

✓ Corrective actions
✓ Project charter
✓ Change committee
✓ Integrated change control
✓ Project selection methods
✓ Project management plan
✓ Work authorization system
✓ Change control system
✓ Project management information system
✓ Configuration management system
✓ Change request

> ✍ Study this chapter again when you finish the rest of the knowledge areas.

Chapter 5 - SCOPE

> *Minds of moderate caliber ordinarily condemn everything which is beyond their <u>range</u>.*
> François de la Rochefoucauld (1613-1680). French writer.

In this chapter we will study project scope management with the intent of defining <u>WHAT</u> work needs to get done to achieve a successful project.

When you finish this chapter, you will have learned the following concepts:
- ✓ Project scope vs. product scope
- ✓ Scope planning
- ✓ Scope management processes
- ✓ Collect requirements
- ✓ Define scope
- ✓ Work breakdown structure
- ✓ Verify scope
- ✓ Control scope

Project Scope vs. Product Scope

Generally project scope is confused with product scope. We could say that the project scope is broader than the product scope.

The **product scope** refers to the characteristics and functions of the product or service. For example, we want to produce a laptop that weights less than 1 lb., with 1,000 GB of hard disk, 40 GB of memory, and standalone battery for one year.

On the other hand, the **project scope** refers to defining all the processes and work needed to provide the product with all the required characteristics and functions. For example, define all the work and the processes that must be followed to have the computer on time including all their requirements.

Project and product scope

Scope planning

Scope planning is done during the process of developing the project management plan to define how the scope management processes will take place.

> ✎ *If you do not plan it, you will not be able to execute it!*

Remember that the project management plan requires iterations and interrelations with the different knowledge areas. When planning the scope, most probably the project management plan will have little detail, but at a minimum should have the following:
- ✓ Phases or project lifecycle
- ✓ Which processes and tools will be used in the project
- ✓ How configuration management will be done

> ✎ *Scope planning requires various <u>iterations</u>.*

As a result of scope planning we will get:

↗ **Project Scope Management Plan**

The scope management plan is a document explaining how:
- ✓ To prepare the scope statement
- ✓ To create and approve the WBS
- ✓ To perform scope verification
- ✓ To process and approve scope changes

> ✎ *The resources responsible for executing the tasks should participate in the elaboration of the scope management plan.*

Scope management processes *

To achieve a successful project we need to implement scope management processes that ensure that all the work, and only that work is performed.

> ✎ *We should deliver to the client what was requested, no more, no less!*

These processes will help us avoid adding changes that did not go through integrated change control and in this way prevent unsolicited work ("gold plating").

We will develop the five scope management processes that are distributed among the planning, and monitoring and controlling process groups as presented in the following table.

Scope Processes

	Initiation	Planning	Executing	Controlling	Closing
Integration	1	1	1	2	1
Scope		. Collect Requirements . Define Scope . Create WBS		. Verify Scope . Control Scope	
Time		5		1	
Cost		2		1	
Quality		1	1	1	
HR		1	3		
Communications	1	1	2	1	
Risks		5		1	
Procurements		1	1	1	1
TOTAL	**2**	**20**	**8**	**10**	**2**

The five scope management processes are:

1. **Collect requirements:** document the stakeholders' needs to convert them into project requirements.

2. **Define** scope: develop the detailed scope statement, the <u>what</u>.

3. Create **the work breakdown structure** (WBS): <u>decompose</u> the project in smaller pieces.

4. **Verify** scope: seek formal scope acceptance from the client or sponsor.

5. **Control** scope: manage scope changes.

* Project Management Institute, Ibidem.

Collect requirements

To be able to comply with the project objectives, it is necessary to define and document all the stakeholders' needs and expectations (sponsor, client, etc.).

> ✍ *Collecting and managing the requirements of the stakeholders is critical to achieve a successful project.*

The process of collecting requirements includes managing the client's expectations, which are the basis of the WBS.

What do I need to start?

⬇ Project charter and scope statement

⬇ Stakeholders registry

What tools can I use?

✂ **Interviews, questionnaires, surveys, observation**

✂ **Focus** groups: a moderator coordinates an interactive discussion among the key project stakeholders.

✂ **Work sessions** to define the product requirements: For example, in the software industry joint application development (JAD) sessions are performed. In the manufacturing industry they are known as quality function deployment (QFD).

✂ **Creativity** techniques: brainstorming, mind mapping, Delphi technique, etc.

   ✂ **Delphi** technique: the team members that will be interviewed are physically separated to minimize the interpersonal influences. The experts' opinions are processed by a general coordinator maintaining their involvement anonymous. The coordinator informs the reasons that justify the different opinions and requests that they re-evaluate their responses to deepen the analysis. This iterative feedback process continues until there are no more changes to make.

✂ Group **decision making** techniques: unanimity, majority (+50%), plurality (even if it does not reach 50%, the majority vote is selected), dictatorship (what the boss says).

✂ **Prototypes**: elaborate a tangible preliminary version of the final product to obtain early feedback about the project requirements. For example, 3D videos, mock ups, samples, etc.

> ✍ Usually, *the most difficult thing in the process of collecting requirements is to understand the blurry needs of the client during the initial phases. To mitigate this inconvenience the following is recommended:*
>   *1) Iterative feedback between designers and client*
>   *2) Preliminary prototypes (trial and error)*
>   *3) Involve upper management in the collection of requirements*
>   *4) Convert the team into pseudo clients (indwelling)*

What do I get at the end of the process?

↗ **Requirements documentation:** project justification, objectives, product functionality, quality, security, acceptance criteria, impact of the project in other areas, assumptions, constraints, etc.

Requirements documentation - Example

Project Name: **Chañares de la Luna**
Localization: Mendoza
Last Revision Date: 08-20-2012
Requirement: Hotel with wine cellars among vineyards
Requested by: Ray Schef (Sponsor)

1. **Justification**
   Attract investors of high income interested in wine tourism.
2. **Project objectives**
   Recover the investment in 5 years
   Achieve an annual internal rate of return of 30%
3. **Product objectives**
   Vineyards capable of producing high quality premium wines
   Hotel that respects the environment
4. **Functional requirements**
   Circular vineyards
   Hotel constructed with materials from the region: rock, wood, and clay
5. **Non-functional requirements**
   Biodynamic vineyards
   Bio-sustainable hotel
6. **Quality requirements**
   Organic certification for the vineyard
   4 stars category rural tourism hotel
7. **Acceptance criteria**
   Full production vineyards in 5 years
   Hotel opened to the public in 5 years
8. **Assumptions**
   Dollar inflation does not surpass 10% annually
   Current foreign tourists' tendency stays the same
9. **Constraints**
   The vineyards and hotel localization is the Uco Valley
   Existing laws do not allow clay construction

⊅ Requirements management plan: How will the requirements be documented and communicated? What will be the process to monitor and control requirements? Who will make changes to the requirements and how? How will the requirements be prioritized?

⊅ Requirements traceability matrix: table that links each requirement with its objective, to be able to monitor and control it, throughout the project lifecycle. In addition to linking each requirement with an objective, it usually includes a link with the strategy, scope and design.

Requirement card

#3	Requirement XXX
Date	
Version	
Description	
Justification	
Objective	
Responsible	
Priority	
Status (open, cancelled, deferred, approved)	
Due date	
Acceptance criteria	

Define scope

In the process of defining the scope we dig deeper in the level of detail of the project and product scope.

What do I need to start?

↓ Project charter

↓ Requirements documentation

What tools can I use?

✂ **Product Analysis**: analyze the established product objectives by the client or sponsor and convert them into tangible project requirements.

✂ **Brainstorming** to identify alternatives

✂ Work **Sessions**

What do I get at the end of the process?

↗ **Project Scope Statement**

The project scope statement defines the necessary deliverables and tasks to create those deliverables. It thoroughly details the deliverable description, analyzes whether the preliminary assumptions are valid, explains the project boundaries, etc.

Scope Statement - Example

Project Name: Chañares de la Luna
Last Revision Date: 10-15-2012
Prepared by: Paul Leido (Project Manager)

1. Brief project description
Chañares de la Luna is a project located in Mendoza, aimed at the world of wine tourism. The project consists of a hotel with a wine cellar inside a 50 acre landscape, with 30 acre planted to produce high quality wines.

2. Product scope
30 acre planted with malbec, cabernet franc and chardonnay varietals
8 acre to maintain Chañares forests, hotel, and recreation areas
Bio-sustainable concept hotel
2,400 meter square hotel distributed in 2 blocks: 1 principal area of 800 m^2 with dining room, living room, underground wine cellar, spa, swimming pool, and general services; and 16 rooms with 100 m^2 immersed within the vineyards.

3. Deliverables
Start-up: Business Plan, Web Page, brochures and presentations
Sub-projects: architectural, vineyards, forestation
Preliminary plan: Work breakdown structure, schedule, budget, responsibility matrix, communications plan, quality management plan, procurement management plan, risk response plan
Planted vineyards
Constructed and equipped hotel

4. Acceptance criteria
100 shares sold in the next 3 years
Full production vineyards in 5 years
Hotel opened to the public in 5 years

5. Exclusions
Wine club formation
Hotel administration

6. Assumptions
An exchange rate of Euros/Dollar of +/- 20% is maintained
Dollar inflation does not surpass 10% annually
The municipality authorizes the hotel construction
Current foreign tourists' tendency stays the same

7. Constraints
The vineyards and hotel localization is in the Uco valley
Existing laws do not allow clay constructions
Malbec plant must be requested 18 months in advance

8. Preliminary identified risks
Lack of shares sales, increment of country risk, anti-vineyard law, lack of electrical energy supply, weather change with increased hail-storms, road destruction by weather problems

9. Approval requirements:
Chañares de la Luna Corp CEO and CFO will approve the project deliverables. Any change in the preliminary scope defined in this document requires the sign-off of the CEO and CFO.

Create the Work Breakdown Structure

The process to create the work breakdown structure (WBS) consists of dividing the project in smaller components to facilitate the project planning.

In general, many organizations have the bad practice to skip this process while planning their projects and they start decomposing the project at the activity level, which does not help for a successful project.

What do I need to start?

↓ Scope statement

↓ Requirements documentation

What tools can I use?

✂ **Decomposition:** divide the project into smaller components

What do I get at the end of the process?

↗ **Work breakdown structure (WBS):** an organizational chart where the project is sub-divided into smaller components.

↗ **WBS dictionary**: where the WBS terms are explained

↗ **Scope baseline**: the scope statement, the WBS and its dictionary. What is not in here is not part of the project.

WBS Example

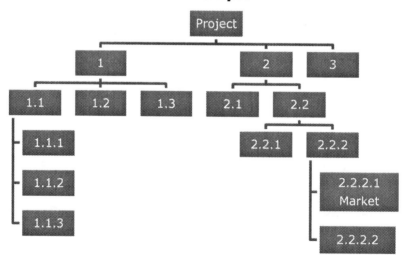

> ✎ *Work package:* the lowest division of the WBS. The grey boxes in the previous example.
>
> ✎ *Control accounts*: places in the WBS used to measure the progress of the scope, schedule, or costs. Each control account includes one or more work package.

The first WBS hierarchical level could be the project lifecycle. For example, in the oil sector the first level is usually displayed with the following division: feasibility, selection, definition, execution, and operation.

WBS - Oil Project Example

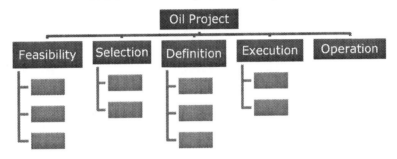

However, the WBS does not have any relation with the sequence of its components. For example, the following figures present WBS examples where the first hierarchical level does not have any relation with the lifecycle.

WBS – Tourism Program

> ✎ *The WBS does not include activities.*

WBS –Construction

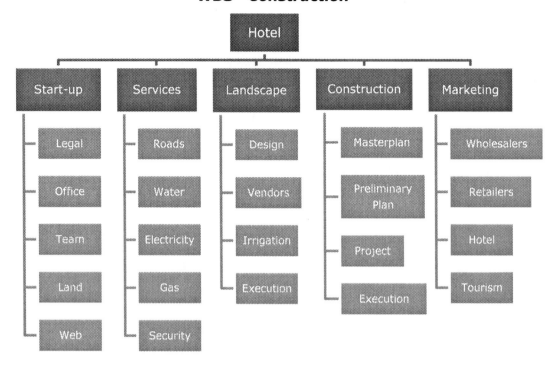

In how many levels should the project be decomposed?

It should be divided down to the level where the costs and schedule can be precisely estimated for each work package. However there is no need to go overboard with the subdivisions. The WBS is part of the plan and a plan is only useful if it gets implemented. Having too many divisions will not help in managing and control the project; therefore, it wouldn't be appropriate.

> ✍ *Divide the project in as many packages as needed and possible for a better management.*

Some **advantages** of using the WBS are:
- ✓ Have an integrated vision were the team quickly understands their place in the project
- ✓ Serve as the estimation basis for time, costs, human resources and risks
- ✓ Facilitate the communication
- ✓ Facilitate the integrated change control

> ✍ *The WBS creation is an excellent team building activity.*

The WBS does not have enough space to explain what each term means. Therefore, it is important to complement it with the WBS dictionary where the detailed terms for each component can be found.

WBS Dictionary - Example

Id # 2.2.2.1	Control Account # 2.2	Last Revision Date 7/15/12	Responsible Jess Gon
Description: Perform a market study research for natural juices				
Acceptance criteria: the report must contain at the minimum the imports from each United Kingdom country for the last 5 years				
Deliverables: multimedia presentation and a written report				
Assumptions: the client delivers the list of sales before 8/15/12				
Assigned resources: 2 analysts, 1 consultant and 3 notebooks				
Duration: 65 days				
Milestones: 08/15/13 – Preliminary report approved by the Sponsor 09/20/13 – Multimedia presentation to stakeholders 10/12/13 – Final report approved by the client				
Cost: $ 32,920				
Dependencies: Before #1.2.3 and after #3.4.1				
Project Manager´s Signature:				

Once the WBS is ready, the activities and tasks related with each component can be planned, like we will see in the next chapter.

📖 Exercise 5.1 – WBS

You are responsible to create the work breakdown structure for Program X. For this, you will need a lot of collaboration from the rest of the team. First, you divide the Program in four Projects and then you divide some of the Projects in other smaller components, as presented on the following table.

Program	Project	Components	Human resources	Estimated duration
X	1	1.1	30	30 days
		1.2	20	15 days
		1.3	10	15 days
	2	2.1	5	20 days
		2.2	15	10 days
	3	3.1	10	5 days
		3.2	10	5 days
	4		30	45 days

a) Draw the WBS for this program.
b) What would be the project duration?
c) Put real names to the projects and components, based on a real case that you are currently working on.

🖐 Take 15 minutes to solve this exercise.

Answer to Exercise 5.1

a) WBS for the Program

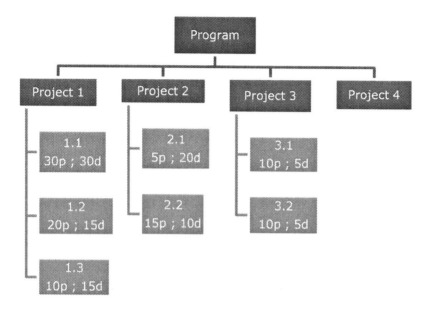

b) The WBS is not used to estimate the project duration. To estimate the project duration it will be necessary to identify the activities, sequence them, and estimate the resources and the duration for each activity. However, the WBS components can be used to approximately estimate resources and duration for each work package as it was presented in the WBS of point a). It serves to have a relative idea of the magnitude of each work package.

c) WBS for the construction project

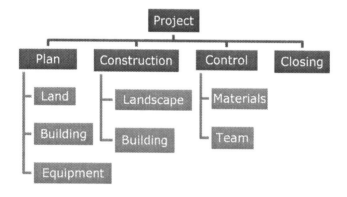

> 👆 Do not forget to complete this answer with the WBS of a personal project.

Verify scope

The process of verifying the scope is part of the Monitoring and Controlling process group. This process can be performed at the end of each project phase and should always be performed at the end of the project.

What do I need to start?

↓ **Requirements** documentation and its traceability matrix

↓ Scope statement, **WBS**, and WBS dictionary

↓ Validated **deliverables**

What tools can I use?

✂ **Inspections or audits**: validate that the deliverables meet the specifications and document the completion of each deliverable

What do I get at the end of the process?

↗ **Accepted deliverables** by the client and sponsor

↗ Change requests and updates

> ✎ *The main objective of verifying the scope is to ensure that each deliverable is being completed in a proper manner. Also, it is a proactive process that allows for recommending corrective actions before delivering the final product to the client.*

Control the scope

During verifying the scope it is ensured that the deliverables are being completed. On the other hand, the process of controlling the scope consists of ensuring that the deliverables defined in the project are being performed, no more no less.

What do I need to start?

↓ Plans: scope, changes, configuration, requirements

↓ Work performance reports

↓ Requirements and traceability matrix

What tools can I use?

✂ **Variation analysis**: study if the deviations in the scope, compared with the baseline, are significant enough to apply corrective actions.

What do I get at the end of the process?

➚ Work performance metrics

➚ Change requests

➚ Updates to the scope baseline and others

✎ *When managing scope changes it should be ensured that any modification is performed through the integrated change control.*

✎ *Scope corruption: when a scope change is performed without going through the integrated change control.*

Summarizing the scope

The following figure summarizes the main inputs, outputs, and interrelations of the scope management processes.

Integrating scope management

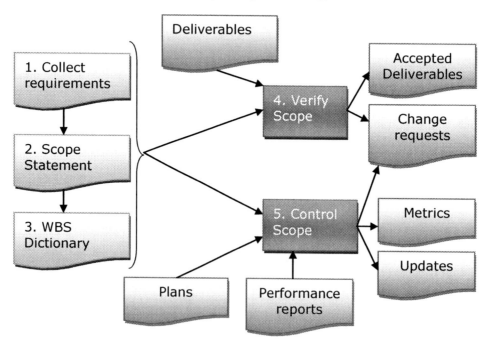

Exam 5 – Scope

> **Number of questions**: 15
> **Time to respond**: 15 minutes
> **Passing score**: 80% (12 correct answers)

1. What tools would you use during the verify scope process?
    A.   Observation
    B.   Variation analysis
    C.   Expert judgment
    D.   Inspection

2. Which of the following items has a higher hierarchy level within the WBS?
    A.   Activities
    B.   Work packages
    C.   Planning package
    D.   Control account

3. You are finalizing the process of creating the work breakdown structure. One of the results you will obtain from this process is to establish the scope baseline. The following statements are part of the scope baseline EXCEPT for:
    A.   Work breakdown structure (WBS)
    B.   Scope statement
    C.   WBS dictionary
    D.   Requirements documentation

4. In which of the following statements can be said that there was scope corruption:
    A.   The project manager studied the causes of the variation and discovered that the differences against the original plan are very significant
    B.   Features were added to the product without the authorization of the client or sponsor
    C.   The configuration management system had delays in the authorization of changes due to a system outage
    D.   While reviewing all the change requests corruption problems appeared

5. The project charter and the scope statement are finalized. The sponsor wants to start the planning processes as soon as possible. The project manager does not want to forget the importance of the verification process. When should the scope be verified?
    A.   When the sponsor defines the detailed scope statement
    B.   Before closing the contract
    C.   At the end of each project phase
    D.   When the main deliverable is complete

6. After finalizing the project charter for the development of a luggage transfer project in an airport, the project manager has been assigned. Also, the sponsor delivered the scope statement to the project manager. The first thing the project manager should do is:
   A.   Create the work breakdown structure (WBS)
   B.   Develop the detailed scope statement
   C.   Define the scope management processes
   D.   Check if the rest of the stakeholders know the scope statement

7. The project manager will use the work breakdown structure (WBS) during the project execution. What use will the WBS have?
   A.   Serve as the basis for the estimating resources, time, and costs
   B.   Establish the roles and responsibilities of the team members for each work package
   C.   Show the dates for each work package
   D.   Communicate with the stakeholders

8. The project manager and his team completed the scope definition process. During the next project stage the team will consider applicable all of the following, EXCEPT for:
   A.   Decompose the project in work packages
   B.   The team and project manager should participate in the next stage
   C.   Sequence the work packages
   D.   Check that the degree of work decomposition is enough

9. In regards to the project and product scope we could say that:
   A.   The project scope defines and controls what is included and not included in the project
   B.   The product scope includes the necessary processes to supply the product with all the required characteristics and functions
   C.   The project scope is based on defining the characteristics and functions of the product
   D.   First we have to plan the project scope to be able to define the product scope

10. A government agency contacts the project manager to add certain changes to the project scope. The project manager asks for written details and then works on the process of controlling the scope by updating the various baselines. What tool did the project manager probably used?
   A.   Inspection
   B.   Decomposition
   C.   Variation analysis
   D.   Expert judgment

11. The work breakdown structure (WBS) for a cosmetic products project is created. The company's top management and all the project stakeholders formally approved the WBS. Now the client requires a scope change that costs $157,800, which represents a 30% of the total cost. The client argues that a company seller promised him over the phone this project characteristic before finishing the WBS. Who should pay for the change?
    A.   The company that manages the project
    B.   The client
    C.   No one. The change should not be implemented
    D.   The company and the client

12. In a project to install last generation automatic elevators, the main deliverable and the test results were sent to the client to get his formal approval. However, 25 days have passed and the client is nowhere to be found. The project manager has tried to communicate with the client many times, but he is not returning phone calls. What is the best thing to do?
    A.   Stop the project until the client formally approves the deliverables
    B.   Request general management's assistance
    C.   Ask the client why is he not returning the calls
    D.   Document the facts in the issues log

13. During the implementation of a module in an information systems project, verify scope would be:
    A.   Test the performance of an installed software module
    B.   Manage changes to the project schedule
    C.   Decompose the WBS in work packages to review the scope with the client
    D.   Perform a cost benefit analysis to determine if we should proceed with the installation of the next module

14. All of the work to produce the project deliverables defined in the contract was completed. The cost performance index (CPI) is 1.1 and the schedule performance index (SPI) is 0.95. All of the quality inspections were satisfactory. There is no issue without resolution. Most of the resources have been already applied to other projects. The sponsor and the project manager want to verify the project scope with the client, when a stakeholder notifies them that the client wants to make a significant change to the scope. What is the first thing the project manager should do?
    A.   Request the client a description of the changes to be made
    B.   Cordially explain to the client that at this point of the project is not possible to add changes because the resources were already assigned to other projects
    C.   Meet with the project team to analyze implementation alternatives for the new scope
    D.   Evaluate the cost and schedule impact

15. In a food technology project, the project manager is using a set of new tools for project management. One of the tools that she is using is the WBS dictionary. What is this good for?
    A.   Define the project activities
    B.   Develop the scope statement
    C.   Control the addition of extra functionality to the product (Gold Plating)
    D.   Analyze the stakeholders' expectations

Lessons learned

- ✓ Product scope
- ✓ Project scope
- ✓ Control scope
- ✓ Scope corruption
- ✓ Control account
- ✓ Define scope
- ✓ Decomposition
- ✓ WBS dictionary
- ✓ Scope statement
- ✓ Work breakdown structure
- ✓ Scope baseline
- ✓ Work packages
- ✓ Requirements
- ✓ Verify scope

CHAPTER #6

TIME

Chapter 6 - TIME

> *There was never a __time__ where there would not be time.*
>
> Saint Agustin (354-439), Bishop and philosopher.

Do your projects always end on the estimated time? If the answer is NO, pay attention to this chapter where we will see many tools to manage effectively the project schedule. Conversely, if the answer was YES, make a quick review of the theoretical topics that may get you on the exam.

When you finish the chapter, you will have learned the following concepts:
- ✓ Time management processes
- ✓ Define activities
- ✓ Sequence activities
- ✓ Estimate activity resources
- ✓ Develop the schedule
- ✓ Critical path and slack
- ✓ Control the schedule

Time management processes *

We will develop the six time management processes, which are distributed within the "Planning" and "Monitoring and Controlling" process groups.

Time Processes

	Initiating	Planning	Executing	Controlling	Closing
Integration	1	1	1	2	1
Scope		3		2	
Time		. Define activities . Sequence activities . Estimate activity resources . Estimate activity durations . Develop schedule		Control schedule	
Cost		2		1	
Quality		1	1	1	
Human Resources		1	3		
Communications	1	1	2	1	
Risk		5		1	
Procurement		1	1	1	1
TOTAL	**2**	**20**	**8**	**10**	**2**

* Project Management Institute, Ibidem.

The six time management processes are:

1. **Define** activities: identify each one of the activities that need to take place in order to achieve a successful project.

2. **Sequence** activities: analyze what types of dependencies exist within the different activities.

3. Estimate activity **resources**: determine the resources available to perform an activity.

4. Estimate activity **durations**: estimate the time to complete activities.

5. Develop the **schedule**: analyze the integration existing between the sequence, the resources, the constraints, and the duration of each activity.

6. **Control the schedule**: administer changes to the schedule.

Define activities

The first input to manage the project due dates is to define in detail each one of the activities to perform.

What do I need to start?

↓ Scope baseline: scope statement, WBS, and the WBS dictionary

> *♪ The scope statement is an input to most of the processes in project management. Therefore, it will not be mentioned again in all the processes in this book.*

What tools can I use?

✂ **Decomposition**: subdivide the work packages on the WBS into activities.

✂ **Rolling wave planning**: plan in detail the activities closer in time, for example the next 12 months, and plan at an aggregate level those activities that will be performed later on.

✂ **Templates** of activities used in similar projects.

> *⌖ When the scope of the project is still vague, you can use control accounts or planning packages on the WBS to estimate at an aggregate level.*

Planning components on the WBS

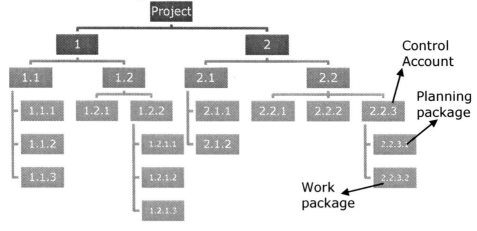

> ✎ The planning packages are located on the WBS below the control accounts and above the work packages (last level of the WBS)

What do I get at the end of the process?

↗ **Activity list** with its attributes

Activity attributes

WBS identifier	3.4.1
Name	Market study
Code	3.4.1.2
Description	Estimate tourists coming into the country
Predecessor activity	3.4.1.1
Successor activity	3.4.1.3
Dependency relation	Discretional
Leads or lags	Start when 3.4.1.1 has advanced 50%
Resource requirements	1 licensed in commercialization and 1 notebook
Constraint date	Not finish after 08-15-2011
Constraints	Maximum budget of 50 hours
Assumptions	A government database is accessed
Responsible person	Diana Rep
Perform location	+C Office
Effort level	Prorated

↗ **Milestone** list: schedule including important events or deliverables.

> ✎ Although activities have a beginning and an end, milestones do not have duration. For example, a milestone would be the signing of the contract on September 15 at 10:00 am.

Sequence activities

The process of sequencing activities consists of determining dependencies between them. In other words, what do I do first and what comes next.

What do I need to start?

⬇ Activity list, activity attributes, and milestone list

What tools can I use?

✂ **Schedule network templates** of other similar projects.

✂ **Precedence Diagramming Method (PDM)**: the activities are represented in each node and the arrows indicate precedence. It is also known as AON (activity on node).

Precedence diagram

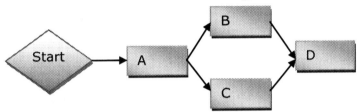

The precedence diagram allows four types of dependencies within the activities: finish to start (FS), finish to finish (FF), start to start (SS), and start to finish (SF). The latter is not used, being the finish to start relation the most used.

Types of dependencies of PDM

- Finish to start: B starts when A finishes

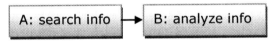

- Finish to finish: B cannot finish until A finishes

- Start to start: B cannot start until A starts

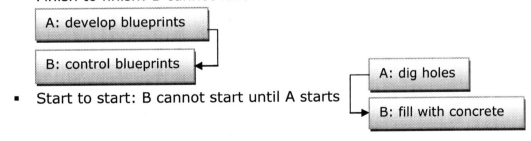

- Start to finish: B cannot finish until A starts (not used).

> ✎ *Arrow Diagramming Method (ADM): the activities are represented with arrows and the circular nodes are events. It is also known as AOA (activity on arrow). This method is hardly used, so it is unlikely that you will see this in the exam.*

Arrow diagram

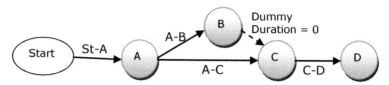

✂ **Dependency determination**: define which type of dependency exists between the activities. There are three types of dependencies: mandatory (hard logic), discretionary (soft logic), and external. For example:

- **Mandatory sequence**: I cannot put the floor until the

- **Discretionary sequence (or chosen)**: I can perform the legal feasibility study before the economic feasibility study, but it can be the other way around.

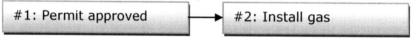

- **External sequence**: we cannot install the gas until the government approves the permit.

| #1: Permit approved | → | #2: Install gas |

✂ Applying **leads and lags**. For example:

- **Lead**: the economic feasibility study can start when the legal feasibility study is 50% advanced.

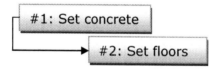

- **Lag**: the economic viability study must start 30 days after finishing the legal viability study.

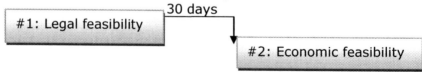

What do I get at the end of the process?

    ↗ **Project schedule network diagram**: all the project activities and their sequence from start to finish. It could be in the PDM or ADM format, as illustrated in the following figures. However, most software packages these days utilize the PDM format, with the activity on node.

Network Diagram (PDM)

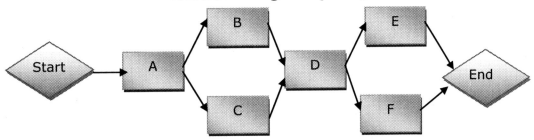

Network Diagram (ADM)

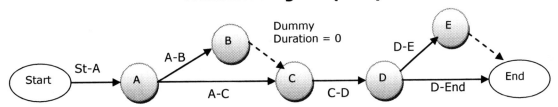

> ✎ *The ADM and PDM methods have the limitation of not allowing conditional programming. For example: iterations between activities (looping) or conditional sequences (activity A can start only when the Sun is out). To do conditional programming, you could utilize GERT (Graphic Evaluation and Review Technique).*

Estimate activity resources

Before you can estimate each activity's duration, it is necessary to predict the resources that will be available and will be needed for each activity. For example, the duration will not be the same for an activity in which I have five people at my disposal than one where I only have two people available.

On the other hand, generally there is a minimum of resources needed to perform an activity. For example, to put steel beams in place it is required, at a minimum, a saw to cut the steel.

What do I need to start?

 ↓ Activity list with their attributes

 ↓ **Resource calendar**: When will resources be available? For how long will they be available? What capabilities and abilities do the available resources have?

What tools can I use?

 ✂ **Alternatives analysis**: analyze the different alternatives of resources that can be used to perform the same activity.

 ✂ **Estimating data of resources published** on specialized journals. For example, report from the Construction Chamber.

 ✂ **Bottom-up resource estimating**: first you break down the activity work into smaller components; then you estimate the necessary resources for the smaller components; and finally you add all the resources from the bottom all the way to the top.

Bottom-up resources estimating

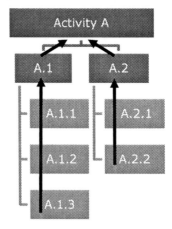

✂ Project management **software**: there are diverse software package that can be used to estimate the resources needed for each activity.

What do I get at the end of the process?

↗ Activity **resource requirements**: quantity and type of resource for each activity.

↗ **Resource breakdown structure**

Example of a resource breakdown structure

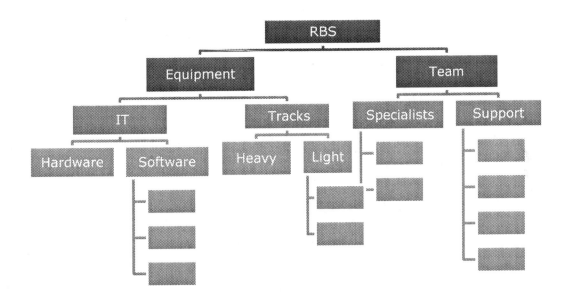

Estimate activity duration

Estimating the duration of each one of the activities requires great effort and has a high risk of obtaining incorrect estimates.

☺ Parkinson's Law: Work expands so as to fill the time available for its completion. In other words, if I am told that my activity can be delivered in 30 days, although it can be done in a few days, with luck I will deliver it on the 30th day.

What do I need to start?

↓ Activity list with their attributes

↓ Resource requirements and availability

What tools can I use?

✂ **Analogous** estimating: estimating is done by comparing other similar activities performed in previous projects. It is also known as top-down estimating. This is usually the fastest and most economic technique, but is also the most inaccurate.

✂ **Reserve analysis**: add time reserves to activities as a contingency (see risk chapter).

✂ **Parametric estimating**: utilize parameters based on historical information in order to estimate the duration of a future activity.

📖 Exercise 6.1 – Parametric estimation of times

In your company, the activity of filling out forms has previously been done many times. The activity's duration depends on the amount of forms that have to be filled out.

You want to estimate the duration of the project's activity that consists of filling out 10 forms.

The historical registers are presented on the following table.

Forms filled (X Variable)	Duration in hours (Y Variable)
5	18
2	7
15	53
10	**47**
1	3
15	50
14	40
2	6
4	10
11	30
5	16
14	40
16	59
9	30
5	14
11	35
9	25
16	48
14	43

a) What would be the duration to fill out 10 forms with an analogous estimate?

b) What would be the duration of the same activity with a parametric estimate?

Answer to Exercise 6.1

a) Based on the historical register of how long it took to fill out 10 forms in the past, we could estimate by analogy a duration of 47 hours the next time we have to perform the same activity.

b) To perform a parametric estimation, we will utilize all the historical information and will apply the ordinary least square method to estimate the future.

Steps in Excel to apply this method:
1. Fill out variable "X" data on the first column
2. Fill out variable "Y" data on the second column
3. Select the whole range of data
4. Click on Insert / Scatter graphic
5. Click on some of the dots on the graphic
6. Right-Click on one of the dots of the graphic
7. Click on Add Trendline
8. Type of trend: linear. Select: Display Equation on chart and Display R-squared value on chart
9. Close

After these steps, we will obtain the following information:

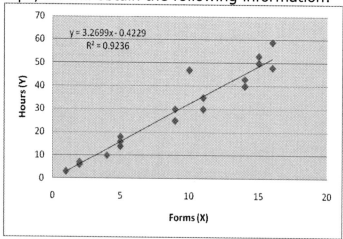

The value of R^2 = 0.92 indicates that the "X" variable (# of forms) is explaining the "Y" variable (hours) in 92%. R^2 values greater than 0.7 indicate the data is acceptable for a projection of the future.

Replacing the unknown of 10 forms (X = 10) on the equation, you obtain the following:

Y = 3.2699 x 10 – 0.4229 = 32.28

This means that the most likely estimate in case of filling out 10 forms is closed to 32.28 hours, with a confidence level of 92%. We can conclude that utilizing an analogous estimation is less accurate when there is not enough information about the activity. In this example, it would be more accurate to use a parametric estimate that takes into consideration all the historical information.

✂ Three-point estimate (PERT): it consists on estimating the duration of an activity utilizing the Pessimistic, Most likely, and Optimistic estimates. This technique is known as PERT: Program Evaluation and Review Technique.

In the PERT technique, the activity's time is considered a random variable just like a Beta probability distribution, as shown in the following figure.

Beta Distribution

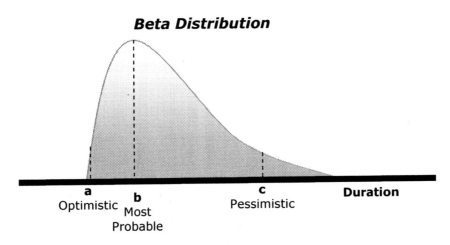

The formulas behind the PERT distribution are:

Mean	$M = \dfrac{a + 4m + b}{6}$
Standard Deviation	$\sigma = \dfrac{b - a}{6}$
Variance	σ^2
Project duration	$\Sigma\,M$ (from critical path activities)
Project Variance	$\Sigma\,\sigma^2$ (from critical path activities)

For example, if the work team estimates that the optimistic duration of an activity is 4 days, the most likely duration is 7 days, and the pessimistic scenario is 16 days. Applying the PERT formulas, you obtain the following:

Estimated Duration = (4 days + 4 x 7 days + 16 days) / 6 = 8 days

Standard Deviation= (16 days – 4 days) / 6 = 2 days

☺ When estimating the duration of an activity, Murphy's Law will always show up: the most likely estimate will always be the most improbable.

And what is the standard deviation of an activity used for?
Assuming that we could repeat that activity hundreds of times, because of the statistical law of large numbers, that activity's distribution will surely approximate a standard normal.

Standard Normal Distribution

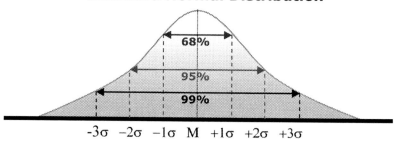

-3σ −2σ −1σ M +1σ +2σ +3σ

Applying the statistical laws of the standard normal distribution, we obtain the following:

- There is a 68.26% probability that the duration of the activity is within the mean +/- 1 standard deviation.

- There is a 95.46% probability that the duration of the activity is within the mean +/- 2 standard deviations.

- There is a 99.73% probability that the duration of the activity is within the mean +/- 3 standard deviations.

> ✎ It is not the intent of this book to go in depth into statistical demonstrations. If you want to know the reasoning behind these statistical relations, I recommend the book "Statistics for Business Economics" by Anderson, Sweeney & Williams.

Going back to our example where the mean was 8 days, with a standard deviation of 2 days, we would obtain that there is a:

- 68.26% probability that the duration of that activity is within 8 +/- 2, meaning between 6 and 10 days.

- 95.46% probability that the duration of that activity is within 8 +/- 4, meaning between 4 and 12 days.

- 99.73% probability that the duration of that activity is within 8 +/- 6, meaning between 2 and 14 days.

Suppose that we are in a simple project with three critical activities.

Extending the three-point estimate calculations of an activity, the results for a project are on the table below.

Activity	Optimistic	Most likely	Pessimistic	PERT	σ	σ^2
A	2	3	10	4	1.33	1.77
B	4	7	16	8	2	4
C	3	5	13	6	1.67	2.79
TOTAL		15		18	N/A	8.56

Project duration = 18; Project variance = 8.56
Project Standard deviation = $\sqrt{8.56}$ = 2.92
Duration range 68% = 18 + -   2.92 = 15.08 ; 20.92
Duration range 95% = 18 + - 2 x 2.92 = 12.16 ; 23.84
Duration range 99% = 18 + - 3 x 2.92 =   9.24 ; 26.76

It is worth mentioning that statistically is not correct to add the activities' standard deviations. What should be done is add the variances for each activity. Once we obtain the total variance for the project, we can calculate the standard deviation for the project by getting the square root of the total variance.

> ✍ On the exam, there could be a question about calculating PERT for an activity on a project. You will hardly see PERT calculations for a project with many activities.

📖 Exercise 6.2 – Three-point estimate

You will meet with your team to estimate with better precision a project's duration.

On this project we do not have many historical data that indicate precisely how long each activity will take. Therefore, you will work with three time estimates for each activity: the best, the Most likely, and the worst.

On the following diagram, the project scheduling is summarized representing the activities on node (AON). In turn, in each node you will see the 3 estimates for each activity. For example, activity A could have a duration of 4 weeks in the best case scenario, 6 weeks is the Most likely, and 8 weeks in the worst case scenario.

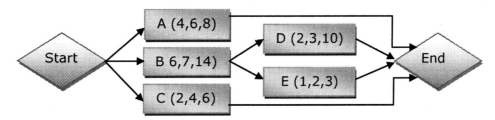

a) Using PERT, estimate the duration for each activity on the project.
b) What is the duration of the project?
c) What would be the project's range of duration with a 95% probability?

✋ Take 15 minutes to solve this exercise.

Answers to Exercise 6.2

a) The duration for each activity is presented on the PERT column on the following table.

Activity	Min.	Most Probable	Max.	PERT	SD	VAR
A	4	6	8	6	0.67	0.44
B	**6**	**7**	**14**	**8**	**1.33**	**1.78**
C	2	4	6	4	0.67	0.44
D	**2**	**3**	**10**	**4**	**1.33**	**1.78**
E	1	2	3	2	0.33	0.11
			Total	**12**	**Var**	3.56
					SD	**1.89**

b) To calculate the duration of the project you should not add the duration of all the activities. Instead, only add the duration of those activities that are part of the critical path (the longest path). In this example, there are 4 paths:
  - Start – A – End = 6 weeks
  - Start – B – D – End = 12 weeks
  - Start – B – E – End = 10 weeks
  - Start – C – End = 4 weeks

As you can observe, the longest path is made of the critical activities B and D, for which duration is 12 weeks.

On the other hand, A has a slack of 6 weeks, C has a slack of 8 weeks, and E has a slack of 2 weeks. Later on, we will look in more detail critical path and slack issues.

c) The project's total variance is obtained adding the variances for the critical activities B and D, meaning 1.78 + 1.78 = 3.56. The standard deviation for the project is 1.89 weeks, which is obtained by getting the square root of the variance. With the total duration of 12 weeks and the standard deviation of 1.89 weeks, we obtain the following:
  - There is a 95.46% probability that the duration of the project is within 12 +/- (2 x 1.89) = between 8.23 and 15.77 weeks.

What do I get at the end of the process?

➚ **Activity duration estimates**

Develop schedule

Schedule development consists of integrating all the parts that we have seen here: activities, sequences, resources, and durations.

What do I need to start?

- ↓ Activity list and their attributes
- ↓ Network diagram
- ↓ Requirements and resource availability
- ↓ Activities duration

What tools can I use?

- ✂ **Critical path method**: identify which are the critical activities that are part of the longest path of the project. In the following section we will explain this tool in detail.

- ✂ **What-if scenario analysis**: perform simulations of how the project schedule will change if any affecting variable changes. For instance, the Monte Carlo simulation (see risks chapter).

- ✂ **Critical chain method**: modify the project schedule taking into account resource constraints. The traditional critical path is modified taking into account the resource limitations by adding time buffers, which are activities that do not require work and consider each activity's risk of resource availability.

> ✎ *If a project's resources would always be available in unlimited amounts, then the project's critical chain would be the same as its critical path.*

- ✂ **Resource leveling**: modify the project scheduling to improve the efficiency in resource allocation.

> ☺ *You cannot kick the corner, hit a header, and intercept the ball as a goalkeeper, all at the same time.*

📖 Exercise 6.3 – Resource leveling

You must add to the project scheduling the personnel requirements to perform each one of the activities.

As you can see on the following network diagram and table, the necessary human resources and each activity's duration have been added.

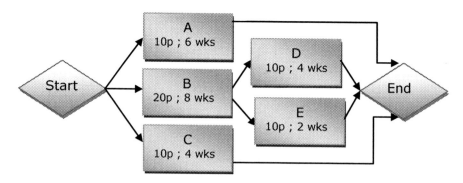

Activity	1	2	3	4	5	6	7	8	9	10	11	12
A	10	10	10	10	10	10						
B	20	20	20	20	20	20	20	20				
C	10	10	10	10								
D									10	10	10	10
E									10	10		
Resources	40	40	40	40	30	30	20	20	20	20	10	10

Activities D and E should be performed once activity B is finished.

The project requires 40 resources in weeks 1-4, 30 resources in weeks 5-6, 20 resources in weeks 7-10, and 10 resources in the last 2 weeks. If you assign all company personnel to this project (40 resources) during the first few weeks, you will not be able to perform any other activity during that period, and this is very risky for the company. On the other hand, it is not possible for this project to take longer than 12 weeks, because the Sponsor will not allow it.

How would you level the resources to fix this problem and use less than 40 resources in the project?

Activity	1	2	3	4	5	6	7	8	9	10	11	12
A												
B												
C												
D												
E												
Resources												

✋ Take 10 minutes to solve this exercise.

Answers to Exercise 6.3

First of all, given the constraint that the project cannot take longer than 12 weeks, the critical activities B and D should not be modified. The options would be to delay the start of A or C, as presented on the following tables:

Leveling 1

Activity	1	2	3	4	5	6	7	8	9	10	11	12
A					10	10	10	10	10	10		
B	20	20	20	20	20	20	20	20				
C	10	10	10	10								
D									10	10	10	10
E									10	10		
Resources	30	30	30	30	30	30	30	30	30	30	10	10

Leveling 2

Activity	1	2	3	4	5	6	7	8	9	10	11	12
A	10	10	10	10	10	10						
B	20	20	20	20	20	20	20	20				
C							10	10	10	10		
D									10	10	10	10
E									10	10		
Resources	30	30	30	30	30	30	30	30	30	30	10	10

In each of these alternatives, the project can be done utilizing a maximum of only 30 resources, which improves the efficiency in relation to the 40 resources situation.

> ✎ Many project management software packages allow for automatic resource leveling. However, software packages do not think and will choose any leveling, leaving the fact that there can be better alternatives by considering factors like weather, personnel availability, etc.

On the other hand, other leveling options that will also use a maximum of 30 resources could be the ones presented on the following tables:

Leveling 3

Activity	1	2	3	4	5	6	7	8	9	10	11	12
A							10	10	10	10	10	10
B	20	20	20	20	20	20	20	20				
C	10	10	10	10								
D									10	10	10	10
E									10	10		
Resources	30	30	30	30	20	20	30	30	30	30	20	20

Leveling 4

Activity	1	2	3	4	5	6	7	8	9	10	11	12
A	10	10	10	10	10	10						
B	20	20	20	20	20	20	20	20				
C									10	10	10	10
D									10	10	10	10
E									10	10		
Resources	**30**	**30**	**30**	**30**	**30**	**30**	**20**	**20**	**30**	**30**	**20**	**20**

However, these solutions would not be effective for the following reasons:

- It is less effective to manage resources with ups and downs: 30 resources, then 20 resources, then again 30 resources, etc. It is preferred to have leveled projects with a pace that is either increasing, decreasing, or constant, instead of leveling with ups and downs.

- Activities that were not critical and had slack, when moved to the final week, they became critical. This added the unnecessary risk of not meeting the project deadlines.

📖 Exercise 6.4 – Resource constraints

After working firmly on rescheduling the project to improve the efficiency in the allocation of resources, you achieve a schedule that consists of finishing the project in 12 weeks utilizing 30 resources, as shown in the following table:

Activity	1	2	3	4	5	6	7	8	9	10	11	12
A	10	10	10	10	10	10						
B	20	20	20	20	20	20	20	20				
C							10	10	10	10		
D									10	10	10	10
E									10	10		
Resources	30	30	30	30	30	30	30	30	30	30	10	10

You send the project schedule to your boss for its approval and he says:

I really have to congratulate all of you for great tools that you have learned and implemented after reading Paul Leido's book. The plan that you have developed is very well presented. However, you have made a terrible error: you will only have 20 resources per week available to perform this project!

a) Which of the triple constraint variables can change in this project if it can only be done with 20 resources?

b) How would the project schedule change if you only have 20 resources per week available?

Activity	1	2	3	4	5	6	7	8	9	10	11	12	13	14	15	16	17	18
A																		
B																		
C																		
D																		
E																		
Resources																		

✋ Take 10 minutes to solve this exercise.

Answers to Exercise 6.4

a) If the budget is cut off (e.g.: the available resources were lowered), you could extend the project deadline. You can also lower the scope, the quality, or the client satisfaction.

b) Under the assumption that the variable being modified is the schedule, one of the possible solutions for this problem could be the one presented on the following table:

Activity	1	2	3	4	5	6	7	8	9	10	11	12	13	14	15	16
A									10	10	10	10	10	10		
B	20	20	20	20	20	20	20	20								
C													10	10	10	10
D									10	10	10	10				
E															10	10
Resources	20	20	20	20	20	20	20	20	20	20	20	20	20	20	20	20

In this solution, you obtained a minimum of 16 weeks duration. However, considering the resource limitation, all the activities are critical because if any of them is delayed, the whole project gets delayed due to having only 20 resources available.

- ✂ **Schedule compression**: it consists of shortening the project schedule without modifying the scope. Two of the most used techniques for schedule compression are crashing and fast-tracking.

  - ✂ **Crashing**: add more resources to the project in order to shorten the duration. In general, this technique implies higher costs. The key is how to obtain the maximum schedule compression at the minimum cost.

  - ✂ **Fast-tracking**: perform activities in parallel to accelerate the project. In general, this technique adds risks to the project.

> ☺ *Last minute Crashing: find out one minute before the dead-line that we can crash the project adding more resources.*

> ☺ *Irrational crashing: add resources that will not speed-up the project. For example, two jockeys running the same horse will not make it get to the end line any faster.*

Exercise 6.5 – Compression

Your project has a negative slack of three days. On the following table you have the critical activities that could be crashed in order to shorten the project's duration.

Activity	Estimated duration	Duration with compression	Reduction in days	Cost of compression ($)	Daily cost ($)
A	5	4	1	5,000	5,000
F	4	2	2	8,000	4,000
J	12	9	3	12,000	4,000
M	8	6	2	4,000	2,000
L	10	9	1	7,000	7,000

Which activities would you crash to avoid a negative slack?

✋ Take 5 minutes to solve this exercise.

Exercise 6.6 – Alternatives for schedule compression

The estimated duration for the project is 27 months, as presented in the following diagram.

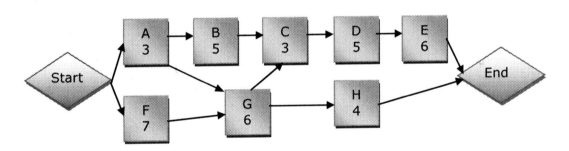

General management has given you a maximum finish deadline of 24 months. What alternatives do you have to shorten the project duration to 24 months?

✋ Take 10 minutes to think of different alternatives.

Answers to Exercise 6.5

The alternatives to shorten the project duration by 3 days are:

Activities	Total Cost	Daily Cost
A-F	13,000	9,000
A-M	**9,000**	7,000
F-L	15,000	11,000
J	12,000	4,000
M-L	11,000	9,000

The most economical alternative to shorten the project duration by three days is to crash activities A and M, with a total cost of $9,000. The daily cost data is not relevant to solve this exercise, because it does not represent the lowest total cost to achieve the objective.

Answers to Exercise 6.6

The different paths of the project are:

A-B-C-D-E   = 22 months
A-G-C-D-E   = 23 months
A-G-H   = 13 months
F-G-C-D-E   = 27 months
F-G-H   = 17 months

The critical path is F-G-C-D-E = 27 months. The rest of the paths have slack, that is, they could be delayed a few weeks without delaying the project. Therefore, we should look for schedule compression alternatives for the activities that are part of the critical path.

On the following table there are some alternatives to shorten the project duration.

Alternative	Comment
Perform D and E in parallel (fast-tracking)	Assumption: there is no dependency between activities D and E
Crash D by moving resources from H to D	Assumption: the resources from H have the abilities needed to perform D
Reduce scope of activity E	Warning: it will surely affect client satisfaction
Add resources to activity C	Assumption: there are qualified resources to perform C
Lower quality standards for the activities on the critical path	Cut quality is always an option, but it can affect client satisfaction or add the risk of defective products
Negotiate so the project ends in 27 months	Many times this is not viable
Do more with the same resources working overtime	This is not an option during planning. It is worthwhile to keep those extra hours as a contingency plan

Are you ready to answer the following two questions related to schedule compression?

? **1)** *You have to finish the following project 4 weeks ahead of schedule.*

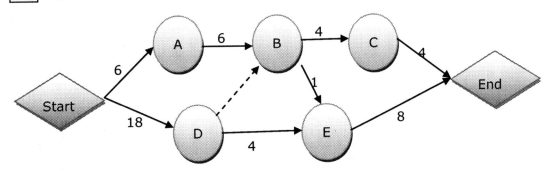

Which of the following options you think is the best alternative?

   A. Assign one person with a lot of experience to activity Start-D in order to finish that activity in 14 weeks. However, this person costs an additional $10,000.

   B. Eliminate part of activity E-End in order to save $5,000 and shorten duration by 2 weeks.

   C. Move resources from activity A-B to activity B-E in order to save $2,000 and shorten A-B's duration by 2 weeks.

   D. Eliminate activity B-C in order to save $15,000 and shorten duration by 4 weeks.

👋 Think before looking for the answer.

? **2)** *The General Manager has told you that you must finish the project three weeks ahead of schedule. What should you do?*

   A. Consult with the sponsor

   B. Compression

   C. Inform the Manager about the impact to the project

   D. Fast-tracking

Answer 1: A

The critical path is Start – D – E – End

Item	Answer	Explanation
A	True	This is the only option that complies with the objective of shortening the project duration by 4 weeks.
B	False	We need to cut 4 weeks.
C	False	This would increase the duration of A-B in order to decrease the duration of B-E, which is not on the critical path.
D	False	B-C is not on the critical path. Furthermore, if you eliminate the scope there could be client dissatisfaction.

Answer 2: C

Before thinking about crashing or fast-tracking, the PM should inform about what is the impact of any proposed change to the project.

We can summarize the different alternatives to shorten the project schedule in the following table.

How to shorten the schedule?	Impact on the project
Fast-tracking	Increases risks Requires more time from the PM
Compression	Increases costs Requires more time from the PM
Decrease scope	Saves time and costs Decreases client satisfaction
Cut quality	Could save time and costs Increases risks

What do I get at the end of the process?

↗ Project **Schedule**: it can be in either one of the following formats: milestones schedule, bar chart, or network diagram.

Milestones Schedule

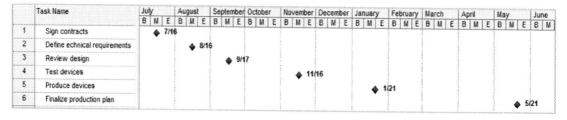

144

> ⋏ *The milestones diagram is the most adequate format to present to top management. We should not abuse manager's valuable time with detailed explanations of Gantt charts.*

Bar chart (Gantt)

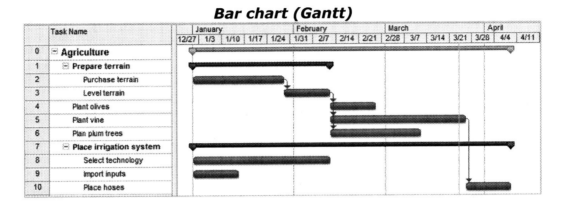

> ⋏ *The Gantt chart is the most adequate format for the PM and the project team to manage the project.*

Network diagram

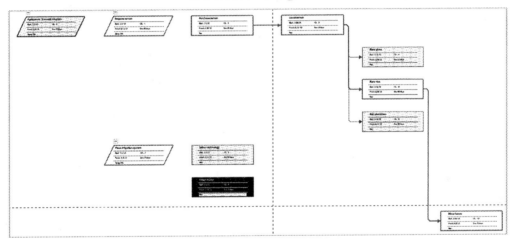

↗ **Schedule baseline**: the starting and finishing dates for the activities in the project schedule are established, accepted, and approved.

> ⋏ *The schedule baseline must be accepted and approved by the project management team.*

↗ **Schedule data**: document that includes all the information about the milestones, the activities and their attributes, resource histogram, resource leveling alternatives, contingency reserves, assumptions, constraints, etc.

Critical Path Method

The critical path method is a well used tool for the development of the project schedule.

Suppose that we want to use scheduling tools for a hospital startup. After asking the experts on these topics, we identified all the activities, and estimated the duration and sequence of each one of them. The project information is presented in the following table:

Name	Activity	Duration	Predecessor
1 – A	Select personnel	12	
2 – B	Select location	9	
3 – C	Select teams	10	1
4 – D	Make blueprints	10	2
5 – E	Install services	24	2
6 – F	Interview personnel	10	1
7 – G	Buy equipment	35	3
8 – H	Build hospital	40	4
9 – I	Install information systems	15	1
10 – J	Install equipment	4	5, 7, 8
11 – K	Train personnel	6	6, 9, 10

On the other hand, we have applied AON scheduling techniques to make the project network diagram as follows, with the name of the activity and its duration in each node.

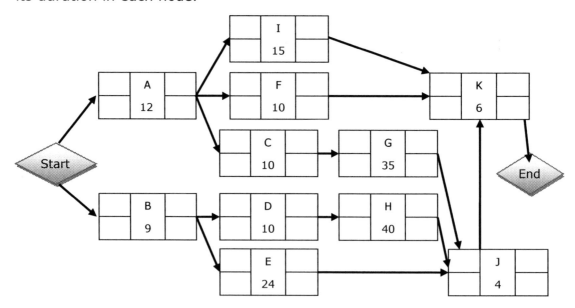

? What is the project's duration?

What is the critical path?

What is the slack for each activity?

Firstly, we will fill out the network diagram's upper spaces with the activity's early start (ES) date and the early finish (EF) date for the activity.

Early Start and Early Finish Dates

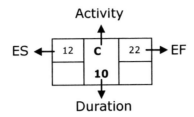

For example, activity C can start when activity A is finished. Activity A does not have a predecessor, thus it starts on day 0 and it lasts 12 days, so it finishes on day 12, at the earliest. Activity C can start when A is finished, with an early start date on the same day 12, it lasts 10 days and it ends on day 22, at the earliest.

Following this same logic with the rest of the activities, we completed the network diagram as follows.

Forward pass

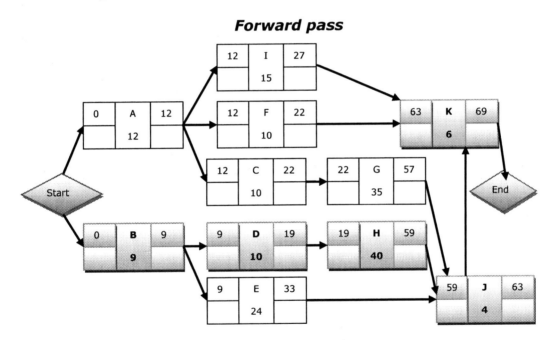

It is worth mentioning that the activities that have more than one predecessor start, at the earliest, on the early finish date of the predecessor with the longest duration. For example, J is preceded by G which finishes on day 57, H which finishes on day 59, and E which finishes on day 33. Therefore, J can start, at the earliest, on day 59.

On the other hand, if we analyze all possible paths of this project we will obtain the following:

- A – I – K = 33 days
- A – F – K = 28 days
- A – C – G – J – K = 67 days
- B – D – H – J – K = 69 days
- B – E – J – K = 43 days

We can then conclude that the critical path, the longest path, is B-D-H-J-K with 69 days.

> ✎ *The near critical path is the "almost" critical path. In this example, it would be the path A-C-G-J-K of 67 days.*

We have analyzed the critical path from the start until the end (forward pass) and in the upper right quadrant of activity K we can observe the total project duration of 69 days.

We will now analyze the network diagram in the inverse form, that is, from the end until the beginning (backward pass). For this, we will fill out the lower quadrants for each activity, with the late finish (LF) date and the late start (LS) date.

Late Start and Late Finish dates

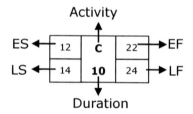

For example, if activity C can finish on day 24 at the latest, with 10 days, it will be able to start on day 14 at the latest.

To be able to do a backward pass we have to start from the last activity, which in our example is J. We already know that J finishes on day 69, which we will assume is the late finish date. When we subtract its duration of 6 days, the late start date will be on day 63.

After that, activities I, F, and J, which precede K, will have a late finish date of 63 days.

Following this same logic, we obtain the following network diagram.

Backward pass

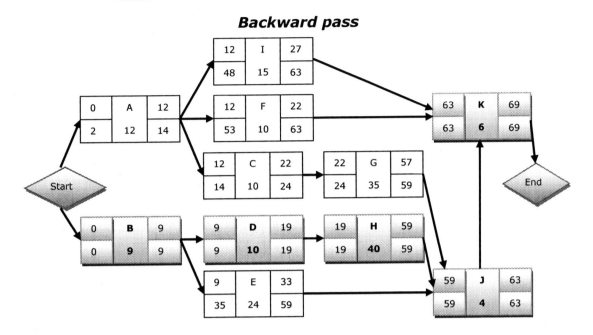

Why do I need all this calculations?

To determine each project activity's slack.

The **total slack** of an activity is the amount of time that this activity can be delayed without changing the project duration. This can be obtained with either one of the following equations:

$$\text{Total slack} = LS - ES$$

$$\text{Total slack} = LF - EF$$

☺ *The formula starts with LS or LF, because we are always late.*

For example, the slack for activity I is 36 days and this is obtained by:

$$LS - ES = 48 - 12 = 36 \text{ days}$$

or

$$LF - EF = 63 - 27 = 36 \text{ days}$$

This means that activity I can be delayed up to 36 days without affecting the total project duration of 69 days. More than 36 days of delay in activity I will affect the total project duration.

Furthermore, there are other definitions for slack that we should know:

- **Free slack**: the amount of time an activity can be delayed without causing slippage (delay) to the early start date of any of its successors.

Keeping with our example of the hospital, the free slack of activity A is 0, because any delay will cause a slippage start of its successors I, F, and C. However, activity F has a free slack of 41 days, which is the maximum amount of time that it can be delayed, without delaying the start of its successor K.

- **Project slack**: the amount of time the project can be delayed without delaying the published finish date.

For example, if a contract has been signed with the Client to build the hospital in 90 days and the plan indicates 69 days, we have a project slack of 21 days.

> ✎ *The project slack can be negative. For example, the finish date according to the plan is 69 days, whereas the date established on the contract with the client is 60 days. In this case the project total slack is -9 days.*

Now, the simplest way to analyze the project duration, the critical path, and each activity's slack would be to use a project management software package. For example, with MS Project we could have all this information in 5 minutes.

MS Project – Critical Path and Slack

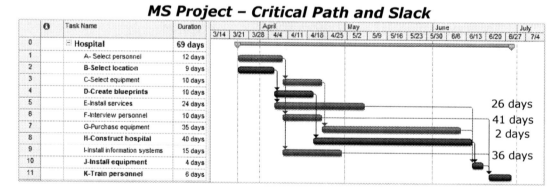

> ✎ *It is not the intent of this book, neither the PMP® Exam, to discuss tools to use project management software packages.*

Unfortunately, when you take the PMP® Exam you will not have any software available and you must solve the exercises by hand, utilizing the manual techniques that we will see in the following exercises.

📖 Exercise 6.7 – Arrow Diagramming Method (ADM)

Based on the following table, draw the network diagram and answer the questions that follow.

Activity	Duration (Weeks)
Start-A	4
Start-B	8
A-C	3
B-C	2
B-E	1
C-D	2
C-E	Dummy
E-End	4
D-End	3

a) What is the critical path?

b) What is the impact on the project if activity E-End increases by 1 week?

c) Which activities must finish before E-End starts?

d) If the Client requests that the project ends 3 weeks ahead of schedule, what is the project slack? Does the critical path changes?

It is not necessary to dedicate too much time to solve this diagramming technique, due to the fact that AOA it is practically not used anymore.

Answer to Exercise 6.7

The network diagram for this project is the following:

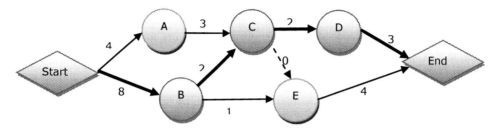

a) The possible paths for this project are:

Start-A, A-C, C-D, D-End	= 12 weeks
Start -A, A-C, C-E, E-End	= 11 weeks
Start -B, B-E, E-End	= 13 weeks
Start -B, B-C, C-D, D-End	= 15 weeks
Start -B, B-C, C-E, E-End	= 14 weeks

The longest path (critical path) is Start-B, B-C, C-D, D-End (15 weeks).

b) If activity E-End increases one week, duration of the different paths will be as follows:

Start-A, A-C, C-D, D-End	= 12 weeks
Start-A, A-C, C-E, E-End	= 12 weeks
Start-B, B-E, E-End	= 14 weeks
Start-B, B-C, C-D, D-End	= 15 weeks (Critical Path)
Start-B, B-C, C-E, E-End	= 15 weeks (Critical Path)

Did you think that there is no impact on the project because the duration does not change? That is incorrect, because you must analyze the impact on all the triple constraint variables. Now we have two critical paths, which mean that the impact to the project is that the risk of not finishing on time increases.

c) The activities that precede E-End are: Start-A, A-C, Start-B, B-C, B-E.

Did you think it was only B-E? Incorrect! The rest of the activities must also finish so E-End can start.

You thought it was C-E? Incorrect! That is not an activity, but a dummy activity with duration 0 that is used to indicate sequence.

d) If the client requests that the project ends 3 weeks ahead of schedule, the critical path does not change. However, we will have a negative project slack of 3 weeks: Client (12 weeks) – Plan (15 weeks) = -3 weeks

📖 **Exercise 6.8 – Precedence Diagramming Method (PDM)**

Based on the following table, draw the network diagram and answer the questions that follow:

Activity	Duration (days)	Predecessor
A	2	
B	4	A
C	6	A
D	5	B
E	3	C and D

a) What is the duration of the project?

b) What is the slack for activity B?

c) What is the slack for activity C?

d) What is the slack for the path with the greatest slack?

e) What is the impact to the project if activity C lasts 8 days?

f) Going back to the original data, the sponsor adds activity F with 7 days. This activity must end before E starts and it must start after C finishes. What is the project duration now?

🖐 Take 15 minutes to solve this exercise.

Answer to Exercise 6.8

The network diagram for this project is the following:

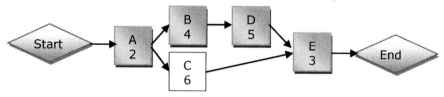

a) The possible paths are:
   Start-A-B-D-E-End = 14 days (Critical Path)
   Start-A-C-E-End   = 11 days (Path with Slack)
   The project duration, based on the critical path, is 14 days.

b) Activity B is on the critical path; therefore, it does not have any slack. In other words, it has a slack of 0 days.

c) Activity C has a slack of 3 days.

Critical path (14 days) – Path with slack (11 days) = 3 days of slack.

The long way to solve this, taking into account the calculations of ES, EF, LS, and LF, is presented in the following diagram:

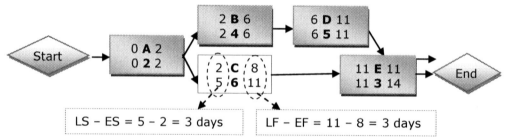

d) The path with the greatest slack, Start-A-C-E-End, has a slack of 3 days.

Critical path (14 days) – Path with slack (11 days) = 3 days of slack.

e) If activity C lasts 8 days, the slack for that path decreases to 1 day, which means that the project is more risky.
Critical path (14 days) – Path with slack (13 days) = 1 day of slack.

f) When activity F is added, the new network diagram is as follows:

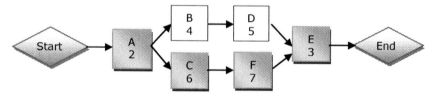

The critical path is A-C-F-E and the project duration is 18 days.

Control Schedule

The last process related to time management is Control Schedule, which belongs to the Monitoring and Controlling process group.

What do I need to start?

* ⬇ Schedule
* ⬇ Work performance information

What tools can I use?

✂ **Performance reviews**: to compare the real durations in relation to the schedule baseline and evaluate if the changes are significant. You can use Earned Value Management, as explained in the next chapter.

In many projects, status reports are obtained asking team members: *"how are you doing?"* And the answer always is: *"Doing well!"*

Warning! Asking for the percentage of work completed is not worth it if it is not accompanied with tangible deliverables. In those projects where it is difficult to obtain tangible partial deliverables before finalizing the activity, the following rules are very useful:

> * 50/50 Rule: the activity is considered 50% complete if it is already started and the other 50% is only assigned when finished.
> * 20/80 Rule: 20% is assigned at the beginning and 80% at the end.
> * 0/100 Rule: you only inform 100% at the end, any other time the activity is informed at 0%.

✂ **Variance analysis**: you analyze the cause for the variances and determine whether or not there is the need to implement corrective actions.

✂ **Project Management Software.** For example, with MS Project you can obtain bar charts that can be compared to the baseline.

Bar Chart

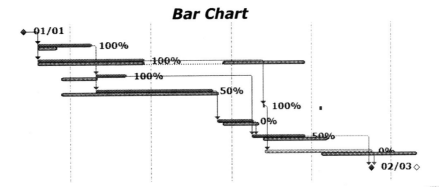

✂ **Resource leveling**

✂ **What if** scenario analysis: analyze different scenarios to adjust the schedule changes to its original baseline.

✂ Schedule **compression**: accelerate delayed activities adding more resources (compression) or perform activities in parallel (fast-tracking).

✂ Adjusting **leads and lags**: accelerate the leads or reduce the lags to manage the schedule delays in relation to its baseline.

✂ **Scheduling** tools: update the schedule to reflect the real advance and pending tasks.

What do I get at the end of the process?

Similar to all the other control processes, the outputs for this process are:

↗ Work performance measurements. For example, the schedule performance index (SPI) and the cost variance (CV), indicators that we will explain in the next chapter.

↗ Change requests

↗ Updates (processes, plan, activities, schedule, baseline)

Summarizing time management

In the following figure we summarize the main inputs, outputs, and interrelations of the time management processes.

Integrating Time Management

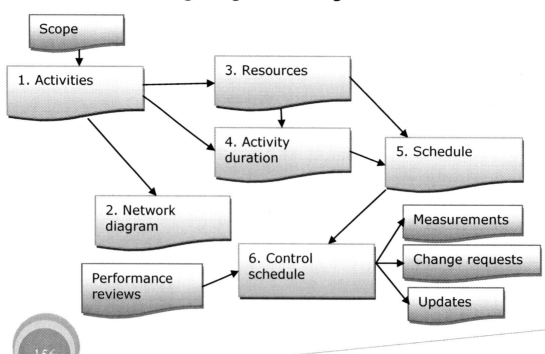

Exam 6 – Time

Number of questions: 15
Time to respond: 15 minutes
Passing score: 80% (12 correct answers)

1. Based on the following table, what is the critical path for this project?

Activity	Duration (weeks)	Predecessor
A	10	Start
B	8	Start
C	4	A
D	7	A, B
E	10	B
F	8	C, D
G	10	D, E
H	8	F, G

    A.   ADFH
    B.   ADGH
    C.   BDGH
    D.   BEGH

2. Based on the table on question 1, what is the slack for activity A?
    A.   It has no slack
    B.   1 week
    C.   5 weeks
    D.   - 1 week

3. Based on the table on question 1, what happens with the project if activity F extends 3 weeks over what it was scheduled?
    A.   The project duration will extend for 3 weeks
    B.   The project becomes more risky
    C.   The project will have a negative slack
    D.   The project will not be affected

4. You need to shorten the project's duration to be able to comply with the contract signed with the client. The options that are being evaluated by the project team are compression or fast-tracking. Which of the following statements is correct?
    A.   Compression will add risks to the project
    B.   Fast-tracking will add costs to the project
    C.   Compression will extend even more the project deadlines
    D.   Fast-tracking will add risks to the project

5. An architecture company is working on the design of a new bridge that will cross a big river. However, the company's main architect had to leave the project to attend a personal emergency. This takes the schedule performance index to 0.8 because there is no blueprint data backed up and the specialist is required to sign the blueprints. This causes a delay on the finish date of the project. This is an example of:
   A.   Compression
   B.   Mandatory Dependency
   C.   External Dependency
   D.   Slow Execution

6. You are the project manager for a project that consists of performing a publicity campaign for a new women's perfume. You have finalized the WBS with a good level of detail. You are holding a meeting with your work team to start with the process of estimating the duration of the activities. Which of the following options will not be of much help in this meeting?
   A.   Project charter
   B.   Constraints
   C.   Assumptions
   D.   Identified risks

7. You are the project manager for the development of a new technology to cure myopia related problems. In conjunction with the project team, you have identified three activities that are part of the critical path. In addition, you have estimated three durations for each activity as presented in the following table. What is the estimated duration for this project using a range of two standard deviations?

Activity	Duration		
	Pessimistic	Most likely	Optimistic
A	2	3	10
B	3	6	9
C	3	5	13

   A.   14 - 16
   B.   11.29 – 20.71
   C.   13.64 – 7.92
   D.   2 - 13

8. In a project for the production of computer sensors, the building phase requires the design phase to be completed first. This is an example of this type of dependency:
   A.   Mandatory
   B.   External
   C.   Discretional
   D.   PERT

9. The project manager is evaluating alternatives of sequencing project activities utilizing the precedence diagramming method (PDM) or the arrow diagramming method (ADM). What is the difference between these two methods?
   A.   ADM is also known as AOA, whereas PDM is also known as GERT.
   B.   PDM allows two types of dependencies between activities, whereas ADM allows four types of dependencies between activities
   C.   Currently, ADM is more widely used than PDM
   D.   PDM places activities on nodes and ADM places activities on arrows

10. Which of the following precedence relations is the one that a project manager would LEAST use for the precedence diagramming method?
    A.   Start to Start
    B.   Finish to Finish
    C.   Start to Finish
    D.   Finish to Start

11. You are the project manager in a company that provides energy distribution services. You have finalized the planning processes and have completed the milestone diagrams and bar charts. In what scenario would you recommend utilizing a milestone diagram instead of a bar chart?
    A.   During the executing phase
    B.   To present to management
    C.   To communicate to the work team members
    D.   For the risk analysis

12. For a project activity you have estimated three durations: Pessimistic = 20; Optimistic = 9; Most likely = 15. What would be the variance for this activity based on the three-point estimate?
    A.   1.67
    B.   3.36
    C.   4.50
    D.   There is not enough information for the calculation

13. What would be the tool LEAST used by a project manager to control the project schedule for the launching of a new product to market?
    A.   Resource leveling
    B.   What if analysis
    C.   Schedule compression
    D.   Three-point estimate

14. One of the network diagramming methods is called GERT (Graphic Evaluation Review Technique). Which of the following propositions better describes this method?
    A.   Conditional diagramming method
    B.   Precedence diagramming method (PDM)
    C.   Precedence determination
    D.   Critical chain method

15. You are developing the project schedule, so you have to clarify to the rest of the team some basic concepts of network diagrams. Which of the following statements is correct?
    A. The network diagram will change whenever the starting date changes
    B. There is only one critical path in projects
    C. The project cannot have a negative slack
    D. The critical path can include dummy activities

Lessons Learned

- ✓ 50/50 Rule; 0/80 Rule; 0/100 Rule
- ✓ Activity on node (AON)
- ✓ Analogous estimation
- ✓ Bar charts
- ✓ Bottom-up estimating
- ✓ Compression
- ✓ Critical chain method
- ✓ Critical path method
- ✓ Decomposition
- ✓ Dependencies: finish-start, finish-finish, start-start, start-finish
- ✓ Dependencies: mandatory, discretional, external
- ✓ Fast-tracking
- ✓ Leads and lags
- ✓ Milestone diagram
- ✓ Near critical path
- ✓ Network diagram
- ✓ Parametric estimation
- ✓ PERT
- ✓ Planning package
- ✓ Precedence diagramming method (PDM)
- ✓ Resource breakdown structure
- ✓ Resource leveling
- ✓ Rolling wave planning
- ✓ Schedule compression
- ✓ Slack: total, free, of the project
- ✓ Status report
- ✓ Three-point estimate
- ✓ Variance analysis
- ✓ What if analysis

CHAPTER #7

COST

Chapter 7 - COST

> *Watch for the small <u>costs</u>, a small leak can sink a great ship.*
>
> Benjamin Franklin (1706-1790) United States statesman and scientist

All projects are limited by a budgetary constraint. Cost management is an area with various technical notions that a good PM should know to achieve successful projects.

When you finish this chapter, you will have learned the following concepts:
- ✓ Cost management plan
- ✓ Cost types
- ✓ Cost management processes
- ✓ Activities' costs
- ✓ Budget
- ✓ Control costs
- ✓ Earned value management (EVM)
- ✓ Net present value
- ✓ Internal rate of return
- ✓ Payback rule

Cost management plan

The PM and his team should plan how to manage the project management costs, answering the following questions:

- How to **manage** the project according to budget?

- What is the **level of accuracy** of the cost estimates? A rough order of magnitude (ROM) precision level varies between +-50%; while a definitive estimate ranges between +-10%.

- Which are the **connections** of each cost group with the WBS control accounts?

- Which are the allowed cost variance **limits** or **thresholds**?

- How to manage cost **variances**?

- How and when to perform **value analysis**?

> ✎ *Value analysis or value engineering: look for the most economic alternatives to perform the work.*

- What cost management **processes** will be used?

- How is the costs **life cycle**? For example, you could save costs completing a few blueprints during the design phase of a construction project, but this saving may increase future costs in the execution phase with permanent changes during construction.

Costs life cycle

Feasibility $ | Selection $$ | Definition $$$ | Execution $$$$ | Operation $$$

> 🐦 *Saves $ in early project stages could increase costs later on.*

Cost types

There are different cost types; here we mention the main ones.

- **Variable costs:** depend on the production volume. For example, raw materials. The more sneakers are produced, the more shoe laces are needed.

- **Fixed costs:** do not change with the production volume. For example, rentals. Regardless of the production volume of a golf club factory, the rent paid for the factory place will stay the same.

- **Direct costs:** can directly be attributed to the project. For example, the costs of a trip to exclusively promote a new beauty lotion.

- **Indirect costs:** benefit various projects and generally, the exact ratio that should go to each project cannot be identified. For example, the structure costs (accounting, electricity, telephone, PMO, etc.).

- **Opportunity costs:** the opportunity cost of a resource is the best alternative left aside. When estimating the activities' costs, not only should the cash outflow be included, but also the opportunity cost for each resource.

- **Sunk costs:** costs that were already accrued and will not change with the decision of proceeding or not with the project.

> ☝ *Sunk costs should not be considered in the project economic analysis.*

To discuss the concepts of opportunity cost and sunk costs, think of the answer to the following four questions.

1. *Project A has a $25,000 profit and project B has a $30,000 profit. What is the opportunity cost of choosing project A?*

2. *You performed a market study that cost $10,000. You put 50% cash down and you will pay the other 50% with a check after 120 days. What value should you consider as a project cost to decide whether to proceed or not with the project?*

3. *You have two investment alternatives of similar risk: bonds that yield 8% annually and a mutual fund that yields 11% annually. What is the opportunity cost of capital to use in a new project with similar risk than the others?*

4. *The original project budget was $100. The actual progress is 40% and you have already spent $300. Would you consider the $200 in excess to decide whether or not to proceed with the project?*

✋ Think 5 minutes on the answers before reading the following table.

Question	Answer
1	$30,000. The incremental cost to choose A is $5,000, but if I choose A, I leave aside $30,000, and that is the opportunity cost.
2	$0. The $10,000 have to be paid whether or not the project proceeds. The 50% that will be paid in the future is a sunk cost because it was accrued and has to be paid even if the project does not proceed.
3	11%. The best investment alternative is 11%. That is the opportunity cost or discount rate to be used in projects with similar risks.
4	NO. The $300 are already a sunk cost. To decide whether the project should proceed, you have to analyze the future cost versus the future project benefits. For example, if the estimated benefits are $150 and the future costs are $120, the project must proceed; although, from an accounting perspective $270 are lost ($150 - $120 – $300). It is best to lose $270 than $300, in case you decide not to proceed with the project.

Other concepts related to costs are:

-   **Working Capital:** necessary amount of money to cover the project's operational costs until the cash inflows start. One way to calculate the working capital emerges from the difference between current assets and current liabilities.

> ✎ The majority of the projects require working capital to finance the natural gap that is produced between the occurrence of operational expenditures and cash inflows.

- **Accounting Depreciation:** decrease in the book value of an asset according to accounting criteria. The depreciation is tax deductible from the earnings.

  o **Linear depreciation**: the same amount is depreciated every year. For example, a $1,000 investment for which its accounting useful life is 20 years has a depreciation of $50 per year ($1,000 / 20 years).

  o **Accelerated depreciation**: higher amounts are depreciated on the early years. For example, a government that subsidizes the purchase of capital goods, could allow an accounting depreciation of 50% the first year, 30% the second year, and 20% the third year.

- **Economic depreciation:** variation of the market value of an asset. For example, a new $1,000 computer has a 5 year accounting depreciation, or 20% annually. After a year of the computer purchase, its market value is $300; therefore, it had an economic depreciation of 70%, even though the accounting depreciation is only 20%.

- **Law of diminishing returns:** when incrementing the utilization of resources, production increases at a decreasing rate. For example, in a bicycle assembly project, when you duplicate plant personnel from 5 to 10, the production of bicycles increases from 100 to 140. In the area of diminishing returns, costs increase at an increasing rate.

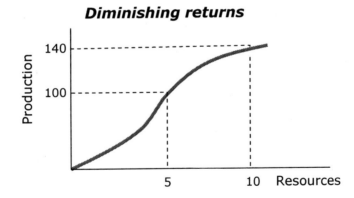

Diminishing returns

Cost management processes *

In the following sections we will develop the three cost management processes that are distributed among the planning and monitoring and controlling groups as presented on the following table.

Cost management processes

	Initiating	Planning	Executing	Controlling	Closing
Integration	1	1	1	2	1
Scope		3		2	
Time		5		1	
Cost		. Estimate Costs . Determine Budget		Control Costs	
Quality		1	1	1	
HR		1	3		
Communications	1	1	2	1	
Risks		5		1	
Procurements		1	1	1	1
TOTAL	2	20	8	10	2

The three cost management processes are:

1. **Estimate costs:** calculate the costs of each resource to complete the project activities.

2. **Determine budget:** add the costs of all the project activities across time.

3. **Control costs:** influence over the cost variances and manage the budget changes.

> ⌦ *In small projects, estimate costs and determine budget could be done in just one process.*

Estimate costs

Once we have the cost management plan, the resources' costs of each of the project activities are estimated.

What do I need to start?

⬇ **Scope** baseline: statement of scope, WBS, and WBS dictionary

⬇ Plans: **schedule, human resources,** and **risks**

Initially, you may not have the human resource plan and the risk plan; however, the estimate costs process is iterative and will be perfected as we gather more information from the different project areas.

> ✎ *At the moment of estimating the project costs we should not forget the costs related with:*
> *- Quality processes and risk management*
> *- Project manager's time*
> *- Training to the project team*
> *- Office and PMO expenses*

What tools can I use?

✂ **Analogous** estimating: use costs from previous projects to estimate the costs of the next project.

✂ **Bottom-up** estimating: decompose the activities in smaller components to estimate with more accuracy each of the inferior parts and then add up the costs from bottom up.

Bottom-up estimating

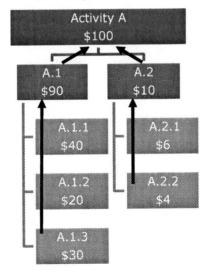

📖 Exercise 7.1 – Analogous and bottom-up estimating

On the following table specify the advantages and disadvantages of the different methods to estimate activities costs.

Analogous estimating	
Advantages	**Disadvantages**

Bottom-up estimating	
Advantages	**Disadvantages**

✋ Take 5 minutes to complete the answer.

Answer to exercise 7.1

Analogous estimating	
Advantages	**Disadvantages**
+ Fast and Cheap	- Low accuracy
+ Project or activity's detail is not needed	- Assumes all projects are the same
Bottom-up estimating	
Advantages	**Disadvantages**
+ More accurate	- Slower and costly
+ Commits team members because they participate in the estimation	- Tendency to use estimates without foundation when the activities are not well known
+ Provides the basis for monitoring and controlling	- Requires plenty of project information for its implementation

☺ *Estimate costs with M.O.D. basis: Method of the oscillating digits, the "handometer" or the "so-so" gesture made with our hands to communicate approximation.*

✂ **Parametric** estimating: use historic information to estimate future costs. They could be simple models, such as estimating the construction costs based on historic cost values per constructed m^2; or more complex econometric models where the construction costs depend on various variables such as m^2, localization, weather, etc.

A parametric estimation could also be performed using linear regression. For example, in the following figure a positive correlation is observed between the produced quantities (X variable) and the total costs (Y variable).

Parametric estimating

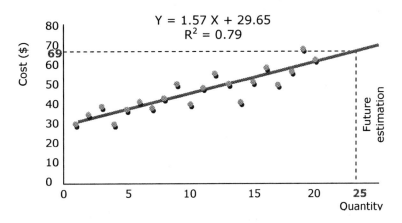

Based on historical data, we want to estimate the future costs for a production of 25 units.

Applying the ordinary least squares method, a correlation coefficient, R^2, of 0.79 is obtained, which means that variable X is explaining, with a 79% approximation, the behavior of variable Y.

The following equation is obtained:

$$Y = 1.57\ X + 29.65$$

This means that:

$$\text{Total Cost} = 1.57 \times \text{quantity} + \text{fixed cost}$$

Where $1.57 is the variable cost per each unit produced and $29.65 is the fixed cost.

With this information the total cost for a 25 unit production can be estimated in the following manner:

$$\text{Total cost} = \$1.57 \times 25\ \text{units} + \$29.65 = \$68.90$$

📖 Exercise 7.2 – Parametric cost estimating

You want to show off your parametric estimating knowledge helping your brother in law, who owns a bakery. Your brother in law's company, The Bakery Corp., produces cakes with its own brand and sells them to supermarkets. The majority of the company's costs can be classified as fixed and variable costs. However, the accounting records for the gas costs do not allow discrimination between fixed and variable costs.

The bakery has a warehouse of 2,000 m^2 and 4 ovens to produce different varieties of cakes. Last year all ovens had an average gas consumption of 429 cubic meters (m^3) per month. The monthly gas consumption and costs are registered in the following table and figure.

Monthly gas consumption and costs

Month	m^3 (X)	Cost $ (Y)	Month	m^3 (X)	Cost $ (Y)
Jan	110	505	Aug	330	1,560
Feb	250	1,200	Sep	210	1,025
Mar	440	1,710	Oct	370	1,560
Apr	720	2,700	Nov	550	1,950
May	400	1,720	Dec	810	2,830
Jun	540	1,870	**Total**	**5,150**	**20,450**
Jul	420	1,820	**Average**	**429**	**1,704**

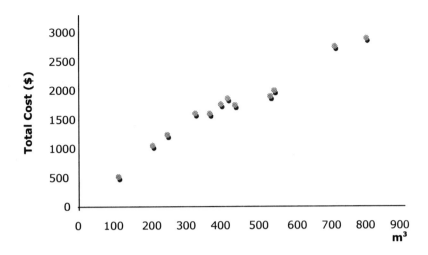

It is estimated for the next year that the cake production will increase 30% because the company signed contracts with two additional supermarkets. To increase the cake production the ovens will be operating more hours per day. The technicians estimate an increment of 20% in the monthly gas consumption.

1. What is the fixed charge per gas consumption?

2. What is the variable cost per consumed m^3?

3. What is the total annual cost for the gas consumption for next year?

Steps to make the calculation in Excel:
1. Load X variable data in the first column
2. Load Y variable data in the second column
3. Select the range of data
4. Click Insert / Scatter graphic
5. Click on any point of the graphic
6. Right click your mouse
7. Add a trend line
8. Type of trend: linear
9. Select show equation and R squared
10. Close

Take 15 minutes to solve the exercise.

Answer to Exercise 7.2

After applying the ordinary least squares method using Excel, the information shown on the following figure is obtained:

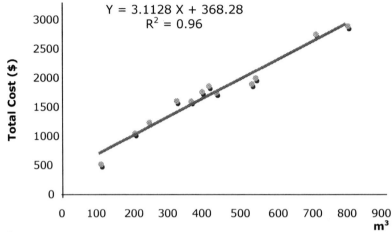

The 0.96 R^2 indicates a significant statistical correlation. On the other hand, the equation provides information about the variable and fixed costs.

1. The fixed charge is $368.28 monthly.

Note: Because the data series is monthly the fixed cost is monthly. If the series was annual the fixed cost would be annual, and if the series was daily, the fixed cost would be daily.

2. The variable costs are $3.1128 for every m^3 of gas consumed.

3. Next year, a 20% increase in gas consumption is expected; therefore, the annual estimated consumption is 6,180 m^3 (5,150m^3 + 20% x 5,150m^3).

For this gas consumption, the total annual cost will be $23,656 ($3.1128 x 6,180 m^3 + $368.28 x 12 months).

The following table presents the estimated monthly costs, considering the seasonality, assuming that for each month the gas consumption increases 20% in relation with that same month of the previous year.

Month	m3 (X)	Cost $ (Y)	Month	m3 (X)	Cost $ (Y)
Jan	132	779	Aug	396	1,601
Feb	300	1,302	Sep	252	1,153
Mar	528	2,012	Oct	444	1,750
Apr	864	3,058	Nov	660	2,423
May	480	1,862	Dec	972	3,394
Jun	648	2,385	**Total**	**6,180**	**23,656**
Jul	504	1,937	**Change %**	**+20%**	**+16%**

✂ Determine the resources' **rates**: request quotes, consult databases, and published price lists. For example, in construction projects publications with average item prices are usually used.

✂ Three point estimating or **PERT**: like for the estimation of an activity duration, the PERT technique can be applied to estimate costs as well.

Estimated cost = (a + 4 x b + c) / 6
Standard deviation = (c – a) / 6
Where: *a* is the optimist, *b* is the most probable, and *c* is the pessimistic

For example, the technicians estimate that the cost of an activity will be $180 (optimistic), $240 (most likely), and $360 (pessimistic). Therefore, the estimated cost per the three point estimating technique would be $250, the standard deviation would be $30, and there is a 95% probability that the cost be in a $190 and $310 range (mean +/- 2 standard deviations).

✂ **Reserve** analysis: add an additional cost reserve for contingency over those foreseen but uncertain events. In other words, add a contingency reserve over those known-unknowns that have residual risk.

For example, it could be that any of the team members get sick and we would have to contract another person to replace that person on the project, which would increase cost for that activity. However, we do not know for sure when would this occur and over which activities. If we add a reserve to each project activity, we could be over estimating it; therefore, a general project reserve is recommended.

One of the tools used to add a general reserve is the Monte Carlo simulation.

Let us see the example on the following table, which has three critical activities (A, B, C), of which the most likely cost is $10 each.

Contingency reserve

Activity	Minimum	Most likely	Maximum	Maximum reserve
A	$7	$10	$13	$3
B	$7	$10	$13	$3
C	$7	$10	$13	$3
Total	**$21**	**$30**	**$39**	**$9**

Let us assume that in the event an operator assigned to one activity gets sick, we will have an additional cost of $3 (maximum cost of $13). On the other hand, if some employee has a higher than normal productivity, the cost for that activity could decrease by $3 (minimum cost of $7).

A way of assigning the contingency could be to add $3 to each activity, which would represent a total reserve of $9. This would be an over estimation of the reserve since it is least likely that all operators get sick and none of them be more productive.

Using a software to run the Monte Carlo simulation, such as Crystal Ball or @Risk, we would obtain a contingency reserve of $6, after entering to the software that each activity has a triangular distribution of ($7, $10, $13) and perform thousands of random simulations (like it is explained in the risk chapter).

Therefore, a $6 reserve for the whole project, without specifying to which activity it corresponds, is more exact than a $9 reserve, assigning $3 more to each activity.

> ☝ *The contingency reserves are part of the total budget and the PM may administer them without upper management authorization.*

✂ **Cost of quality**: costs to ensure the quality of the project. Include all prevention and evaluation costs (compliance costs) and failure costs (non-compliance costs), like we will explain in the quality chapter.

✂ **Software**: worksheets, simulators, statistical tools, etc.

✂ **Bid** proposals analysis: estimate the project costs based on the vendor offers.

When the bidder can select only one part of the proposal, it is important to discriminate the cost of each deliverable individually since there can be scale economies that make the sum of the parts not coincide with the whole project, like it is presented on the following figure.

Price of each deliverable vs. project

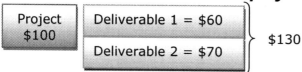

What do I get at the end of the process?

↗ Activity **cost estimates**: human resources, materials, equipment, services, installations, contingency reserves, inflation adjustments, etc.

↗ **Basis of estimates**: support information for the estimates. Document that justifies how the cost estimates were performed, justifications for the assumptions used, specifications of the accuracy range used (for example -10% to +10%), etc.

Determine budget

During the process of preparing the budget the project cost baseline is established.

What do I need to start?

⬇ Scope baseline: statement, WBS and its dictionary

⬇ Cost estimates and basis of estimates

⬇ Schedule and resource calendars

⬇ Contracts

What tools can I use?

✂ **Cost aggregation**: add the project activities' costs distributed across time.

✂ **Reserve** analysis: add a contingency reserve for the known risks or a cost management reserve for those unplanned changes caused by unforeseen risks.

> ☞ *The management reserve is part of the total budget and the PM requires authorization before using this reserve.*

> ☞ *The management reserves are not part of the cost baseline and are not considered for the earned value technique calculations.*

Contingency reserve and management reserve

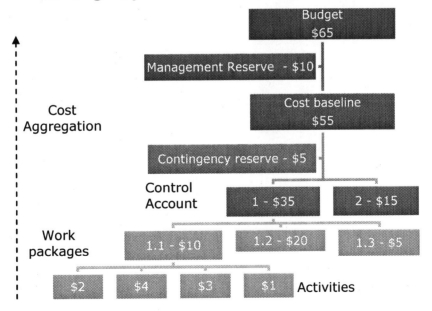

✂ **Analogous or parametric** estimating: use historical information to estimate future budgets.

✂ **Funding limit** reconciliation: analyze if the estimated budget expenditures are coherent with the available funding. For example, if the bank approved a $10 million credit line to finance the project, but will deliver a maximum of $2 million per year, it must be verified that the budget does not exceed that funding limit.

Funding limit

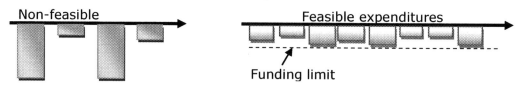

Non-feasible   Feasible expenditures

Funding limit

> ✎ *Large expenditure variations should be avoided for a better project management. It is preferred that the expenditures be consistently increasing or decreasing.*

What do I get at the end of the process?

↗ **Cost baseline**: it is made out of the accumulated project budget. For example, in the following table and figure the project cost baseline is presented with two items. On month 4 the total budget is $600, but the accumulated budget or baseline is $2,250.

Cost Baseline

Item	Month 1	Month 2	Month 3	Month 4	Month 5	Month 6
Personnel	300	400	500	500	500	200
Materials	100	150	200	100	100	50
TOTAL	400	550	700	600	600	250
Accumulated	400	950	1,650	2,250	2,850	3,100

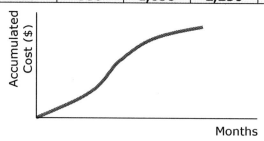

Months

> ✎ *The baseline is similar to an "S" because the majority of the budget is used during the project execution.*

↗ **Funding requirements**: required monies to fund the project across time.

Control costs

During the project cost control process, actions such as the following take place:

✓ Manage and influence changes

✓ Monitor periodically the project cost progress

✓ Verify that the expenditures do not exceed the authorized funding

✓ Ensure the use of integrated change control

✓ Report the approved changes to the stakeholders on time and with quality

> ⌕ *Any cost increment in relation to the approved budget, should be authorized through the integrated change control.*

What do I need to start?

↓ Cost performance baseline

↓ Funding requirements

↓ Work performance reports

What tools can I use?

✂ **Earned value management**: evaluate the project status in relation with its baseline to analyze the progress of project time and cost (see next session).

✂ **Forecasting**: re-estimate periodically the estimated cost at the end of the project.

✂ **To-complete performance index (TCPI)**: estimate how much I should adjust expenditures to meet the approved budget.

✂ Performance **reviews** and variance analysis: compare the actual project performance with its cost and schedule baseline.

What do I get at the end of the process?

↗ Work performance measurements: the status and deviations from its baselines.

↗ Budget forecasts: the cost estimate at the end of the project.

↗ Change requests and updates

Earned Value Management (EVM)

Earned value management (EVM) is a tool, used during the monitoring and controlling process group, to evaluate the project performance during its execution.

This tool is used to control the integrated management of scope, time, and cost. To perform earned value it is required to calculate three values:

- PV: Plan Value

- AC: Actual Cost

- EV: Earned Value or budgeted cost of work performed (BCWP)

To explain this technique we will analyze a very simple car development project, which activities are design, construction, and test as presented in the following figure.

Car project

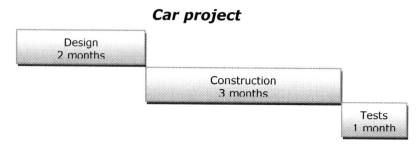

Planned value (PV)

The following table presents the project budget and its baseline, or the planned value (PV) for each activity. For example, the total PV at the end of month 4 is $7,000 (accumulated budget). The total PV at the end of the last month always coincides with the total project budget, in this example $10,000.

Planned value (PV)

Activity	Month 1	Month 2	Month 3	Month 4	Month 5	Month 6	Total
1. Design	1,500	1,500					**3,000**
2. Construction			2,000	2,000	2,000		**6,000**
3. Tests						1,000	**1,000**
Total	**1,500**	**1,500**	**2,000**	**2,000**	**2,000**	**1,000**	**10,000**
Accumulated (PV)	**1,500**	**3,000**	**5,000**	**7,000**	**9,000**	**10,000**	**-**
Accumulated%	15%	30%	50%	70%	90%	100%	-

> ⌕ The PV coincides with the cost baseline, in other words the accumulated budget.

Actual cost (AC)

Once the project is in execution, the actual cost (AC) or the actual cost of work performed (ACWP) should be calculated. The following table indicates the actual costs for each activity up to month 4.

Actual cost (AC)

Activity	Month 1	Month 2	Month 3	Month 4	Month 5	Month 6	Total
1. Design	1,000	1,000					2,000
2. Construction			2,000	4,000			6,000
3. Tests							
Total	1,000	1,000	2,000	4,000			
Accumulated (PV)	1,000	2,000	4,000	8,000			-
Accumulated%	10%	20%	40%	80%			-

Traditional budget analysis

If simple cost variance analysis methods are applied, when the AC is compared with the PV, we could say that at month 3 the PV ($5,000) is higher than the AC ($4,000), which would indicate that the project is well because we have spent less than the estimated. On the other hand, on month 4 the PV ($7,000) is smaller than the AC ($8,000), which could seem as a problem for spending $1,000 more than the budget.

Difference between PV and AC

	Month 1	Month 2	Month 3	Month 4	Month 5	Month 6
PV	1,500	3,000	5,000	7,000	9,000	10,000
AC	1,000	2,000	4,000	8,000	?	?
PV - AC	500	1,000	1,000	-1,000	?	?

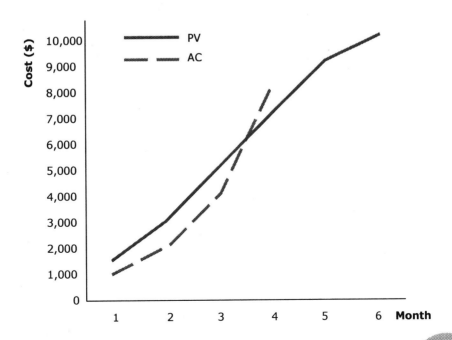

However, comparing only the PV against the AC is incorrect, because this partial information does not allow knowing how efficiently the resources have been used. For example, if on month 4 the car was completed in perfect conditions, having spent only $8,000 is very good, because we have spent $2,000 less than what has been budgeted for this car ($10,000). In addition, the project was completed two months earlier than expected (month 4 instead of month 6).

On the other hand, if in month 4 we have not completed any activity, having spent $8,000 is excessive and the project is on the edge of failure.

Therefore, it is not correct to compare PV with the AC, because this does not account for the project schedule status. To be able to correctly evaluate the project performance it is necessary to know the activity level of progress.

Earned value (EV) or budgeted cost of work performed (BCWP)

To be able to estimate the budgeted cost of work performed or the earned value (EV), it is necessary to collect information about the work actually accomplished of each project activity. Then, the percent complete is converted in the monetary value when it is multiplied by the total budgeted cost of each activity.

The activities' percent complete is presented on the following table. This information is generally provided by the person responsible for executing each of the project activities. The earned value is obtained by multiplying the activities percentages of completion by their respective total budgeted cost, like it is presented on the following table.

Percent complete and earned value (EV)

Activity	Month 1	Month 2	Month 3	Month 4	Month 5	Month 6	Total
1. Design	60%	100%	100%	100%			**3,000**
2. Construction			20%	50%			**6,000**
3. Tests							**1,000**
Earned value (EV)							
1. Design	1,800	3,000	3,000	3,000			
2. Construction			1,200	3,000			
3. Tests							
Total	**1,800**	**3,000**	**4,200**	**6,000**			
% Completed	18%	30%	42%	60%			

Budgetary deviations

Once the EV is calculated, the project budgetary deviations can be properly monitored. The following figure summarizes the information on the previous tables, and it is very useful to control the project budget.

PV, AC and EV

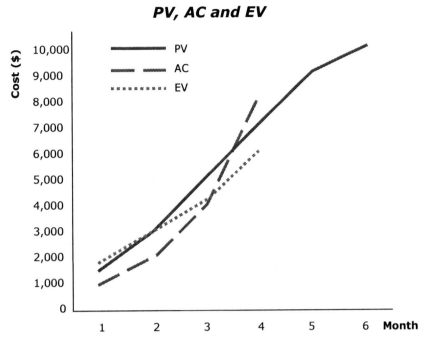

For example, if all project activities are analyzed as a whole, it is observed than on month 4 a value of $6,000 has been worked (EV) and $8,000 have been spent (AC). Therefore, $2,000 more than what has been worked has been spent, which indicates a project cost problem.

At the end of month 4 the EV is $6,000 when according to the plan $7,000 should have been performed (PV), which indicates a delay in execution.

Cost analysis

To analyze cost deviations, the earned value (EV) should be compared with the actual cost (AC). This comparison can be done through the **cost variance (CV)**, or through the cost performance index (**CPI**).

☞ Cost Variance: CV = EV – AC

☞ Cost Performance Index: CPI = EV / AC

In our example, at the end of month 4, the cost variance is -$2,000 ($6,000 - $8,000). A negative CV indicates inefficiency because there is more spending than work performed. On the other hand, a positive CV indicates efficiency.

A similar analysis can be done with the cost performance index (CPI). On this case the CPI is 0.75 ($6,000/$8,000). If the CPI is less than 1, it is showing inefficiency because there is being more spent than work performed. When the CPI is higher than 1 it indicates efficiency in the resource utilization.

Cost variance analysis

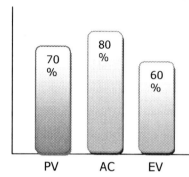

At the end of month 4:
AC = $8,000 ; EV = $6,000
CV = EV − AC = -2,000
CPI = EV / AC = 0.75 ⇒ Inefficiency

This analysis should be done periodically for each activity, during the project execution. On the following table we can evaluate the cost performance of the project activities at the end of month 4.

Cost variance analysis

Activity	PV	AC	EV	CV = EV - AC	CPI = EV / AC
1. Design	3,000	2,000	3,000	1,000	1.50
2. Construction	4,000	6,000	3,000	-3,000	0.50
Total	**7,000**	**8,000**	**6,000**	**-2,000**	**0.75**

Analyzing the cost variance (CV), it can be concluded that in the design activity we have spent $1,000 less than what has been worked (CV = 1,000). On the other hand, the cost performance index for this activity is higher than 1 (CPI = 1.5), which is good because it indicates efficiency.

The construction activity has budgetary problems because we have spent $3,000 more than what has been worked (CV = -3,000), and a less than 1 cost performance indicates inefficiency (CPI = 0.5).

Schedule analysis

To evaluate appropriately the schedule progress compliance with the project times, it is necessary to compare the EV with the PV. This comparison can be done through the **schedule variance (SV)** or the **schedule performance index (SPI)**.

☞ Schedule variance: SV = EV − PV

☞ Schedule performance index: SPI = EV / PV

Using the same example, on month 4 the SV is -$1,000 ($6,000 - $7,000), indicating that the project is delayed. On the other hand, a positive SV would indicate that the project is being executed faster than expected.

A similar analysis can be done with the SPI. In our example it is 0.86 ($6,000/$7,000). If the SPI is less than 1 it shows a delay, if it is greater than 1, it would indicate that is being executed faster than planned.

Schedule variance analysis

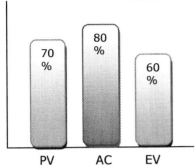

At the end of month 4:
PV = $7,000 ; EV = $6,000
SV = EV – PV = -1,000
SPI = EV / PV = 0.86 ⇒ Delay!

Analyzing the activities separately, according to the following table, it can be concluded that the design activity has a SV equal to 0, which indicates that the activity is complete and its SPI is equal to 1. In regards to the construction activity, it is delayed because its SV is -$1,000 and its SPI is .75.

Schedule variance analysis

Activity	PV	AC	EV	SV = EV - PV	SPI = EV / PV
1. Design	3,000	2,000	3,000	0	1
2. Construction	4,000	6,000	3,000	-1,000	0.75
Total	**7,000**	**8,000**	**6,000**	**-1,000**	**0.86**

> ✍ *The earned value analysis formulas always start with EV. Variance is a subtraction and index is a division.*

Forecasting

The terminology used for forecasting is the following:

- Budget at completion (**BAC**)
- Estimate at completion (**EAC**)
- Estimate to complete (**ETC**)

➢ *Forecasting based on original budget*

Assumption: regardless of the efficiency or inefficiency of what has been spent up to the moment, the cost of the remaining work will stay as it was originally budgeted.

EAC = AC + (BAC – EV)
EAC = $8,000 + ($10,000 - $6,000) = $12,000
ETC = EAC – AC = $12,000 - $8,000 = $4,000

➤ Forecasting based on actual CPI

Assumption: the future expenditures will stay at the same efficiency or inefficiency level as it has been demonstrated up to the moment.

Using the previous example, the CPI at the end of month 4 is 0.75 ($6,000/$8,000), because $6,000 worth of work was performed and $8,000 were spent. This index could be interpreted as having worked 25% less than expended (-$2.000/$8.000), or that we spent 33.33% more than what was worked ($2,000/$6,000).

Under the assumption that this inefficiency will stay across time, we could estimate in a simple manner that the project will end up at a 33.33% higher cost than what was originally planned. On this example, the original estimated cost at the end of month 6 was $10,000; therefore, the estimated cost at the end of the project would be $13,333. This result can be obtained with the following equation:

EAC = BAC / CPI

EAC = $10,000 / 0.75 = $13,333

This would be the same to say that:

EAC = AC + (BAC – EV) / CPI

EAC = $8,000 + ($10,000 - $6,000) / 0.75 = $13,333

ETC = EAC – AC = $13,333 - $8,000 = $5,333

☝ _Simple and fast formula to estimate costs at completion:_

EAC = BAC / CPI

➤ Forecasting considering the CPI and the SPI

Assumption: future costs will depend on the actual inefficiency of the CPI and the SPI, given that the schedule delays will also affect costs.

EAC = AC + ((BAC – EV) / (CPI x SPI))

EAC = $8,000 + (($10,000 - $6,000) / (0.75 x 0.86) = $14,202

ETC = EAC – AC = $14,202 - $8,000 = $6,202

You may consider any other proportion to weight the CPI and SPI indices. For example, you may use 80% CPI and 20% SPI. On this case the result would be:

EAC = AC + ((BAC – EV) / (80% x CPI + 20% x SPI))

EAC = $8,000 + (($10,000 - $6,000) / (0.6 + 0.172) = $13,181

ETC = EAC – AC = $13,181 - $8,000 = $5,181

> ### Forecasting based on a new estimate

A more accurate way, but also slower and more costly, to estimate the costs at completion, would be the following:

EAC = AC + New estimate for remaining costs

If the project team feels that the CPI for each of the remaining activities is not relevant to forecast the future costs, the estimated cost at completion would be the cost spent to date plus an updated budget for the remaining tasks.

In our example the cost at completion could be estimated in the following way:

Activity	AC	ETC	Explanation
1. Design	$2,000	$0	It is already completed
2. Construction	$6,000	$6,000	The remaining 50% will be as the AC
3. Tests	?	$1,500	Labor costs increased
Total	$8,000	$7,500	$15,500 = EAC

To-complete performance index (TCPI)

This index measures the relation between what is left to be done and the remaining funds. It indicates the necessary cost efficiency to achieve the BAC (or the EAC).

TCPI = (BAC – EV) / (BAC – AC)

TCPI = ($10,000 - $6,000) / ($10,000 - $8,000) = $4,000 / $2,000 = 2

This means that we should improve the cost efficiency a 100% to be able to only spend the originally planned $10,000. In other words, decrease to half the costs; instead of spending the $4,000 that are left to work, we should only spend $2,000 to stay within the original $10,000 budget.

If the company confirms that it is impossible to meet the BAC, it may approve a new EAC as the most probable project estimated cost. For example, if $15,500 EAC is estimated, the TCPI should be modified in the following manner:

TCPI = (BAC – EV) / (EAC – AC)

TCPI = ($10,000 - $6,000) / ($15,500 - $8,000) = $4,000 / $7,500 = 0.53

This means that we can only spend an additional 47% (1 – 0.53) of the remaining funds to meet the modified budget of $15,500. In other words, we can only spend an additional $3,500 (47% x $7,500) of the remaining work ($4,000) to meet the ETC.

📖 Exercise 7.3 – Earned value management – Construction

The estimated budget of your next construction project is the following:

Activity / Month	1	2	3	4	5	6	7	8	Total
1. Market study	40	20							60
2. Define Strategy			40						40
3. Construct local				100	100	100	400		700
4. Equipment								200	200
TOTAL	40	20	40	100	100	100	400	200	1000
Baseline									

Up to month 6 the actual costs were the following:

Activity / Month	1	2	3	4	5	6	7	8	Total
1. Market study	40	30							70
2. Define Strategy			40						40
3. Construct local				100	150	200			450
4. Equipment									
TOTAL	40	30	40	100	150	200			560
Accumulated									

Up to month 6 the project % complete was the following:

Activity / Month	1	2	3	4	5	6	7	8	Total
1. Market study	50%	100%	100%	100%	100%	100%			100%
2. Define Strategy			100%	100%	100%	100%			100%
3. Construct local				20%	40%	60%			60%
4. Equipment						0%			0%
Earned value									
1. Market study									
2. Define Strategy									
3. Construct local									
4. Equipment									
Total									

a) Analyze the total project cost deviations at the end of month 6

b) Analyze the total project schedule deviations at the end of month 6

c) Forecast the total project costs at the end of the project and the variance at completion (VAC)

d) Calculate the TCPI

🖐 Take 15 minutes to solve this exercise

📖 **Answer to exercise 7.3**

Planned value (PV)

Activity / Month	1	2	3	4	5	6	7	8	Total
TOTAL	40	20	40	100	100	100	400	200	1000
Baseline = PV	40	60	100	200	300	400	800	1000	

Actual cost (AC)

Activity / Month	1	2	3	4	5	6	7	8	Total
TOTAL	40	30	40	100	150	200	?	?	560
Accumulated = AC	40	70	110	210	360	560	?	?	

Earned value (EV)

Activity / Month	1	2	3	4	5	6	7	8	PV
1. Market study	50%	100%	100%	100%	100%	100%			$60
2. Define Strategy			100%	100%	100%	100%			$40
3. Construct local				20%	40%	60%			$700
4. Equipment						0%			$200
Earned value									
1. Market study	30	60	60	60	60	60			
2. Define Strategy			40	40	40	40			
3. Construct local				140	280	420			
4. Equipment						0			
Total = EV	30	60	100	240	380	520			

a) Total project costs deviations at the end of month 6:

$CV = EV - AC = \$520 / \$560 = -\$40$

Inefficiency. We have spent $40 more than what has been worked.

$CPI = EV / AC = \$520 / \$560 = 0.93$

For every dollar spent we have worked $0.93

b) Total project schedule deviations at the end of month 6

$SV = EV - PV = \$520 / \$400 = \$120$

The project is moving fast. We have worked $120 more than what was planned.

$SPI = EV / PV = \$520 / \$400 = 1.3$

The project is moving 30% faster than planned.

c) Total cost at the end of the project, assuming we keep the same inefficiency:

$EAC = BAC / CPI = \$1,000 / 0.93 = \$1,075$

$VAC = EAC - BAC = \$1,075 - \$1,000 = \$75$

We estimate spending $75 more than what was originally budgeted.

d) $TCPI = (BAC - EV) / (BAC - AC) = (\$1,000 - \$520) / (\$1,000 - \$560)$

$TCPI = \$480 / \$440 = 1.091$

A 9.1% cost efficiency improvement is needed to be able to meet the original $1,000 budget. Or we should decrease costs by $40 until the end of the project and in addition finish the remaining work based on the original budget.

📖 <u>**Exercise 7.4 – Earned value management –"Pine-trees" Project**</u>

You have been assigned to plant 4 pine trees. The estimated duration to plant each pine tree is 1 day, with an estimated cost of $100 per pine.

You will not be able to fast track activities; therefore, you will be able to plant a pine tree only if its predecessor pine was already planted.

The project report at the end of day 3 is as follows:

PLAN	↑	↑	↑	↑
	Day 1	Day 2	Day 3	Day 4
Cost planned	$100	$100	$100	$100
ACTUAL	↑	↑	↑	
Progress	100%	100%	40%	0%
Actual cost	$100	$120	$30	

You may observe that pine tree 2 finished later than planned, which delayed the start of pine tree 3. At the end of day 3, pine 3 has only a 40% progress.

Complete the following table with the project status.

Indicator	Calculation	Answer	Interpretation
PV			
EV			
AC			
BAC			
CV			
CPI			
SV			
SPI			
TCPI			
EAC			
ETC			
VAC			

✋ Take 10 minutes to solve this exercise

Answer to exercise 7.4

Indicator	Calculation	Answer	Interpretation
PV	PV1 + PV2 + PV3	$300	We should work for a $300 value
EV	100% x PV1 + 100% x PV2 + 40% x PV3	$240	We have completed $240 of the total work
AC	AC1 + AC2 + AC3	$250	We have spent $250
BAC	PV total	$400	The total budget is $400
CV	EV - AC	-$10	We have spent $10 more of what we have worked
CPI	EV / AC	0.96	We only obtain $0.96 for every $ invested
SV	EV - PV	-60	The project is slow
SPI	EV / PV	0.80	We have only completed an 80% of what was planned
TCPI	(BAC-EV) / (BAC – AC)	160/150 = 1.067	We should decrease 6.7% of the remaining funds to spend $400
EAC	BAC / CPI	$416.67	The estimated cost at completion is $416.67
ETC	EAC - AC	$166.67	There is $166.67 left to spent to complete the project
VAC	BAC - EAC	-$16.67	We estimate to spend $16.67 more than what was budgeted

Summarizing earned value management

The following table presents the main formulas and their earned value technique interpretation.

Name	Formula	Interpretation
Cost variance (CV)	EV - AC	> 0 Efficient < 0 Inefficient
Schedule variance (SV)	EV - PV	> 0 Fast < 0 Slow
Cost performance index (CPI)	EV / AC	For every $ spent we have worked $____
Schedule performance index (SPI)	EV / PV	We are progressing at a ___% of what was planned
To-complete performance index (TCPI)	(BAC-EV) / (BAC – AC)	How much we should adjust costs to meet the BAC
Estimate at completion (EAC)	BAC / CPI	How much will be the project cost at the end of the project
Estimate to complete (ETC)	EAC - AC	How much more will the project cost
Variance at completion (VAC)	BAC - EAC	Difference between the budget and what we expect to spend

? *The CPI of an agricultural project is 1.4 and the SPI is 0.8. This means that we are receiving $1.4 for each invested dollar. However, we are only at 80% of where we should be according to plan. What is the best thing to do?*

    A. *Use less resources to decrease costs*
    B. *Report to the client that the project is delayed*
    C. *Compress the schedule*
    D. *Fast track activities*

> ✎ *Approximately 5 exam questions include earned value calculations and an additional 5 questions require knowing earned value management concepts.*

Answer:

Alternative	Explanation
A	False. Since the CPI is higher than 1, there is no cost problem.
B	It could be true if options C and D weren't available.
C	True. Because the CPI is positive, we could increment the cost for a compression and in that way accelerate the project.
D	It could be if option C was not available, given that by fast tracking activities you add risk to the project.

Financial decision methods

During the project initiating processes, different financial decision techniques are used to select among different project alternatives. Moreover, the budget is complemented with financial indicators to evaluate the project profitability.

The financial techniques mostly used during the project formulation and evaluation are:

- Net present value (**NPV**)
- Internal rate of return (**IRR**)
- Investment payback rule (**IPR**)
- Cost benefit ratio

> ✎ *None of these financial indicators are explained in the PMBOK® Guide. There might be approximately 3 conceptual questions about these financial criteria.*

Explaining in detail these financial indicators is outside the scope of this book. We will briefly explain what is most important of each of these concepts.

➢ Net present value (NPV)

The net present value (NPV) measures the project profitability in present value of money, after recovering the initial investment and opportunity cost of money. The formula to calculate the NPV is the following:

$$NPV = NB_0 + \frac{NB_1}{(1+i)} + \frac{NB_2}{(1+i)^2} + \dotsb + \frac{NB_n}{(1+i)^n}$$

Where,
NB: Net benefit
NB_0: Net benefit at moment 0 (initial investment).
i: interest rate or discount rate

A project will be profitable if the present value of the net cash flow is positive.

> ✎ *Rule of thumb when using NPV:*
> *If NPV > 0 => Profitable project => Invest*
> *If NPV < 0 => Non-profitable project => Do not invest*

The NPV measures, in today's money, how much richer is the investor by investing on that project instead of in its best alternative.

Let us assume that a company can invest its money in projects that yield 8% annually. The project definition indicates that a $50,000 investment is required to obtain a $10,000 NPV. Is it convenient to proceed with this project?

From a financial point of view, every time the NPV is positive, it is convenient to proceed with the project. The $10,000 NPV means that the investor recover the $50,000, the 8% annually during the project life ($4,000 per year), and obtains an additional $10,000 at present value.

➢ Internal rate of return (IRR)

The internal rate of return is the discount rate that makes the NPV equal to zero. This indicator measures the project profitability in percentage terms. When the IIR is higher than the discount rate (opportunity cost of money or interest rate), the project is profitable.

> ✎ *Rule of thumb when using IRR:*
> *If IRR > interest rate => Invest*
> *If IRR < interest rate => Do not invest*
> *Assumption: At the beginning negative project cash flows and later positive cash flows*

A simple way of calculating the IRR is with Excel:

1. Construct the project's net cash flow

2. Select the values of the net cash flow

3. Insert / Function / Financial / IRR

4. Bingo! You will get the IRR.

☺ *How is the project IRR calculated? There are priceless things in life, for everything else there is Excel.*

For example, if a project has an IRR of 15% annually and the best alternative is to put the money in a 10% annual rate, the project should proceed.

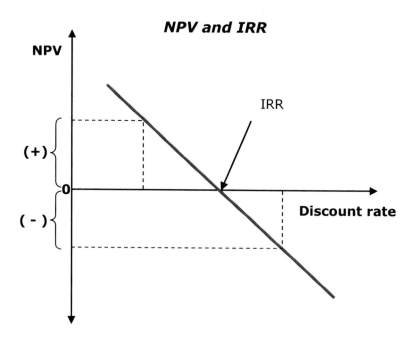

If the discount rate increases, the NPV decreases

📖 **Exercise 7.5 – NPV and IRR**

You want to select between two investment projects. The net cash flow for each project is presented in the following tables.

North Project

Project	Year 0	Year 1	Year 2	Year 3	Year 4	Year 5
NORTH	-140,000	7,000	20,000	25,000	60,000	90,000

South Project

Project	Year 0	Year 1	Year 2	Year 3	Year 4	Year 5
SOUTH	-140,000	61,000	52,000	44,000	15,000	10,000

a) What decision should you take if the minimum return demanded for your projects is 10% annually?

b) How does the decision change if the discount rate for your investments is only 5% annually?

c) What is the internal rate of return for each project?

✋ Take 10 minutes to solve this exercise, but do not waste time in the IRR calculation.

Answer to exercise 7.5

a) NPV of each project with an annual discount rate of 10%:

NPV North $= -140{,}000 + \dfrac{7{,}000}{1.1} + \dfrac{20{,}000}{1.1^2} + \dfrac{25{,}000}{1.1^3} + \dfrac{60{,}000}{1.1^4} + \dfrac{90{,}000}{1.1^5}$

NPV North = $-1,461

NPV South $= -140{,}000 + \dfrac{61{,}000}{1.1} + \dfrac{52{,}000}{1.1^2} + \dfrac{44{,}000}{1.1^3} + \dfrac{15{,}000}{1.1^4} + \dfrac{10{,}000}{1.1^5}$

NPV South = $7,942

Project North is not profitable because we lose $1,461. We should not proceed even if it is the only alternative.

Project South is profitable. We earn $7,942, after recuperating the $140,000 and the 10% of $140,000 during 5 years. Therefore, the best alternative is to invest in Project South.

b) NPV of each project with an annual discount rate of 5%:

NPV North $= -140{,}000 + \dfrac{7{,}000}{1.05} + \dfrac{20{,}000}{1.05^2} + \dfrac{25{,}000}{1.05^3} + \dfrac{60{,}000}{1.05^4} + \dfrac{90{,}000}{1.05^5}$

NPV North = $26,283

NPV South $= -140{,}000 + \dfrac{61{,}000}{1.05} + \dfrac{52{,}000}{1.05^2} + \dfrac{44{,}000}{1.05^3} + \dfrac{15{,}000}{1.05^4} + \dfrac{10{,}000}{1.05^5}$

NPV South = $23,445

Project North is profitable. We earn $26,283, after recuperating the $140,000 investment and the 5% of $140,000 during 5 years.

Project South is profitable. We earn $23,445, after recuperating the $140,000 investment and the 5% of $140,000 during 5 years.

Given that both projects have a positive NPV using the 5% discount rate, we should choose Project North for being more profitable.

c) What is the internal rate of return for each project?

The following is obtained using Excel or a financial calculator:

Project North IRR = 9.704% annually

Project South IRR = 12.933% annually

It is observed that the IRR for North is less than the IRR for South, then we may conclude that Project South is better than North. However, to calculate which project is more profitable we must calculate the NPV. For example, for an annual 10% discount rate Project South turned out to be better than North, while for an annual 5% discount rate, Project North is more profitable than Project South.

The IRR is the discount rate that makes the NPV equal to zero. Demonstration:

$$NPV\ North = -140{,}000 + \frac{7{,}000}{1.09704} + \frac{20{,}000}{1.09704^2} + \frac{25{,}000}{1.09704^3} + \frac{60{,}000}{1.09704^4} + \frac{90{,}000}{1.09704^5} = 0$$

$$NPV\ South = -140{,}000 + \frac{61{,}000}{1.12933} + \frac{52{,}000}{1.12933^2} + \frac{44{,}000}{1.12933^3} + \frac{15{,}000}{1.12933^4} + \frac{10{,}000}{1.12933^5} = 0$$

> ✎ *The IRR is not a good indicator to select among projects. However, when taking the exam, if you do not have the NPV information, you should assume that the project with the highest IRR is the best.*

📖 Exercise 7.6 – Project selection per NPV

Based on the data from the following table, which project would you select as the best?

Project	Inversion ($)	NPV ($)
A	100	100
B	50	80
C	30	30
D	20	20
E	60	-20

🖐 Take 5 minutes to solve this exercise

Answer to exercise 7.6

To answer which project is the best we need more information about the project typology and the budgetary constraint.

a) Assuming independent projects without constraints in investment funds, we should pursue all projects with a positive NPV (A, B, C, D) and do not invest on project E because it has a negative NPV.

b) Assuming independent projects with a budget constrained to $100, we should evaluate the different project combinations that maximize the sum of their respective NPVs. On this example, it is convenient to invest the $100 on projects B, C, and D to obtain a NPV of $130 ($80 from B + $30 from C + $20 from D).

c) Assuming excluded and non-repeatable projects among each other, without constraints on the capital investment, we should select the project with the highest NPV (Project A).

Do you prefer project B because the NPV compared to the investment is better than with project A? You forgot that the NPV already considers the recovery of the investment; therefore, you should select project A to obtain a NPV of an additional $100 over the recovery of the investment, instead of B where you would only earn $80.

> **Investment payback rule (IPR)**

The payback rule measures the number of years needed to recover the investment with the net benefits. In other words, the IPR indicates in how much time the investment will be recovered.

Based on the data in the following table, which project would you select?

Project	Year 0	Year 1	Year 2	Year 3	IPR (years)
A	-5000	2000	3000	3000	2
B	-5000	5000	0	0	1
C	-5000	4000	1000	5000	2

Did you like project B because its IPR is shorter? Be careful! Project B will have a negative NPV, regardless of the discount rate.

The IPR is frequently used, because every businessman wants to know how long it will take to recover their investment. There is no defined criterion that mentions what should be the optimum IPR for a project. For example, in projects of significant technology change, short IPRs are demanded (1 or 2 years), while in agricultural projects, a 10 to 30 years IPR may be

reasonable. How much time to wait to cut down a forest? How many years a rum in an oak barrel before going out to market? Once more time, the common response is "It depends!"

> ✎ The IPR demanded from projects to make an investment is a very arbitrary criterion.

We should not select a project based on its IPR without first evaluating its NPV. Going back to the example presented above, the following table present the NPV of each alternative if the annual discount rate is 10%.

Project	Year 0	Year 1	Year 2	Year 3	IPR	NPV ($)
A	-5000	2000	3000	3000	2	1,551
B	-5000	5000	0	0	1	-455
C	-5000	4000	1000	5000	2	3,219

As it can be observed, project B recovers the investment in one year, but it would be a bad selection because its NPV is negative. On the other hand, either project A or C recovers the investment in two years, but the NPV for C is better than A.

> ✎ The IPR is not a good indicator to select among projects. However, when taking the exam, if you do not have the NPV or the IRR information, you should assume that the project with the lowest IPR is the best.

➢ Cost benefit ratio

The cost benefit ratio consists of dividing the actual value of the benefits by the actual value of the costs (including the initial investment).

> ✎ Rule of thumb when using the cost benefit ratio B/C:
>
>   If B/C > 1 => Invest (the NPV is positive)
>
>   If B/C < 1 => Do not invest (the NPV is negative)

The B/C ratio is frequently used in health economics and social projects. Nonetheless, this indicator has the same decision making logic as the use of the NPV.

Summarizing cost management

The following figure summarizes the main inputs, outputs, and interrelations of the cost management processes.

Integrating cost management

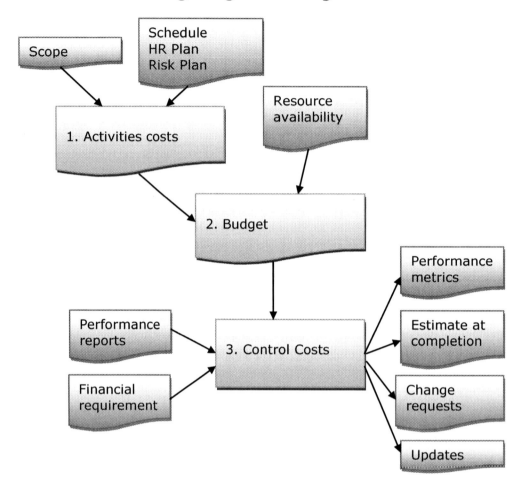

pablolledó
PL projectManagement

Exam 7 – Cost

> **Number of questions**: 15
> **Time to respond**: 15 minutes
> **Pass score**: 80% (12 correct answers)

1. You have been assigned as the Project Manager and should calculate the budget for a tax counseling project for an automobile industry client. Which of the following statements is FALSE?
   A. The management reserve is considered for the earned value calculations
   B. The cost baseline includes a contingency reserve for residual risks
   C. The control account will be at a superior hierarchy level than the work packages
   D. The project budget should include a management reserve

2. Your company needs to purchase a power generator to supply for blackout periods. You will purchase a $4,000 equipment that will last 15 years, if used normally, and with proper maintenance. The accounting useful life for this type of asset is 5 years. If the company applies a linear depreciation method, what will be the depreciation that can be discounted annually from the income tax?
   A. $266.66
   B. $400.00
   C. $800.00
   D. Need more information to respond

3. A project ends with the delivery of a high speed train for a European client. The operational and maintenance costs that the client will face are considered as:
   A. Prorated costs
   B. Variable costs
   C. Sunk costs
   D. Lifecycle costs

Use the following table to answer questions 4 through 6.

End of year	Inflows	Outflows
0	0	100
1	50	40
2	100	20
3	120	20

4. What will be project net present value if the discount rate is 12% annually?
   A. $43.88
   B. $90.00
   C. $190.00
   D. $270.45

5. Based on the information from question 4, what is the project's internal rate of return?
   A. 5.7%
   B. 10.8%
   C. 12.0%
   D. 30.3%

6. Based on the information from question 4, what is the payback rule?
   A. 3 years
   B. 2 years
   C. 1 year
   D. Need more information to respond

7. The Project Manager, along with the project team, established the baseline for an agricultural project at $105 million and an estimated duration of 3 years. In which case would it be acceptable to change the baseline while the project is in execution?
   A. The contracted company increased by 50% the quality management budget
   B. The engineering department productivity is 30% less than expected
   C. The client and the sponsor authorized a $25,000 project scope change
   D. The wholesale price index for various inputs used by the project has increased by 45%

8. A simple and fast way of calculating the estimate at completion for the project, would be to take the budget at completion and divide it by:
   A. Cost variance
   B. Cost performance index
   C. To-complete performance index
   D. Schedule performance index

9. You have been assigned to plant 10 pine trees to sell on the next Holiday Season in December. The planned value for each pine is $5; therefore, the total budget adds up to $50. We are on September and all the pines have been planted at a total cost of $40. What would be the schedule performance index?
   A. 1.25
   B. 0
   C. 0.80
   D. 1

10. You are controlling the costs of a project that surpasses 20 million dollars. The main result that you will get out of this process will be:
    A. Budget
    B. Estimated cost at completion
    C. Financing requirements
    D. Estimated activities cost

11. You are the project manager of a textile production company. Generally the projects end up spending more than budgeted and lasting longer than expected. Therefore, you have decided to improve the planning, and the monitoring and controlling processes. What tool will you use to evaluate the efficiency on the progress of the schedule?
    A. Schedule variance
    B. Gantt chart
    C. Schedule performance index
    D. Estimate at completion

12. A project for the transfer and distribution of electric power is reporting a cost performance index of 0.72. We could say that:
    A. The project gets $0.72 for every spent dollar
    B. It is expected that the total project cost be 72% higher than planned
    C. The project is 28% under the planned value
    D. The project has completed only 72% of what was planned

13. You want to make a trip in your car from Springfield to Dayland. You know that the distance is 1,100 miles, that the actual price of gasoline is $1 per gallon and that your car consumes 10 liters every 100 miles. With this information you decide to estimate the gasoline cost for this trip. What estimating technique would you be using?
    A. Order of magnitude (ROM)
    B. Parametric
    C. Analogous
    D. Definitive

14. You should select between the projects shown on the following table, and have enough money to invest in any of them. These are mutually exclusive projects and once completed cannot be repeated. Which alternative is most convenient?

Project	Investment	NPV	Duration (years)
A	100	50	5
B	50	100	4
C	200	200	10
D	100	20	1

    A. Project A
    B. Project B
    C. Project C
    D. Project D

15. The planned value for activity A is $600, it is 80% complete and its actual cost is $550. Activity B has a planned value of $300, the actual progress is 60%, and its actual cost adds up to $350. Lastly, activity C, with a planned value of $200, is fully complete and its actual cost was $300. The total project budget is $1,100. What is the cost performance index (CPI)?
    A. 1.3953
    B. 0.7167
    C. 1.2791
    D. 0.7818

Lessons Learned

- ✓ Actual cost (AC)
- ✓ Analogous estimating
- ✓ Bottom up estimating
- ✓ Budget at completion (BAC)
- ✓ Cost baseline
- ✓ Cost benefit ratio
- ✓ Cost lifecycle
- ✓ Cost performance index (CPI)
- ✓ Cost variance (CV)
- ✓ Definitive estimating
- ✓ Direct and indirect costs
- ✓ Earned value (EV)
- ✓ Earned value management (EVM)
- ✓ Estimate at completion (EAC)
- ✓ Estimate to complete (ETC)
- ✓ Fixed and variable costs
- ✓ Funding limit
- ✓ Internal rate of return (IRR)
- ✓ Linear and accelerated depreciation
- ✓ Net present value (NPV)
- ✓ Opportunity cost
- ✓ Order of magnitude estimating (ROM)
- ✓ Ordinary least squares method
- ✓ Parametric estimating
- ✓ Payback rule
- ✓ Planned value (PV)
- ✓ Reserve analysis
- ✓ Schedule performance index (SPI)
- ✓ Schedule variance (SV)
- ✓ Sunk costs
- ✓ To-complete performance index (TCPI)
- ✓ Value analysis
- ✓ Variance at completion (VAC)
- ✓ Working capital

CHAPTER #8

QUALITY

Chapter 8 - QUALITY

> *Quality is never an accident; it is always the result of intelligent effort.*
>
> John Ruskin (1819-1900); English writer and critic.

It is very important to dedicate time to quality management in every project to:
- Prevent errors and defects
- Avoid re-work, which implies time and money savings
- Have a satisfied client

When you finish this chapter, you will have learned the following concepts:
- ✓ Basic quality concepts
- ✓ Quality theories
- ✓ Quality management processes
- ✓ Quality planning
- ✓ Cost of quality
- ✓ Quality assurance
- ✓ Continuous improvement
- ✓ Quality control

Basic quality concepts

Quality management implies that the project satisfies the needs for what it was conceived for. For that, the following will be necessary:
- ✓ Convert the stakeholders' needs and expectations into project requirements
- ✓ Achieve client satisfaction when the project delivers what was originally planned and the product meets the real needs
- ✓ Perform preventive actions over inspections
- ✓ Permanently look for perfection: continuous improvement

> ✍ *Definition of quality according to the American Society for Quality:*
> *"The degree to which a project fulfills the requirements"*

> ✍ *Definition of quality according to Dr. Kaoru Ishikawa:*
> *Design, produce, and maintain a product that is the most economic, the most useful, and it always satisfies the consumer.*

? The project manager finds out that one of its team members has created its own process for the installation of hardware. What should the project manager do?

    A. *Thank the team member for creating a new process for the company*
    B. *Analyze if the process is convenient for the company*
    C. *Investigate the project plan to determine if a standard process can be used*
    D. *Evaluate the cost-benefit ratio of the new process*

Rookies in the quality management topic would have answered A or B. However, any expert in quality management would have recognized that the correct answer is C.

? *A client has called to tell us that the house that we delivered does not have an acceptable quality. However, it was never clear on the project scope what "acceptable quality" means for the client. What should you do next time to avoid this inconvenience?*

Answer:

    1. Always define "acceptable quality" and convert it to a project requirement
    2. Establish how quality will be measured
    3. Determine all the necessary work, so the project meets that requirement

? *What has more quality, a used Land Rover or a new Ferrari?*

Before answering, we have to differentiate between "**quality**" and "**grade**". Surely, the new Ferrari has a greater grade of features than the used truck, including 7 speed transmission, cruise control, automatic parking sensors, etc. However, quality is related to the fulfillment of pre-established requirements. For example, if the requirement of minimum quality is defined as "that it does not break in rocky, unpaved roads", surely the used truck is of better quality than the Ferrari. On the contrary, if quality is defined as "top speed of 200 mph", then the Ferrari is better than the truck.

It is worth mentioning that the lack of grade (features) in projects is not a problem, whereas the lack of quality surely is.

? *Which clock has the more exact time, an analog clock without a seconds hand or a digital clock?*

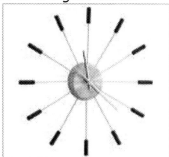 

To answer this question we should distinguish the difference between **accuracy** and **precision**. The digital clock with seconds surely has greater precision, because the analog clock gives us less information. However, accuracy depends on meeting an objective. In this example, if the objective was having the time as the Big Ben, the more accurate clock would be the one with the time closest to the Big Ben, regardless of their precision.

Let us look at another example to see the difference between accuracy and precision. If we throw darts to a target, accuracy will be when we hit the center of the target. Now, if all the darts are off target, but in the same zone, it is said that they were consecutive throws with enough precision.

Accuracy vs. Precision

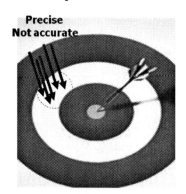

In engineering, science, and statistics, accuracy and precision are not equivalent. Accuracy is the capacity to be close to the target. Precision is the capacity of taking similar samples that are usually measured with the standard deviation.

The PM and its team must plan for the grade of accuracy and precision that the project requires.

Quality theories

It is not the objective of this book to go into detail about the quality theories. In this section, we will briefly explain the contributions of the main quality theorists: Deming, Juran, Ishikawa, and Crosby.

Quality Theorists

W. Edwards Deming (1900-1993)	
Joseph Moses Juran (1904-2008)	
Kaoru Ishikawa (1915-1989)	
Philip Crosby (1926-2001)	

Edwards Deming is one of the pioneers in topics related with quality management. His three most known concepts are:
- ✓ The chain reaction
- ✓ The 14 steps to total quality
- ✓ The continuous improvement cycle ("plan-do-check-act")

Next, we summarize these three concepts in the following figures:

Chain reaction

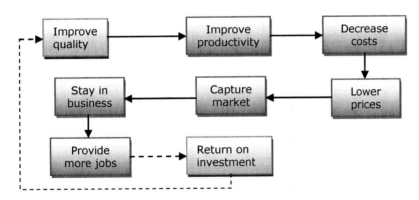

14 Steps to Achieve Total Quality Management

1. Publish the vision, mission, and objectives.
2. Adopt the new philosophy.
3. Understand the purpose of inspections.
4. End the practice of awarding business on the basis of a price tag.
5. Improve constantly.
6. Institute training on the job.
7. Leadership.
8. Innovation.
9. Teamwork.
10. Eliminate exhortations for the workforce.
11. Eliminate arbitrary numerical quotas for the workforce.
12. Allow the workforce to feel pride of workmanship.
13. Promote education and self-improvement.
14. Accept the responsibility and commitment of management.

Continuous Improvement Cycle

First we plan the quality (plan), then we execute (do) the project, then we follow-up (check), and last we control (act) to fix any deviation.

Joseph Moses Juran is recognized primarily for the following:

- ✓ The quality trilogy: 1st Quality planning, 2nd Quality control, 3rd Quality improvement.
- ✓ Made popular the Wilfred Pareto principle - 80/20.
- ✓ Top management must be involved in quality management.
- ✓ Quality is achieved when a product is "fit for use".

Kaoru Ishikawa concentrated on statistical theories for quality control and is recognized for the 7 basic tools of quality:

1. Cause-and-effect diagram: what causes problems.
2. Control charts: variations control.
3. Flowcharts: what is done.
4. Histograms: graphical vision of the variations.
5. Pareto charts: problem ranking.
6. Run charts: historical.
7. Scatter diagrams: relation between variables.

Phillip Crosby was convinced that quality must be understood by everyone. Some of his main contributions are:

✓ Quality is defined as "conformance to requirements".
✓ The system of quality management requires prevention, instead of inspection.
✓ Zero defects is the quality performance standard.

The PMBOK® Guide is compatible with the following quality management theories:

- **Deming, Juran, Ishikawa, Crosby**
- **ISO** (International Organization for Standardization)
- **TQM** (Total Quality Management)
- **Six Sigma**
- Cost of Quality (**COQ**)
- Failure mode and effects analysis (**FMEA**)
- Design reviews
- **Continuous improvement**

Both professional project management and the modern quality management vision recognize the following basic principles:

- Always look for client satisfaction
- Prevention is preferable to inspection
- Process continuous improvement
- Project managers are responsible for bringing resources to have a successful project

*Quality management processes ***

Although in big companies there are departments dedicated to planning, assuring, and controlling quality on projects, the PM, regardless of his expertise level in quality topics, must perform the following actions:

✓ Recommend improvements to the company's quality processes and policies
✓ Establish metrics to measure quality
✓ Review quality before finishing the deliverable
✓ Evaluate the impact on quality whenever there is a change in the triple constraint
✓ Allocate time to perform quality improvements
✓ Ensure that the integrated change control is used

In the following sections we will develop the three quality management processes, which are distributed within the "planning", "executing", and "monitoring and controlling" process groups, as presented on the following table:

Quality management processes

	Initiating	Planning	Executing	Controlling	Closing
Integration	1	1	1	2	1
Scope		3		2	
Time		5		1	
Cost		2		1	
Quality		Plan Quality	Perform Quality Assurance	Perform Quality Control	
Human Resources		1	3		
Communications	1	1	2	1	
Risk		5		1	
Procurement		1	1	1	1
TOTAL	**2**	**20**	**8**	**10**	**2**

The three quality management processes are:

1. **Plan quality**: which standards are relevant and how to comply with them.

2. **Perform quality assurance**: use the necessary processes to fulfill project requirements. In other words, make sure that the quality management plans are being used.

3. **Perform quality control**: supervise that the project is within the pre-established limits.

* Project Management Institute, Ibidem.

📖 Exercise 8.1 – Quality management processes

On the following table, place each item in its corresponding quality management process: Planning, Assurance, Control

Quality audits to evaluate the project's compliance with the standards and processes	
Balance quality needs with the rest of the triple constraint variables	
Look for pre-existing quality standards	
Develop the process improvements plan	
Develop metrics to evaluate quality compliance	
Develop quality standards	
Define the work needed to achieve the quality standards	
Define the quality control lists	
Evaluate project performance in relation to quality standards	
Identify necessary improvements	
Implement approved changes in the baseline	
Continuous improvement	
Recommend changes and corrective actions	
Validate the repaired defects	

🖐 Take 5 minutes to complete the table.

Answers to Exercise 8.1

Quality audits to evaluate the project's compliance with the standards and processes	Assurance
Balance quality needs with the rest of the triple constraint variables	Planning
Look for pre-existing quality standards	Planning
Develop the process improvements plan	Planning
Develop metrics to evaluate quality compliance	Planning
Develop quality standards	Planning
Define the work needed to achieve the quality standards	Planning
Define the quality control lists	Planning
Evaluate project performance in relation to quality standards	Control
Identify necessary improvements	Assurance
Implement approved changes in the baseline	Control
Continuous improvement	Assurance
Recommend changes and corrective actions	Assurance and Control
Validate the repaired defects	Control

Plan Quality

Quality is not incorporated to the project when is already under way by inspection processes. On the contrary, quality is planned, designed, and incorporated before project execution starts.

When planning the quality, it is important to identify relevant quality standards. For example, ISO standards could be useful to not re-invent the wheel.

> ✎ *ISO 9000 Standards*
>
> 1. *Write what we do*
> 2. *Do what we have written*
> 3. *Register what we did*
> 4. *Verify*
> 5. *Act over differences (Improve)*

What do I need to start?

- ⬇ Baselines: scope, schedule, costs
- ⬇ Stakeholder register
- ⬇ Risk register

What tools can I use?

- ✂ **Cost of quality** (COQ)

In the following table we summarize the costs of quality:

Costs	Type	Example
Conformance or compliance	1. Prevent noncompliance	Policies and PROCESSES Maintenance Training Studies
	2. Evaluate product's conformance	Supervision Oversight Control Inspection
Nonconformance or noncompliance	3. Internal failures	Repair defects before they reach the Client Rework and corrective actions Work with excess of inventory Less productivity
	4. External failures (Costs of nonconformance)	Defects detected "after the fact" Fines, warranties, devolutions Discounts, loss of sales

? *Which costs are greater, conformance or nonconformance costs?*

Answer: nonconformance. If not, why dedicate time and resources to quality improvements?

Companies with reactive approaches in topics related to quality management, where they solve problems once they occur, spend approximately 80% in nonconformance costs.

Reactive approach

Prevention	5%
Evaluation	15%
Internal & external failures	80%
TOTAL	100%

Nonconformance costs

- The average business never has any news of 96% of their unhappy clients
- The average client that has had problems, tells 10 other people
- Clients that have solved the problem, tell 5 other people

Source: TARP Worldwide

> ✍ *Work in reducing nonconformance costs in the project planning phase is very feasible. It is better to prevent rather than to cure!*

Companies should work with a proactive approach in terms of quality management, where prevention is more important than inspection.

Reactive vs. Proactive approach

	Reactive	Proactive
Prevention	5%	70%
Evaluation	15%	15%
Internal & external failures	80%	15%
TOTAL	100%	100%

Source: Own elaboration

✂ **Control chart:** is used to evaluate the process behavior throughout time. The client sets tolerance limits and the PM determines the control limits. For example, you sign a contract with the client which allows a maximum of 2% of defect products. The project team determines that more than 1% of defect products, it will be out of control.

> ✍ *Rule of Seven:*
> *It is said that a process is out of control when there are 7 consecutive measures above or below the average.*

Control Chart (X bar)

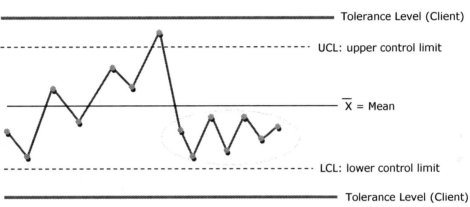

- Tolerance Level (Client)
- UCL: upper control limit
- $\overline{X}$ = Mean
- LCL: lower control limit
- Tolerance Level (Client)

> ✍ The control limits (UCL and LCL) could be out of the tolerance limits, but this is not a proactive approach to quality.

Another type of control chart is the R chart, which measures the amplitude of the variations, or the difference between one measure and the next. In the following figure, we show an X Bar chart and below an R Bar chart.

Control Chart (X Bar and R Bar)

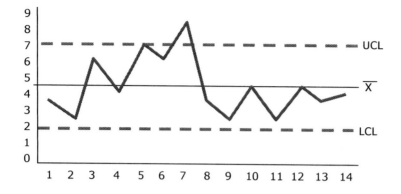

X	R
3.9	
2.5	1.4
5.9	3.4
4.2	1.7
6.8	2.6
5.9	0.9
8.4	2.5
3.9	4.5
2.8	1.1
4.4	1.6
2.9	1.5
4.3	1.4
3.5	0.8
4.0	0.5

X̄	R̄
4.53	1.84

✂ **Benchmarking**: use other studies performed on similar projects to plan the project quality.

✂ **Design of experiments**: evaluate statistically which factors improve quality in the project.

Changing one factor at a time to analyze the impact over the quality of the project could be inefficient. With statistical models we could change every factor in a process simultaneously and evaluate which combination of factors has the greatest impact on quality, all at a reasonable cost. For example, evaluate which combination of suspension and tires produce the least amount of surface wear.

✂ **Statistical samplings**: select part of a population for its analysis, this way we reduce quality control costs relating to not having to investigate the whole population. For example, randomly select 30 doors to control quality over a total of 200 doors.

📖 *Mutually exclusive events:*
The probability of occurrence of an event is not related with another event. For example, when throwing a coin there is a 50% probability of getting "heads" each time it is thrown, regardless of previous results.

> ✎ *Statistically dependent events:*
> *The probability of occurrence of an event affects the probability of occurrence of the next event. For example: playing Bingo.*

✂ **Flowcharts**: uses symbols to describe the steps in a process and the actions that must be done in each step.

ANSI symbols for flowcharts

	Process or activity. Function performed by a person.
	Alternate process.
	Decision or alternative.
	Data. Is generated and fed during the process.
	Document.
	Initiator or Terminator.
	Connector. Link between different parts of the diagram.
	Communication line. Transmit information from one place to another

Flowchart

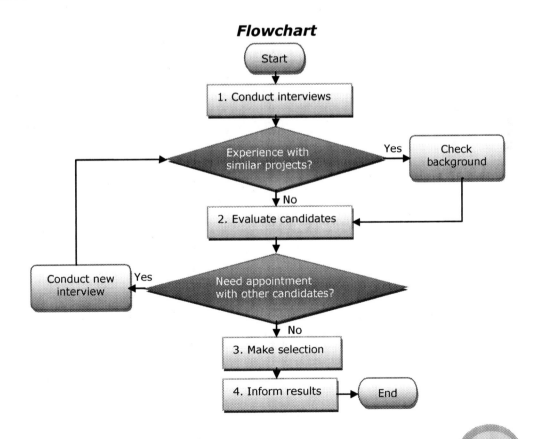

☺ *Joke chart*

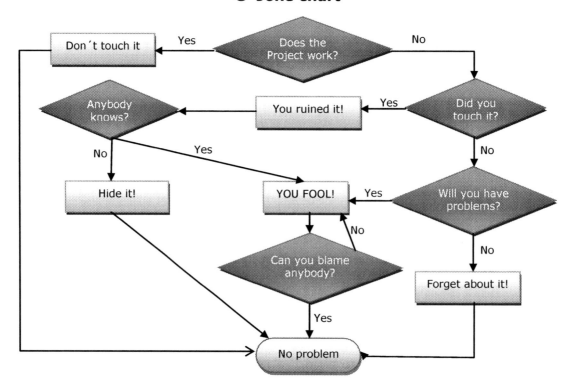

✂ **Additional methodologies and tools**: six sigma, lean thinking, deployment of quality functions, CMMI, affinity diagrams, nominal group technique, matrix diagrams, just in time, etc.

> ✎ *Just in time: decrease the amount of inventory improving quality. Raw materials are delivered just before needed in the manufacturing process.*

What do I get at the end of the process?

➚ **Quality management plan**

➚ **Quality metrics**: objective parameters used to measure the project's quality.

➚ **Quality checklists**: lists used to validate that quality processes are being followed.

Quality checklist

Activity	Acceptance Criteria	Validation Method	Check
Install boiler	Height 3.93 ft +/- 2 in	Tape measure	
Test pressure	120 lbs	Manometer - 2hs	

➚ **Process improvement plan**: identify which processes are good for recognizing non-value added activities.

Quality Assurance

Once the project is in execution, with quality assurance we validate that all processes and standards defined in the quality plan are being implemented.

What do I need to start?

⬇ Quality management plan and process improvement plan

⬇ Quality metrics

⬇ Work performance information

⬇ Quality control measurements

What tools can I use?

> ✎ *The same tools used for quality planning and control, can be used for quality assurance.*

✂ **Quality audits**

Quality audits are performed by the quality assurance department. In case this department does not exist, the PM should perform the audits. With these audits, we respond the following questions: Are quality policies and standards being applied? Are current processes effective and efficient?

✂ **Process analysis**

Whenever a project has repetitive processes, periodic revisions are done in order to follow a continuous improvement process. For example, plan the revision of the software installation process every 10 computers.

> ✎ *You cannot do today's work with yesterday's methods and stay in business tomorrow. Therefore, continuous improvement is necessary.*

There are two great approaches on **continuous improvement**:

1. Improvement or Kaizen: many small improvements
2. Innovation or Kairyo: one big improvement

In the following table, we mention the main characteristics of each one of these approaches.

Continuous improvement – Approaches

Improvement		Innovation	
Kaizen	改善	**Kairyo**	的基本信息
Many small improvements		One big improvement	
HR re-engineering		Process re-engineering	
Small investment		Big investment	
High maintenance		Low maintenance	
Involves everybody		Involves the "chosen ones"	
Conventional experience + PDCA cycle		Technological or organizational innovation	

✎ *Mnemonic rule:*

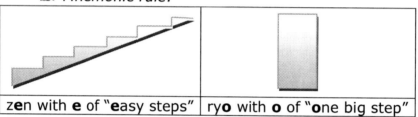

z**e**n with **e** of "**e**asy steps"	ry**o** with **o** of "**o**ne big step"

Continuous improvement – Phases

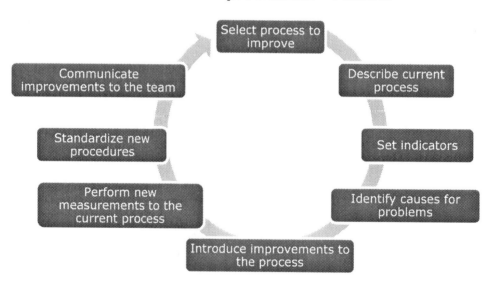

What do I get at the end of the process?

↗ **Change requests**

↗ **Updates**

Quality Control

Unlike quality assurance, which consists primarily of assuring that standards are followed, during the quality control process we verify that the project deliverables are within the pre-defined quality limits.

During the quality control process the PM should ask himself the following:

- ✓ Does the project comply with quality standards?
- ✓ How are we eliminating unsatisfactory results?
- ✓ Will we have a successful project?

Some of the actions taken to control the quality of the project are:

- ✓ Preventive measures to avoid errors in the process
- ✓ Corrective actions to eliminate the root cause of a problem
- ✓ Inspections to avoid errors getting to the client

What do I need to start?

- ⬇ Quality management plan, metrics, and checklists
- ⬇ Deliverables and work performance measurements
- ⬇ Approved change requests

What tools can I use?

- ✂ **Cause and effect diagrams (Ishikawa or fishbone)**: identifies, in a schematic way, the causes of problems. It is usually used during the Plan Quality process, because it is very useful to inspire ideas and generate discussion in order to resolve a problem.

Cause and effect diagram

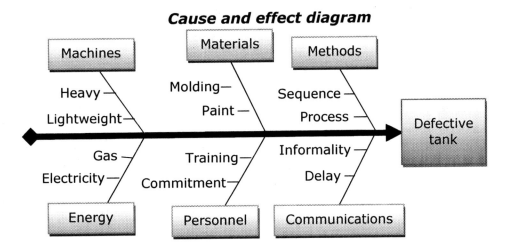

⚔ **Control chart**: used to evaluate the process behavior throughout time, as explained in the Plan Quality section.

📖 **Exercise 8.2 – Control chart**

You work for the company "Close It All", dedicated to the fabrication of doors.

One of their European clients has made an order of 100 doors, each one with a height of 2,500 millimeters. The client will accept doors with an error of up to +/- 10 millimeters.

The company could establish project control limits with ranges greater than what the client requested, but this could be costly. Therefore, the project manager has set a control limit of +/- 5 millimeters.

Up to date, 25 doors have been produced as presented in the following table and figures.

Door	Measure (millimeters)	Variation	Door	Measure (millimeters)	Variation
1	2,504		14	2,503	1
2	2,503	1	15	2,502	1
3	2,500	3	16	2,501	1
4	2,501	1	17	2,503	2
5	2,492	9	18	2,497	6
6	2,503	11	19	2,498	1
7	2,500	3	20	2,503	5
8	2,499	1	21	2,499	4
9	2,501	2	22	2,501	2
10	2,497	4	23	2,502	1
11	2,504	7	24	2,501	1
12	2,501	3	25	2,506	5
13	2,504	3			

Median	2,501.00
Standard Deviation (σ)	2.93

Control Chart (X Bar)

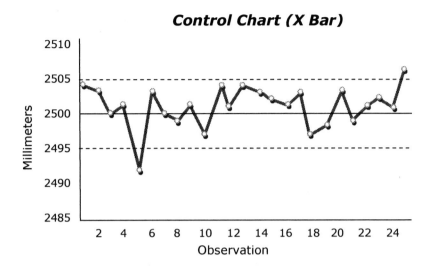

Control Chart (R Bar)

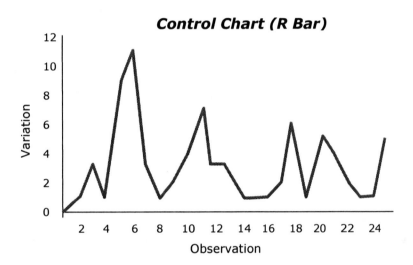

Based on this information, determine the following:

a) Confidence interval of 68.26%
b) Upper control limit (UCL)
c) Lower control limit (LCL)
d) Tolerance levels
e) Places where the process is out of control

✎ Confidence intervals:
Median +/- 1 σ = 68.26%
Median +/- 2 σ = 95.44%
Median +/- 3 σ = 99.73% (2,700 failures every 1 million)
Median +/- 6 σ = 99.99985% (1.5 failures every 1 million)

Answer to Exercise 8.2

a) Based on the median of 2,501 and the standard deviation of 2.93, we could say that 68.26% of the data on that sample are within 2,498.07 and 2,503.93 (2,501 +/- [2 x 2.93]).

b), c), d), and e)

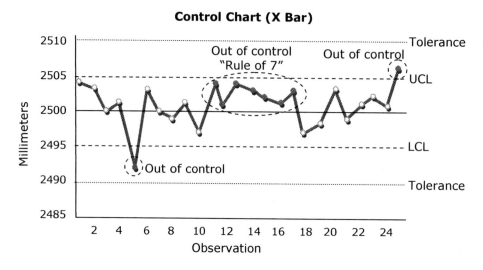

Control Chart (X Bar)

✂ **Flowchart**: describes the steps in a process, as described in the Plan Quality section. It is useful to determine problems in the process and to identify improvement opportunities.

✂ **Histogram**: frequency distributions are represented graphically, grouped by different classes or categories. For example, in the following figure we can observe that the majority of the doors have between 2,502 and 2,504 millimeters.

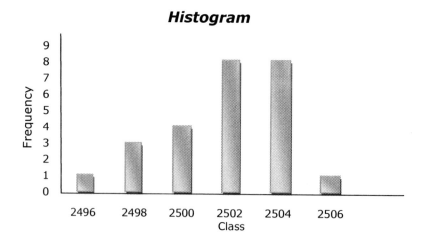

Histogram

When the data sample is big, the histogram could tend to have a standard normal distribution.

Standard Normal Distribution

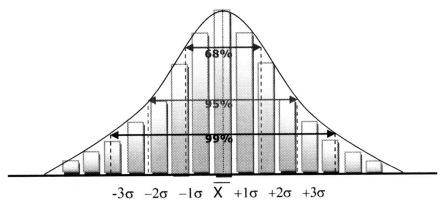

-3σ –2σ –1σ X̄ +1σ +2σ +3σ

📖 Exercise 8.3 – Histogram

Based on the data for the "Close It All company" (previous exercise), graph a histogram. Which frequency distribution does it look like?

Steps in Excel:
1. Install add-in "Analysis ToolPak"
2. Data / Data Analysis
3. Histogram
4. Enter the Input Range and the Bin Range
5. Select only "Chart Output"

Frequency	Class
2,504	2,494
2,503	2,496
2,500	2,498
2,501	2,500
2,492	2,502
2,503	2,504
2,500	2,506
2,499	
2,501	
2,497	
2,504	
2,501	
2,504	
2,503	
2,502	

Histogram

Input
Input Range: $A$1:$A$26
Bin Range: $B$1:$B$8
☑ Labels

Output options
◉ Output Range: $C$10
○ New Worksheet Ply:
○ New Workbook

☐ Pareto (sorted histogram)
☐ Cumulative Percentage
☑ Chart Output

OK
Cancel
Help

Answer to Exercise 8.3

As observed in the histogram, the frequency distribution of the company samples is similar to a standard normal.

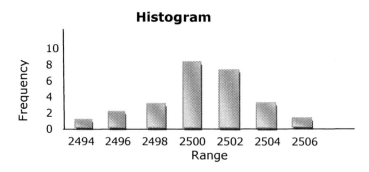

✂ **Pareto chart**: the frequency distribution is represented in a histogram with the causes for the product defects. The usefulness of this tool is that we can easily detect the most important factors that are causing the defects. In other words, it allows separating the "least critical" from the "most non-critical".

> ✍ *Pareto Law or 80/20 Principle:*
> *80% of the problems come from 20% of the causes*

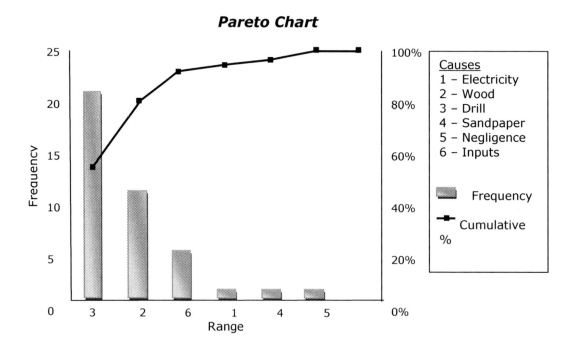

📖 Exercise 8.4 – Pareto Chart

At Close It All, the causes for the last 40 defective doors have been registered, as presented in the following tables.

Door	Cause	Code		Door	Cause	Code
1	Input B	6		21	Drill	3
2	Drill	3		22	Input D	6
3	Wood	2		23	Drill	3
4	Drill	3		24	Wood	2
5	Drill	3		25	Drill	3
6	Electricity	1		26	Wood	2
7	Drill	3		27	Drill	3
8	Wood	2		28	Sandpaper	4
9	Wood	2		29	Drill	3
10	Wood	2		30	Wood	2
11	Drill	3		31	Drill	3
12	Input C	6		32	Wood	2
13	Drill	3		33	Drill	3
14	Drill	3		34	Drill	3
15	Input E	6		35	Wood	2
16	Drill	3		36	Drill	3
17	Drill	3		37	Input A	6
18	Negligence	5		38	Wood	2
19	Drill	3		39	Drill	3
20	Drill	3		40	Wood	2

Graphically represent the 80/20 Pareto principle.

Tip with Excel: Data / Data Analysis / Histogram
In "Bin Range" include the causes.

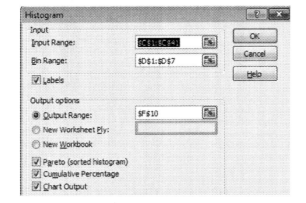

Answer to Exercise 8.4

Cause	Frequency	Cumulative %	Cause	Frequency	Cumulative %
1	1	2.5%	3	21	52.5%
2	11	30.0%	2	11	80.0%
3	21	82.5%	6	5	92.5%
4	1	85.0%	1	1	95.0%
5	1	87.5%	4	1	97.5%
6	5	100.0%	5	1	100.0%
More	0	100.0%	More	0	100.0%

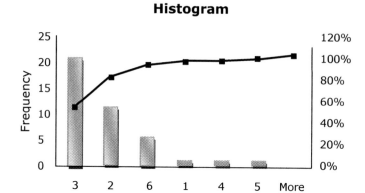

Histogram

We can observe that the main problems "3" and "2" explain 80% of the defective doors.

✂ **Run chart**: it uses historical information to study the evolution of a variable throughout time. This chart can show tendencies, variances, or changes in processes throughout time. For example, with the tendency analysis we can forecast future results over the historic data.

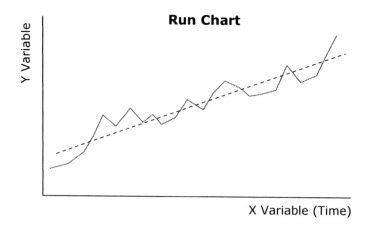

Run Chart

📖 Exercise 8.5 – Run chart

In the following table, we observe the amount of doors that Close It All has sold in the last 24 months.

Month	Sales
1	300
2	302
3	306
4	312
5	321
6	317
7	324
8	319
9	321
10	317
11	320
12	327
13	324
14	330
15	335
16	333
17	329
18	329
19	331
20	340
21	334
22	337
23	345
24	352

What would be the amount of estimated door sales for the next month?

Answer to Exercise 8.5

In the following figure, we present the equation of the trendline that takes the historical information based on the ordinary least squares (OLS) method, as explained on the Time Management chapter.

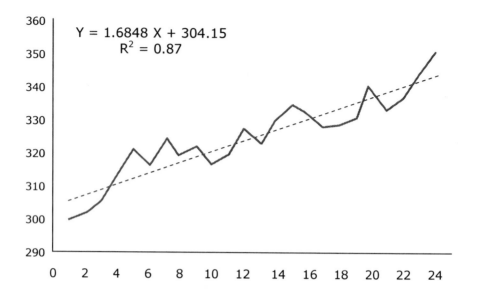

The unknown (X), next month, corresponds to the value 25. Replacing this value on the equation, we obtain the following result:

Y = 1.6848 x 25 + 304.15 = 346.27

✂ **Scatter diagram**: it shows the relation between two variables. The closer the data is to a diagonal, the greater the correlation between the variables.

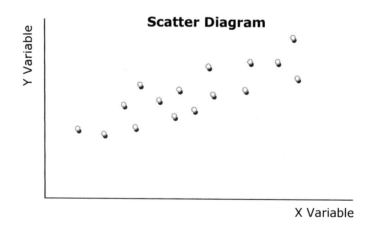

Correlation

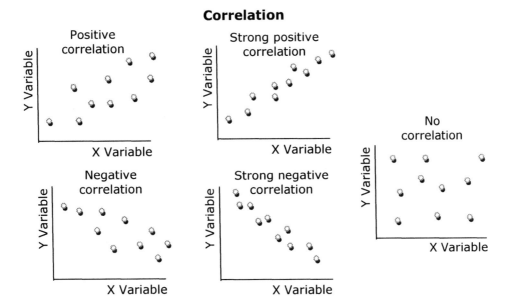

📖 Exercise 8.6 – Scatter diagram

You are worried about your clients complaining when they receive a defective door. Therefore, you have decided to investigate which factors are related to the defective doors.

Intuitively, your team suspects that hot days are the cause for the defects. You take a random sample of 30 days from last year. Then, you find out how many doors produced during those days had defects, based on the client complaints log. Finally, you use the government meteorological registers to know the temperatures (Celsius) in each one of those days.

Observation	Temperature	# Defective Doors	Observation	Temperature	# Defective Doors
1	21	5	16	14	4
2	18	4	17	30	8
3	12	3	18	25	4
4	19	2	19	28	6
5	24	6	20	26	6
6	7	4	21	40	8
7	14	2	22	20	4
8	40	5	23	6	2
9	38	6	24	13	3
10	20	4	25	14	5
11	19	5	26	23	3
12	27	6	27	39	7
13	38	7	28	21	5
14	28	6	29	13	2
15	32	7	30	40	6

Is there any correlation between temperature and defects?

Answer to Exercise 8.6

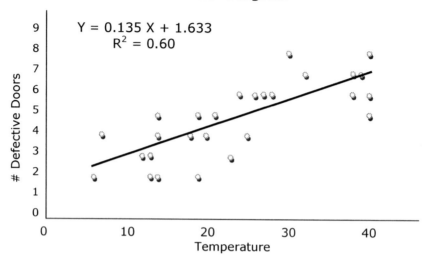

Scatter Diagram

$Y = 0.135 X + 1.633$
$R^2 = 0.60$

The Correlation Coefficient (R^2) of Pearson ascends to 0.60, which indicates that 60% of the defects (Y) can be explained by the temperature (X).

> ✂ **Statistical sampling**: to select part of a population for its analysis, as explained in the Plan Quality section.

> ✂ **Inspection**: product revisions or audits are conducted to evaluate if it is complying with the standards, or to validate the defects that have been repaired.

> ✂ **Approved change requests review**: verify that the changes have been implemented the same way they were approved.

What do I get at the end of the process?
- ↗ Quality control measurements
- ↗ Validated changes and deliverables
- ↗ Change requests
- ↗ Updates

Summarizing quality management

In the following figure we summarize the main inputs, outputs, and interrelations of quality management processes.

Integrating quality management

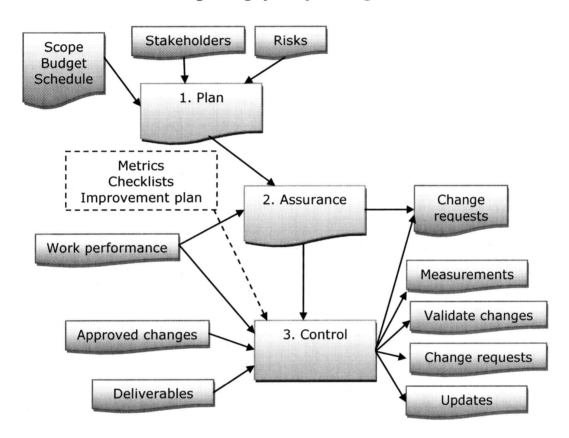

Exam 8 – Quality

Number of questions: 15
Time to respond: 18 minutes
Pass score: 80% (12 correct answers)

1. During the project planning process you want to establish the quality standards and the necessary work to comply with those standards. The team members are evaluating what can cause problems in complying with those standards. Which tool could they use in this planning phase?
    A. Process analysis
    B. Quality audits
    C. Fishbone diagram
    D. Pareto chart

2. You are using a Pareto chart in a heavy load vehicles construction project. This tool helps you to:
    A. Encourage thinking and the search for alternatives
    B. Determine if a process is out of control
    C. Focus on the most critical issues to improve quality
    D. Estimate a future result

3. You and your team are convinced of the importance of prevention over inspection. Therefore, you want to implement a proactive approach to increment the quality conformance costs. Which of the following costs is NOT part of this strategy?
    A. Studies
    B. Rework
    C. Training
    D. Quality policies

4. A project manager from the quality control area is trying to categorize the number of defects that occur in the painting area for the left back door of a Ford. For this, he lists all possible defects on a sheet of paper and requests the quality inspector to mark the sheet each time a defect is found. This is an example of:
    A. Quality metrics
    B. Scatter diagram
    C. Random sampling
    D. Quality checklists

5. A company that sells household appliances is having problems related to the quality in its projects. The company's general management has a policy of solving problems as they appear, instead of preventing them. Which of the following concepts surely is NOT part of the quality policy on this company?
    A. Process improvement training
    B. Plans for the response to devolutions and claims
    C. Work with a greater amount of inventory
    D. Dissatisfied clients

6. Who is the main responsible for the quality management in a technology change project?
A. The quality department
B. The quality manager
C. The project team members responsible for quality assurance
D. The project manager

7. Your company uses a control chart during the manufacturing process. As part of the control process, every week they extract a random sample of 10 pieces. Then, each piece is measured and the difference between the highest and the lowest measurement is graphed in the control chart. How is this value denominated?
A. R Bar
B. Variance
C. X Bar
D. R

8. You are the project manager for the manufacturing of carousels for heavy products. Last week you met with your work team to explain the requirements that need to be fulfilled in the project. In that meeting you clarified that is critical to not deviate from the requirements requested by the client. Which quality process is this?
A. Total quality management
B. Quality assurance
C. Plan quality
D. Quality control

9. All of the following statements are part of the quality audits, EXCEPT:
A. Validate defect repairs
B. Determine if the project activities comply with the processes
C. Identify inefficient processes being used
D. Confirm the implementation of defect repairs

10. The project management team wants to determine what is causing the mortality of some plantations in an agricultural project. They have been able to isolate two variables based on the available information. Which of the following options will help verify if there is a correlation between these two variables?
A. Pareto chart
B. Control chart
C. Flowchart
D. Scatter diagram

11. Nicoshimo Wang has been assigned as the project manager in the Nitzumoto Zelerompe Company. This company sells and distributes microprocessors. During the project execution phase, the Program Manager informs Nicoshimo that the company is going to implement Kaizen technologies as part of its total quality management program. What is the Program Manager referring to?
A. Small improvements to every project
B. One big process re-engineering
C. Small improvements to the product and processes in a continuous base
D. One big technological improvement to increment the project's productivity

12. A product or service category with the same functionality, but with different technical characteristics is called:
    A. Quality
    B. Functionality
    C. Standard deviation
    D. Grade

13. You and your team are working to assure the quality in a project for the construction of vehicles that will use bio-degradable combustibles. Which of the following statements will NOT be necessary to perform this process?
    A. Quality metrics
    B. Approved change requests
    C. Process improvements plan
    D. Work performance information

14. You are the project manager for the confection of ready-made suits for the company TS. To build the project schedule, you have decided to use the Just in Time (JIT) production method. Which of the following options is an advantage of using the JIT method?
    A. Allows members of the project team have control over project materials
    B. Decreases inventory investment
    C. Requires that materials are available in the right moment
    D. Requires approximately 10% of inventory for contingencies

15. You take a random sample of 1,000 products. Then you weight them and you observe that they have a standard normal distribution. Finally, you decide to work with a confidence interval of +/- 3 sigma and you obtain a range between 200-800 grams. Which percentage of products will be included in that range?
    A. 68.26%
    B. 100.00%
    C. 99.73%
    D. 95.44%

Lessons learned - Quality

- ✓ Cost-benefit analysis
- ✓ Process analysis
- ✓ Quality and grade
- ✓ Conformance cost
- ✓ Cost of defects
- ✓ Cost of quality (COQ)
- ✓ Nonconformance cost
- ✓ Standard deviation
- ✓ Cause and effect diagram
- ✓ Run chart
- ✓ Control chart
- ✓ Scatter diagram
- ✓ Flowchart
- ✓ Ishikawa diagram
- ✓ Pareto chart
- ✓ Fishbone diagram
- ✓ Accuracy and precision
- ✓ Out of control
- ✓ Control limits
- ✓ Specification limits
- ✓ Checklists
- ✓ Median
- ✓ Continuous improvement
- ✓ Metrics
- ✓ Quality management plan
- ✓ Process improvement plan
- ✓ 80/20 Rule
- ✓ Run of Seven Rule

CHAPTER #9

HUMAN RESOURCES

Chapter 9 – HUMAN RESOURCES

> *The fact that science has survived for so long depends on psychology; in other words, depends on what human beings wish.*
>
> Bertrand Russell (1872-1970) Philosopher, mathematician, and English writer.

If you want to be a good project manager, you should pay a lot of attention to this chapter. Remember that projects are not only templates, Gantt Charts, and plans. People make successful projects a reality. This is why is so import of knowing how to lead, motivate, and allocate people.

The word "team" will be used to refer to the work team members.

When you finish this chapter, you will have learned the following concepts:
- ✓ Human resources management processes
- ✓ Develop human resource plan
- ✓ Types of power
- ✓ Team roles and responsibilities
- ✓ Acquire project team
- ✓ Develop project team
- ✓ Leadership and motivation
- ✓ Manage project team
- ✓ Conflict management

Human resources management processes *

In the following sections we will develop the human resources management processes, which are distributed among the "Planning" and "Executing" processes as presented in the following table.

---

* Project Management Institute, Ibidem.

Human resources management processes

	Initiating	Planning	Executing	Controlling	Closing
Integration	1	1	1	2	1
Scope		3		2	
Time		5		1	
Cost		2		1	
Quality		1	1	1	
Human Resources		Develop HR Plan	. Acquire team . Develop team . Manage team		
Communications	1	1	2	1	
Risks		5		1	
Procurements		1	1	1	1
TOTAL	2	20	8	10	2

The four human resources management processes are:

1. **Develop human resource plan:** define the roles, responsibilities, and skills of the team members, as well as the communication relationships.

2. **Acquire project team:** obtain the necessary human resources to perform the project activities.

3. **Develop project team:** improve the competencies and interpersonal skills of the team members.

4. **Manage project team:** monitor each person's individual and team performance, and solve the conflicts that usually emerge among team members.

Develop human resource plan

When we plan the needs of the human resources to perform the project activities, we should answer the following questions:

✓ How and when is each person brought on board?

✓ What are their current capabilities and information needs?

✓ What will be their roles and responsibilities?

✓ What will be the work packages assigned to each team member?

✓ When should each person send the reports?

✓ To which meetings should each person attend?

✓ What will be the individual and team incentive plan?

✓ How will we protect the personnel from external contingencies?

✓ How and when will people be released from the project?

What do I need to start?

⬇ Activity resource requirements

In addition, it is necessary to know thoroughly the following:

✓ How are the formal and informal relations in the organization?

✓ What are the cultural or language differences?

✓ What confidence and respect levels exist between persons?

✓ Are there informal partnerships between employees?

✓ What is the organizational structure? Functional, matrix, projectized?

✓ Are there work unions?

✓ What distance separates individuals physically?

✓ What types of power exist in the organization?

> ✎ *Types of power*
> *Formal: hierarchical position in the company*
> *Rewards: authority to manage recompenses*
> *Penalty: authority to manage punishment*
> *Expert: is recognized based on knowledge and formation*
> *Referred: is referred by a superior*

? *What is the best type of power?*
A. Expert
B. Reward
C. Formal
D. Penalty

Generally people think that the best type of power is the formal, but this is not correct. For example, it is a lot more important if the PM is recognized for her knowledge (expert), than if she has a personal card that states that she is the Vice President of Operations.

> ☝ *The best types of power are "expert" or "rewards", while the worst type of power is that which uses penalty and punishment.*

What tools can I use?

✂ **Organization charts and position descriptions**: schemes where each person's job and hierarchical level is explained. These could be hierarchical diagrams, matrix based charts, or text oriented format.

Hierarchical diagram (Matrix organization)

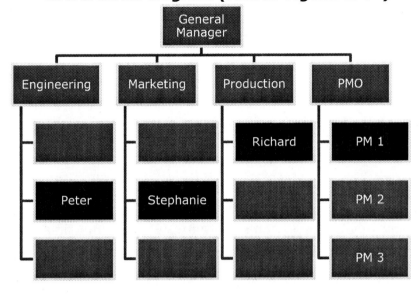

Usually, matrix-based charts are also used as presented in the following examples.

RAM (Responsibility Assignment Matrix)

Activity	Pedro	Marcela	Rogelio
Information research		X	
Market study		X	
Cost benefit analysis			X

X (responsible)

RACI Chart

Activity	Pedro	Marcela	Rogelio
Information research	A	R	C
Market study	A	R	C
Cost benefit analysis	I	A	R

R (responsible); A (accountable); C (consulted); I (informed)

> ✎ The RACI Chart is a type of RAM. The RAM or RACI do not indicate when should each person perform the activity.

Lastly, a text-oriented format could be used to define the roles and responsibilities of each team member.

Text

Role:
Authority:
Responsibility:
Competencies:

✂ **Networking**: for example, organize an informal meeting each Friday evening with the team members, where the company pays for the food and drinks, and nobody wears suit or tie.

✂ **Organizational theories**: provide information about the individual behavior at organizations (open, closed, natural, and rational systems).

What do I get at the end of the process?

↗ **Roles and responsibilities:** role is the appointment or position that a person has in each project activity, while responsible refers to the person that should ensure that the activity is developed in an adequate manner. The person responsible can be someone different from who executes the activity.

📖 **Exercise 9.1 – Roles**

Mark with an X who has the main role in each case: **S**: Sponsor; **M**: Functional Manager; **P**: Project Manager; **T**: Team

Who should get assigned the main role?	S	M	P	T
Product or service formal acceptance				
Analyze assumptions and constraints				
Approve changes				
Approve the project management plan				
Assign resources to the project				
Help identify plan deviations				
Create a change control system				
Meet project objectives				
Give support to the team during execution				
Define quality policies				
Decompose work packages				
Determine the need for corrective actions				
Determine quality metrics				
Establish dependencies and create the network diagram				
Estimate costs and duration for each activity				
Set priorities among projects				
Identify and involve stakeholders				
Report on other projects in execution				
Improve processes				
Negotiate resource availability				
Grant financial resources				
Protect the project from external resources				
Perform the project charter				
Create WBS				
Create a realistic schedule				
Select adequate processes				

🖐 Take 10 minutes to solve this exercise

Answer to Exercise 9.1

We should consider that when we talk about roles there could be more than one person performing the same role.

Who should get assigned the main role?	S	M	P	T
Product or service formal acceptance	x			
Analyze assumptions and constraints				x
Approve changes	x			
Approve the project management plan	x	x		
Assign resources to the project		x	x	
Help identify plan deviations				x
Create a change control system			x	
Meet project objectives			x	
Give support to the team during execution			x	
Define quality policies	x			
Decompose work packages				x
Determine the need for corrective actions			x	
Determine quality metrics			x	
Establish dependencies and create the network diagram				x
Estimate costs and duration for each activity				x
Set priorities among projects	x			
Identify and involve stakeholders			x	x
Report on other projects in execution		x		
Improve processes				x
Negotiate resource availability		x	x	
Grant financial resources	x			
Protect the project from external resources	x			
Perform the project charter	x			
Create WBS			x	x
Create a realistic schedule			x	
Select adequate processes				x

📖 **Exercise 9.2 – Responsibilities**

In the following table, mark who has the main responsibility for solving the following problems.

Who is responsible for solving these problems?	S	M	P	T
During initiation there is no negotiation for obtaining the best resources				
The Project Manager does not have enough authority to make things happen				
The project team does not know who is responsible for the project				
The human resource manager does not know the acquired skills by a team member				
The Functional Manager is not clear on who will be the persons involved in the project				
The project does not have enough funds to be able to develop all of the processes				
The project has a performance index of 0.87				
There was a change in the final product through a formal client request				
A recognition and rewards system for the workers does not exist				
A clear description of the tasks to be performed by each team member does not exist				
A change in the scope of a critical path activity, which will delay the project, occurs				
Additional work, which will increase the estimate at completion, is added to the project				
Three team members have different opinions about the utilization of a new technology				
The commercial manager does not deliver an assistant during the project execution				
A team member does not know when should each task occur due to lack of a schedule				

🖐 Take 5 minutes to solve this exercise

Answer to Exercise 9.2

Who is responsible for solving these problems?	S	M	P	T
During initiation there is no negotiation for obtaining the best resources			x	
The Project Manager does not have enough authority to make things happen	X			
The project team does not know who is responsible for the project	X			
The human resource manager does not know the acquired skills by a team member			x	
The Functional Manager is not clear on who will be the persons involved in the project			x	
The project does not have enough funds to be able to develop all of the processes	X			
The project has a performance index of 0.87			x	
There was a change in the final product through a formal client request	X			
A recognition and rewards system for the workers does not exist			x	
A clear description of the tasks to be performed by each team member does not exist			x	
A change in the scope of a critical path activity, which will delay the project, occurs	X			
Additional work, which will increase the estimate at completion, is added to the project	X			
Three team members have different opinions about the utilization of a new technology				x
The commercial manager does not deliver an assistant during the project execution		x		
A team member does not know when should each task occur due to lack of a schedule			x	

☝ There should only be one responsible for each work package

- ↗ **Organization chart:** establishes the hierarchical level of the team members.

- ↗ **Staffing management plan:** details how the staff will be acquired, the resource histogram, the policy to release and re-integrate resources, the training plans, the policy for recognition and rewards, working agreements, workplace security norms, etc.

Resource Histogram

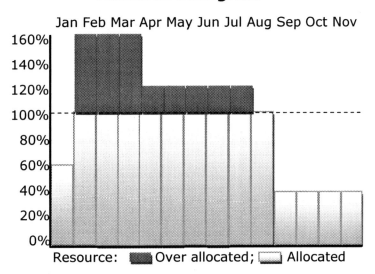

Being explicit in the plan about how resources will be released favors a gradual and anticipated project transition.

On the other hand, it is very important to create a clear rewards schedule, and to comply with what was established.

There are different ways to reward the team without having to increase their salaries, like for example: say thank you, recommend for promotions, communicate good performance, trips, training, assign project activities per each person's preference, etc.

☺ *Non-monetary rewards can be motivating, but do not forget that the incentives that affect your pocket can be very effective. Money makes the mare go!*

Acquire project team

Acquire project team occurs during project execution. However, the project team is required to be able to perform a good planning. How do I plan without having a project team? On big projects not all workers are contracted before the project execution, because this would be inefficient. The project is planned with some key members, and during execution the majority of the workers start coming on board.

During the acquire project team process, the PM should:

✓ Know which persons have been previously assigned to the project

✓ Negotiate to obtain the best possible resources

✓ Know the needs and priorities of the organization

✓ Contract new workers (internal and external)

✓ Know the advantages and disadvantages of virtual projects

> ☞ Do not trust in the **"Halo Effect"** when incorporating team members. For example, because he was a good football player, he will be a good coach.

What do I need to start?

⬇ Roles and responsibilities, Organization Chart, Human Resource Plan.

⬇ Environment: resource availability, capabilities, experiences, project interests, etc.

What tools can I use?

✂ **Pre-assignment**: persons that have already been assigned to the project.

✂ **Negotiation**: negotiate the best resources with the functional managers and other project managers.

✂ **Acquisition**: perform an external or third party contract.

✂ **Virtual teams**: when the persons are not on the same physical place, the project teams can be coordinated remotely with technology such as the Internet or videoconferences.

What do I get at the end of the process?

↗ Project staff assignments

↗ Availability or resource calendars: know exactly the moment in which resources will be available to complete a realistic schedule.

↗ Updates

Develop project team

When the project is in execution you must develop the individual and team capabilities of the project team members.

> ✎ *Develop project team is more beneficial at the early stages, but it should be performed across all project phases*

Here are some key words that a team should <u>improve</u> to achieve high performance: cohes**I**on, tea**M** work, **P**articipation, t**R**ust, c**O**mpetencies, di**V**ersity, and int**E**rrelations.

What do I need to start?

⬇ Project staff assignments, assigned staff, and resource calendars.

What tools can I use?

✂ **Interpersonal skills**: a good PM needs skills such as leadership, motivation, team work, empathy, creativity, etc.

✂ **Training**: formation activities to improve competencies.

✂ **Team building activities**: team work. For example, create the WBS involving some of your team members.

The following figure summarizes the team building stages according to Bruce Tuckman's model.

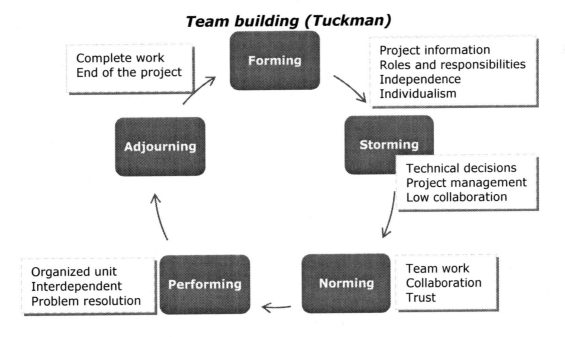

Team building (Tuckman)

✂ **Ground rules**: establish basic rules. For example, turn off cell phones while in meetings, wash coffee cups, etc.

✂ **Co-location**: locate project team members in the same physical working area.

✂ **Recognition and rewards**: use an incentive program to reward positive behaviors. Those rewards where only one winner exists can be detrimental for team cohesion. Instead, it is preferable to grant a reward to whoever surpasses the objectives.

What do I get at the end of the process?

↗ **Team performance assessments**: elaborate reports with the acquired competencies by the workers and the effectiveness of the team.

Leadership

There are different **leadership** styles, such as:

✓ Directing: says what to do.

✓ Coaching: gives instructions.

✓ Supporting: provides assistance.

✓ Delegating: the employee decides on its own.

✓ Facilitating: coordinates with others.

✓ Autocratic: makes decisions without consulting.

✓ Consensus: team problem resolution.

☝ *During project execution the PM has enough information to be able to reach decisions without consensus. Each time there is a problem, he should not call a meeting to reach consensus.*

? *What leadership style is best at project initiation? And during execution?*
A. Directing
B. Coaching
C. Supporting
D. Facilitating

During the initiating process group, a directing leadership style is necessary to set the direction of the project. As we progress over the planning and executing processes, the situational leadership style could be coaching, supporting, or facilitating.

Different leadership styles are presented in the following figures.

Leadership focused on the boss vs. focused on subordinates

Leadership focused on the boss			Leadership focused on subordinates	
+++ Use of authority - - -			- - - Freedom / Empowerment +++	
The PM makes and announces a decision	The PM sells a decision	The PM presents a proposed decision subject to changes	The PM defines the boundaries and asks that others make the decision	The PM allows employees to operate within the boundaries defined by a superior

Situational Leadership (Hersey Blanchard)

Leadership styles

	Supportive behavior

3 Supporting High Support Low Direction	2 Coaching High Support High Direction
4 Delegating Low Support Low Direction	1 Directing Low Support High Direction

Directive behavior

Levels of Development

1 Low Does not know Does not wants	2 Medium Does not know Wants	3 Medium+ Wants Insecure	4 High Knows Wants

Development

☞ *The PM should apply different leadership styles depending on the situation.*

Motivation

There are various doctrines that have studied and continue to study motivation. Below is a summary of the most recognized authors on the subject.

➢ **Maslow** (MASLOW, Abraham. 1954. Motivation and Personality)

People have different hierarchy needs. Until the lower level needs are satisfied, the upper levels cannot be reached.

Maslow's Hierarchy of Needs

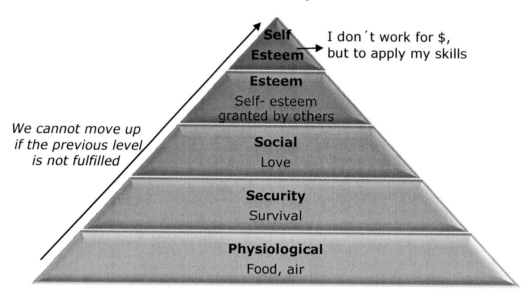

We cannot motivate the esteem of someone if her basic physiological, security, and social needs have not been fulfilled.

➢ **Mc Gregor** (MC GREGOR, Douglas. 1960. The Human Side of the Enterprise)

People belong to one of two categories:

- o X Theory: unable, avoid work, do not want responsibilities, must be controlled by their superiors
- o Y Theory: works without supervision, wants to undertake commitments and progress

Mc Gregor X-Y Theory

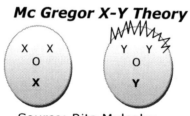

Source: Rita Mulcahy

Which of the two faces is happier? As a rule of thumb you will remember that X is sad, while Y is happy.

You must know each team member's personality well enough to decide on the leadership style to apply in each case. A delegating leadership style with an X person can be less effective, while a very directing style with a Y person can also be counterproductive.

> **Needs Theory** (Mc CLELLAND, David. 1961. The Achievement Motive, Affiliation and Power)

People have three types of needs: achievement, affiliation, and power. Depending on their type of need, it will be the motivation they need.

If it is an achievement need, they will need challenging projects but with achievable objectives, to feel recognized.

On the other hand, if the need is affiliation, they will enjoy working in teams, with other people.

Lastly, the people that need power are leaned towards society and are motivated by leadership; therefore, they should lead other people.

> **Expectancy Theory** (VROOM, Victor H. 1964. Work and Motivation)

People work hard because they expect better performance. From that better performance they expect a reward. With that reward they will satisfy their needs and will go back to work hard to continue the cycle.

Expectancy Theory

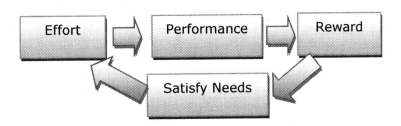

Motivation = (Expectation from action results) x (value of the results)

The worker will stay productive while the reward satisfies her needs; on the contrary, she will not be motivated to keep the efforts.

➢ **Goal setting theory** (LOCKE, Edwin. 1969)

The desire to achieve a goal is the basic source of motivation. Goals motivate and guide our acts and drive us to perform at our best. Goals can have various functions:

✓ Focus the attention and action on the task.

✓ Mobilize the energy and effort.

✓ Increase persistence.

✓ Help in the elaboration of strategies.

➢ **Herzberg** (HERZBERG, Frederick. 1975. The motivation to work)

People are influenced by:

- **Hygiene factors**: salary, security, status, work conditions

- **Motivational agents:** Responsibility, self-esteem, professional development, and recognition

Herzberg

If hygiene factors are not covered, there cannot be motivation. However, if hygiene factors are covered, motivation does not improve, given that we must work on the motivational agents.

➢ **Theory Z – Ouchi** (OUCHI, William. 1981. Theory How American Business can meet the Japanese Challenge)

There are 3 types of enterprises:
- A – Americans
- J – Japanese
- Z

The success of Enterprise Z is based on:

- **Trust**: you do not need to be on top of the employee

- **Close relationships**: good social relationship between boss-employee

- **Politeness**: adapt treatment to each employee

Z enterprises will have more probabilities of success.

Manage project team

During the project's executing process the team is managed with activities such as:

- ✓ Monitor the work team performance
- ✓ Feedback to the team
- ✓ Conflict and issue resolution

What do I need to start?

- ⬇ Assigned staff, roles and responsibilities, organization chart, staffing management plan, team performance.
- ⬇ Project performance reports.

What tools can I use?

- ✂ **Observation and conversation.**
- ✂ **Performance appraisals**: people receive feedback on their project performance. For example, the 360º feedback system, where information about the performance of a particular person is asked from the people that work with her. It is very useful to clarify roles and responsibilities, discover unknown issues, and develop individual development plans.

360º Feedback

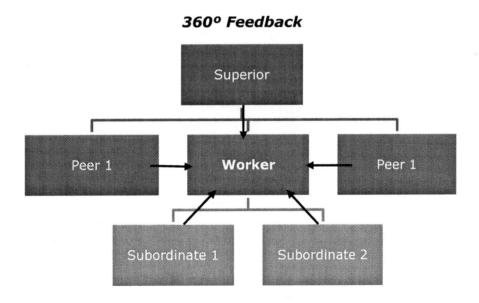

✂ **Conflict management**: conflict management is one of the most important traits of a PM. Conflicts are unavoidable and if different opinions are well managed, they could be positive for the project because they will trigger more creativity and productivity.

? *What is the main source of conflict in projects?*
    A. Schedule
    B. Priorities
    C. Costs
    D. Personalities

✋ Take 1 minute to answer before keep reading.

Did you select personalities? Then, you are blaming people and this is not right. The main cause of conflict is due to schedules, change of priorities, and lack of resources. What usually happens is that, given these causes of conflict, people may have reactions that affect their emotional state. You should consider that the last cause of conflict is personality.

Correct conflict management includes the following actions:

    ✓ Address them early and in private

    ✓ Use a direct and constructive approach

    ✓ Use disciplinary actions only as the last resort

? *What is the most convenient way of conflict resolution?*
    A. Withdrawing or avoiding: step away from conflict
    B. Smoothing or accommodating: emphasize on agreement areas
    C. Compromising: each side should let go of something
    D. Forcing: impose one position over another
    E. Collaborating: seek consensus and compromise
    F. Confronting: treat the conflict as a problem

✋ Take 1 minute to answer before keep reading.

> ✍ *50% of the exam questions are situational conflict management questions.*

Were you wrong again? If you selected collaborating, you have selected a lose-lose alternative, which is not the best. You surely did not select the correct answer, which is confronting. Conflicts are unavoidable and the best way to solve them is facing the problem and finding its root cause. Confrontation is synonym of conflict resolution and that is the best way of finding a win-win solution. The worst answers are forcing and avoiding.

Conflicts Points of Views

Old School	Modern Management
Cause of conflict: - Personality problems - Lack of leadership -	Cause of conflict: - It is unavoidable - Organizational interrelations
Should be avoided	*Could be beneficial*
Resolution: - Physical separation of people - Intervention of upper management	Resolution: - Identify causes - Solve the problem among parties

> ✎ *Conflict management steps:*
> *1. Identify the problem root cause.*
> *2. Analyze the problem.*
> *3. Identify alternative solutions.*
> *4. Implement a decision.*
> *5. Validate if that decision solved the problem.*

✂ **Issue Log:** is a register where you keep track of the occurred conflict and its resolution state.

Project Issue Log

#	Issue	Date occurred	Impacted parties	Proposed resolution date	Status	Resolution date	Applied resolution
13	incentive	2-3-13	Robert	4-5-13	Open		
27	terminology	5-15-13	John/Mary	8-15-13	Closed	7-10-13	Arbitrator

> ✎ *One of the best conflict resolution techniques is holding a face to face meeting with the impacted parties. Then we should register the problem and its possible solution in the project issue log.*

✂ **Interpersonal skills**: leadership, motivation, listening, negotiation, general culture, persuasion to make things happen, etc.

What do I get at the end of the process?

↗ Change requests

↗ Updates

Summarizing human resource management

On the following figure the main inputs, outputs, and interdependencies of the human resources processes are summarized.

Integrating human resource management

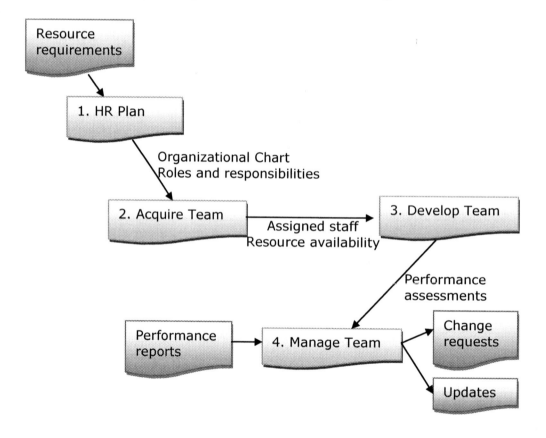

Exam 9 – Human Resources

Number of questions: 15
Time to respond: 18 minutes
Pass score: 80% (12 correct answers)

1. In a project for touristic cabins by the sea shore, the project manager is planning how many persons will be needed during the construction and execution of the cabins. Specialists to complete various work packages will be needed for this project at some point. What tool will surely be used by the project manager to represent the requirements graphically?
   A. Pareto Chart
   B. Responsibility Assignment Matrix
   C. Monte Carlo Simulation
   D. Resource Histogram

2. You are the project manager for the manufacturing of a new balanced food for dogs. The project is very similar to the "Cat Project" that you implemented last year. What method could you use when planning the human resources for the new project?
   A. Use the project management plan from the "Cat Project"
   B. Use the organization chart from the "Cat Project"
   C. Use the "Cat Project" roles and responsibilities descriptions
   D. Use the same project team as in "Cat Project"

3. A project for an alternative source of renewable energy is in its execution stage. The project manager needs to develop the capabilities for the team. One tool that she could use for this purpose is:
   A. Work breakdown structure
   B. Apply the open systems organization theory
   C. Use an issue log
   D. Co-location

4. A project is going through difficult resolution conflicts. The most common causes of conflict in this project could be schedule, priorities, and:
   A. Personalities
   B. Hygiene factors
   C. Resources
   D. Costs

5. In a mining project, the sponsor signed the project charter. What type of power the project manager has as a result of this act?
   A. Referred
   B. Formal
   C. Reward
   D. Expert

6. According to Douglas Mc Gregor, people belong to one of two categories. Based on this, he developed the X-Y Theory. Select the correct answer.
   A. Theory Y managers see their subordinates as creative, imaginative, and open to change.
   B. Theory Y managers know that their subordinates are lazy, irresponsible, and do not want to change.
   C. After the X-Y Theory, Mc Gregor developed the Z Theory.
   D. Theory X managers believe that their subordinates work without supervision and they want to progress.

7. What theory states that the success of an enterprise is based on trust, close relationships between superior and subordinates, and a personalized treatment to each employee?
   A. Theory Z Ouchi
   B. Herzberg's Motivational Theory
   C. McGregor's X-Y Theory
   D. Expectancy Theory

8. Frederick Herzberg, in his motivational theory for people, explains two types of motivational factors: hygiene factors and motivational agents. Examples of motivational agents would be:
   A. Salary and incentives program
   B. Professional development and self-esteem
   C. Vacations and social work
   D. Work place and recognition

9. In a project to maintain Formula One cars, a new mechanic has been assigned as the project leader due to the "halo effect". What does this mean?
   A. An internal pool of resources has been used for this designation
   B. Has been appointed as project leader because he was a good mechanic
   C. Motivational agents of that employee have been considered for this designation
   D. Has been assigned project leader for his referred authority

10. You are involved in the development of the human resource plan for an expansion and remodeling project of an airport. Which of the following statements will not be created in this process?
   A. Organization chart
   B. Staff assignments
   C. Roles and responsibilities assignments
   D. Staffing management plan

11. During the manage project team process, for the performance appraisal we will be using the 360° feedback system. This tool will serve for the following, EXCEPT for:
   A. Clarifying roles and responsibilities of the team members
   B. Discovering unknown issues
   C. Developing individual development plans
   D. Creating a recognition and rewards system

12. In an engineering project, Johnny Tejuno has not finished his work with the excuse that he had received the information from a predecessor activity, with an external dependency that Lucila Gamboa should have delivered. On the other hand, Lucila says that she is not able to finish the task until Johnny provides more details regarding the needs of the project. The project manager tells them: "you better both give something up on this conflict and finish your work by next week." What type of conflict resolution technique is being used?
    A. Confronting
    B. Directing
    C. Smoothing
    D. Compromising

13. The project manager's leadership style should adjust to the level of development of the project team members. In general, this situational leadership should progress in the following way:
    A. Does not know, wants, insecure, knows
    B. Directing, coaching, supporting, delegating
    C. Functional, weak matrix, strong matrix, projectized
    D. Autocratic, facilitator, consensus, delegating

14. According to Abraham Maslow, the highest level that can be achieved on the scale of the hierarchy of needs will be:
    A. Satisfaction of the physiological needs
    B. Achieve survival
    C. Self-Esteem
    D. Esteem

15. The project manager should solve a conflict that involves five team members that are arguing about a solution to a problem with the critical path. The strongest discussion is focused between implementing a fast track or a compression. Which is the best method to solve this problem?
    A. Confronting
    B. Compromising
    C. Avoiding
    D. Smoothing

Lessons Learned

- ✓ Co-location
- ✓ Conflict management techniques
- ✓ Expectancy theory
- ✓ Goal setting theory
- ✓ Ground rules
- ✓ Halo effect
- ✓ Herzberg theory
- ✓ Histogram
- ✓ Issues log
- ✓ Leadership styles
- ✓ Maslow hierarchy of needs
- ✓ Mc Gregor's X – Y theory
- ✓ Needs theory
- ✓ Ouchi's theory Z
- ✓ PM powers
- ✓ Recognition and rewards
- ✓ Roles and responsibilities
- ✓ Roles and responsibilities matrix
- ✓ Situational leadership
- ✓ Sources of conflict
- ✓ Staffing management plan

CHAPTER #10

COMMUNICATIONS

Chapter 10 - COMMUNICATIONS

> *People change and forget to tell each other.*
> Lillian Hellman (1905-1984); American playwright and writer.

A PM's main ability is to communicate. Regardless of your title and in what profession you are specialized, if you do not learn how to communicate effectively, you will not achieve successful projects.

When you finish this chapter, you will have learned the following concepts:
- ✓ Communication processes
- ✓ Identify stakeholders
- ✓ Plan communications
- ✓ Basic communication models
- ✓ Communication channels
- ✓ Distribute information
- ✓ Communication types
- ✓ Performance reports
- ✓ Manage stakeholders expectations

Communication management processes *

In the following sections we will develop the communication management processes, which are distributed among the processes of "Initiation", "Planning", "Executing", and "Monitoring and Controlling" as presented in the following table.

Communication management processes

	Initiation	Planning	Executing	Controlling	Closing
Integration	1	1	1	2	1
Scope		3		2	
Time		5		1	
Cost		2		1	
Quality		1	1	1	
Human Resources		1	3		
Communications	Identify Stakeholders	Plan Communications	. Distribute Information . Manage Stakeholder Expectations	Report Performance	
Risks		5		1	
Procurement		1	1	1	1
TOTAL	**2**	**20**	**8**	**10**	**2**

* Project Management Institute, Ibidem.

The five communication management processes are:

1. **Identify stakeholders**: identify all people or organizations that somehow will be affected by the project.

2. **Plan communications**: determine what will be the project's information needs.

3. **Distribute information**: make information available to stakeholders.

4. **Manage stakeholder expectations**: satisfy stakeholder's requirements and solve conflicts between human beings.

5. **Report performance**: communicate the project's status.

Identify stakeholders

As mentioned at the beginning of this book, project stakeholders are any person or organization whose interests might be affected by the project, either positively or negatively.

Stakeholders should be identified since the beginning of the project in order to analyze their expectations and their power of influence over the project.

> ✎ *Stakeholder identification and management is the key to have a successful project.*

What do I need to start?

⬇ Project charter

⬇ Procurement documents. For example, contracts with suppliers.

What tools can I use?

✂ **Stakeholder analysis**: identify stakeholders' interests, expectations, and power of influence.

Steps for stakeholder analysis

1st - Identify
Roles, area, interests, knowledge, expectations, influence

2nd - Impact
Classify stakeholders by: influence, interests, participation, urgency

3rd - Evaluation
How can they react or influence the project?

In the following figure we present a matrix to classify stakeholders based on their power (influence) and their interests in the project).

Power – Interest Matrix

Source: Adapted from the PMBOK® Guide - 4th edition

What do I get at the end of the process?

↗ **Stakeholder register**: document where all the information about the stakeholders is gathered. For example, name, position, project role, requirements, expectations, power of influence, etc.

↗ **Stakeholder management strategy**: the actions that will be done to gain the stakeholder's collaboration and mitigate negative impacts during the project life cycle.

📖 <u>Exercise 10.1</u> – Stakeholder register and the strategy

What strategies could you use for each stakeholder group?

Stakeholder	Role	Impact	Strategy
Clients	Buy final product	They do not like the product	
Suppliers	Deliver inputs	Delivery delays	
Investors	Finance the project	Not releasing resources	
PM	General coordination	Lack of leadership	
Work team	Execute the project	Lack of communication	
Citizens	Avoid environmental damage	Sue the company	
Government	Establish regulations	Change regulations	

✋ Take 5 minutes to think about all possible strategies for each case

Answers to Exercise 10.1

Stakeholder	Impact	Strategy
Clients	They do not like the product	Implement devolution policies
Suppliers	Delivery delays	Work with more than one supplier
Investors	Not releasing resources	Periodic status reports
PM	Lack of leadership	Training
Work team	Lack of communication	Establish connections
Citizens	Sue the company	Community plans
Government	Change regulations	Sign long term agreements

Plan communications

During the plan communications process, we should be able to answer the following questions:

- What information do stakeholders need?
- When will they need it?
- How many channels are involved?
- Who communicates with whom?
- Who will receive the information?
- How will the information be distributed?
- Who will distribute it?
- What technology will we use?
- How frequent will the communication be?

> ✍ We should not start communicating on the run. Planning communications in an efficient way is being **proactive**.

What do I need to start?

↓ Stakeholder register and their management strategy

What tools can I use?

✂ **Communication requirements analysis**: determine the communication channels and the stakeholders' information needs.

Communication channels determine the project communications' complexity. For example, if there are four stakeholders in the project, we would have six communication channels, as shown in the following figure.

Communication channels

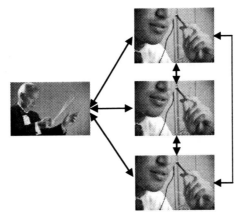

Count the number of arrows
4 persons = 6 arrows = 6 channels

The formula to calculate communication channels is:

> **Communication channels = (n x (n-1)) / 2**
> Where *n* is the number of stakeholders

✂ **Communication technology**: plan what type of technology will be used to distribute the information, taking into consideration the following factors:
  - ✓ Urgency
  - ✓ Actual availability of technology
  - ✓ Personnel competencies
  - ✓ Technological change
  - ✓ Working environment: physical or virtual?

> ✍ *The WBS is an excellent communication tool.*

✂ **Communication models**: communication flows between the transmitter and the receiver.

Behind every message there is a transmitter and a receiver. The transmitter encodes the message before sending it and the receiver decodes it when it is received. The receiver then encodes the message again to send its response to the transmitter, who will decode it.

During each encoding and decoding process, the original message could suffer changes or misinterpretation. This is the consequence of noise in the context, bad encoding, long distances between team members, hostility, languages, cultures, experiences, education levels, etc. In addition, there can be people who can turn themselves into information blockers, with phrases such as: "that is impossible", "what you are trying to do is not feasible", "don't even think about it", "you're dreaming", "that will be expensive", "NO NO NO", etc.

Noise or Information blockers

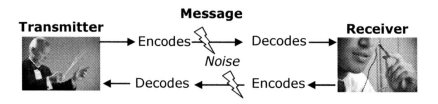

Noise: bad encoding, distances, hostility, language, culture

Blockers: that`s impossible, not feasible, too expensive, No!

Let us see a very simple example of failures in communication in the following figure.

How many columns there are in the figure?

How many columns there are?

Take a minute to look at the figure before moving forward

If you concentrate on the lower part of the figure, you will respond that there are three columns. However, if you focus on the upper part of the figure, you will surely respond that there are two columns. It is not the same to work on a project with two columns, that one with three columns. Is it?

These communication failures between the transmitter and the receiver can create great inconveniences during project management; hence the importance of an effective communication, where:

The transmitter:
1. Encodes the message in a careful and correct manner
2. Selects an appropriate sending method
3. Sends information that is clear and complete
4. Confirms that the message was understood

The receiver:
1. Decodes the message in a careful and correct manner
2. Confirms that the message has been understood through effective listening: observe physical and facial gestures, think what to say before responding, ask questions, and send comments.

Transmitter and Receiver's Responsibilities

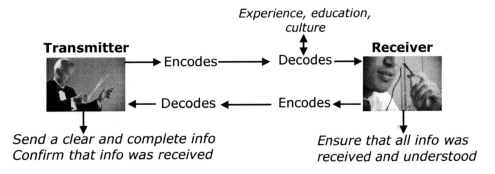

? How much time a project manager dedicates to communications?

? How much time a project manager dedicates to communications?
   A. 50%
   B. 75%
   C. 90%
   D. 100%

? What percentage of communications are non verbal?
   A. 10%
   B. 20%
   C. 60%
   D. 90%

As mentioned in the beginning, the most important ability of a PM is communication. In big projects the PM spends most of its time communicating. Approximately 90% of the time is destined to communications.

A good project manager possesses non verbal communication abilities. For example, the paralinguistic (be aware of the tone of the voice) or the kinesis communication (interpret corporal and facial expressions). Approximately 60% of the communications tend to be non verbal.

✂ **Communication methods**: different alternatives to share information between stakeholders. For example, conduct an interactive or bi-directional meeting, send a unilateral e-mail (push), develop an intranet (pull), etc.

What do I get at the end of the process?

↗ **Communications management plan**: Includes, among others:
- ✓ Communication channels
- ✓ Format and content of the communication type
- ✓ People responsible for communicating
- ✓ People that will receive communications
- ✓ Communications technology that will be used
- ✓ Frequency of communications
- ✓ Glossary of common terms

Communications matrix

| ID # | Activity | Frequency | How | Stakeholder responsability | | | | |
				S1	S2	S3	...	Sn
1	Activity 1	M	M	R	T	A	...	V
2	Activity 2	W	D	S	R	R	...	A
3	Activity 3	Q	F	T	R	R	...	S
....	...	...	...	...	...	...	...	...
n	Activity n	E	S	R	R	A	...	T

References:
Frequency: M (monthly); W (weekly); Q (quarterly); E (eventual)
How: D (document); E (e-mail); M (meeting); F (figure); S (spreadsheet)
Responsibility: T (transmitter); R (receiver); A (approve); S (support); V (validate)

Distribute information

During the project execution, you should implement the communications plan to inform the stakeholders about the progress of the project in due time and form.

What do I need to start?
- ↓ Communications management plan
- ↓ Performance reports

What tools can I use?

✂ **Communication methods and tools**: different alternatives to distribute information. For example: messaging, e-mail, videoconference, databases, press, internet, virtual offices, multimedia presentations, etc.

> ✍ *The PM must ensure that the correct people receive the appropriate information in due time and form.*

When distributing information you must take into account the different communication types:
- Internal: between persons that are part of the project
- External: towards the project's external stakeholders
- Vertical: between boss-subordinate and vice-versa
- Horizontal: between project colleagues
- Formal written: plans, requests, etc.
- Informal written: memos, e-mails, notes
- Formal verbal: presentations
- Informal verbal: meetings, conversations

> ✍ *Recommendations for **effective meetings**:*
> - *Have a clear objective for each meeting*
> - *Program periodic meetings with anticipation*
> - *Distribute the agenda with anticipation*
> - *Establish start and end times; RESPECT THEM*
> - *Assign due dates to each deliverable derived from the meeting*
> - *Document and publish the meeting minutes*

📖 **Exercise 10.2 – Communication types**

Based on the following communication types: Formal written (FW), Formal verbal (FV), Informal written (IW), Informal verbal (IV); complete on the following table the best communication type for each situation.

Situation	Type
Open the supplier's bid terms	
Clarify the sequence of an activity	
Update the communications plan	
Schedule a meeting for design review	
Analyze the root cause for a complex problem	
Send an e-mail to contact a supplier	
Inform a person's bad performance for the first time	
Inform a person their bad performance for the second time	
Instructions to resolve a complex problem	
Presentations to the Director	
Make an announcement in the kick-off meeting	
Make a change in the electrical provisioning contract	
Request additional funds to the sponsor	
Make notes about a telephone call	

✋ Take 5 minutes to solve this exercise

Answers to Exercise 10.2

Situation	Type
Open the supplier's bid terms	FV
Clarify the sequence of an activity	FW
Update the communications plan	FW
Schedule a meeting for design review	IW
Analyze the root cause for a complex problem	IV
Send an e-mail to contact a supplier	IW
Inform a person's bad performance for the first time	IV
Inform a person their bad performance for the second time	FW
Instructions to resolve a complex problem	FW
Presentations to the Director	FV
Make an announcement in the kick-off meeting	IV
Make a change in the electrical provisioning contract	FW
Request additional funds to the sponsor	FW
Make notes about a telephone call	IW

Exercise 10.3 – Distribution methods

When selecting the distribution method, we should consider the following:

a) How many transmitters-receivers are involved: one, few, many?
b) How is the direction: one-way or two-way?
c) What is the complexity of the information: low, medium, high?

Complete the following table:

Situation	a) Transmitter-receiver b) Direction	c) Complexity	Recommended distribution method
Coordination meeting			
Collaboration meeting			
Distribute documents			
Review documents			
Routine memos			
Detailed information			
Negotiations			
Formal requests			
Train teams			

Answers to Exercise 10.3

Situation	a) Transmitter-receiver b) Direction	c) Complexity	Recommended distribution method
Coordination meeting	Few-Few Two-way	Medium	Face to face Teleconference
Collaboration meeting	Few-Few Two-way	High	Face to face Videoconference
Distribute documents	One-many One-way	Low	Intranet E-mail
Review documents	One-many Two-way	Medium	E-mail Photocopy
Routine memos	One-One One-way	Low	E-mail
Detailed information	One-One Two-way	Medium	Face to face E-mail
Negotiations	One-One Two-Way	High	Face to face Videoconference
Formal requests	One-One One-way	Low	Formal letter
Train teams	One-One Two-Way	High	Face to face Videoconference

What do I get at the end of the process?
- ↗ Project notifications to stakeholders
- ↗ Project presentations and progress reports
- ↗ Stakeholder feedback
- ↗ Lessons learned document

Manage stakeholder expectations

The PM is responsible for conducting this process. During this process, project communications are managed in order to satisfy the stakeholder needs and solve the conflicts between them.

> ✎ *The PM should manage the needs and requirements of the stakeholders.*

What do I need to start?
- ↓ Stakeholder register and stakeholder management strategy
- ↓ Communications plan
- ↓ Issues log
- ↓ Change log: document changes and their respective impact to the project

What tools can I use?

✂ **Communication methods**: meetings, telephone calls, e-mail, Skype, adobe connect, etc.

✂ **Interpersonal and management skills**: confidence, conflict resolution, effective listening, attitude towards change, negotiation, oratory, etc.

? Based on the following examples; why do you think the PM should worry about these types of communication?

Situation 1:

Peter is convinced that the scope that was cut from the project should be part of it. Therefore, he will keep pressing until they re-introduce what he wants.

PM: *Peter, I know you want to add other deliverables to the project. The Sponsor has already allocated the funds and has formally signed the final scope. Unfortunately, there is no way back and is not possible to modify the scope. I will appreciate that you do not insist with your request and that you integrate with the rest of the team.*

Situation 2:

Donna, Operations Manager, is furious because project Z will use most of her best human resources, which will delay the execution of her projects.

PM: *We have considered the impact that project Z will have on your projects. I am sure you will understand that this is a strategic project and we need your best resources. To mitigate the impact, I will be requesting the necessary resources two months in advance, and we will keep you informed on the project's progress, in order to liberate your resources as soon as possible.*

Answer:

The PM should always be **proactive** and consider the needs of the stakeholders, even when it is impossible to solve them. This way, you can maintain a fluid communications with the stakeholders and keep the communication channels open.

What do I get at the end of the process?

↗ Updates

↗ Change requests

Report Performance

During the report performance process we compare the actual state of the project in relation to its baselines. The progress reports indicate how resources are being used and tend to include information about the scope, schedule, costs, human resources, risks, and procurement.

What do I need to start?

⬇ Project management plan, with its baselines: scope, schedule and budget.

⬇ Work performance information: deliverables, progress, actual costs, etc.

⬇ Work performance measurements: SPI, CPI, technical performance, etc.

⬇ Budget forecasts: estimated budget at completion.

What tools can I use?

✂ **Variance analysis**: investigate causes and impacts of the deviations between the project status and the baselines.

✂ **Forecasting methods**: predict the project's evolution (schedule, budget, etc.). For example, you could use time series, causal methods, econometric regressions, surveys, forecast by analogy, simulations, etc.

✂ **Communication methods**: for example, project status meetings.

✂ **Reporting systems**: register, store, and distribute information in a systematized way. For example, use software packages that generate project status reports.

What do I get at the end of the process?

↗ Updates and change requests

↗ **Performance reports**: indicate the project's actual situational status and its progress in regards to its baselines. Communicate the estimates of how will the project be at completion (scope, time, costs and quality), considering the up to date information.

In the following table, we present an example of a project's progress report, using earned value management.

Project's progress report

WBS	PLAN	ACTUAL		COSTS			SCHEDULE		
	PV	EV	AC	CV	CV/EV	CPI	SV	SV/PV	SPI
1	10	10	12	-2	-20%	0.83	0	0%	1
2	20	25	15	10	40%	1.67	5	25%	1.25
3	40	30	45	-15	-50%	0.67	-10	-25%	0.75
Total	70	65	72	-7	-11%	0.90	-5	-7%	0.93

Another graphic report that tends to be useful to indicate the schedule and costs evolution is presented in the following figure.

Time and cost progress

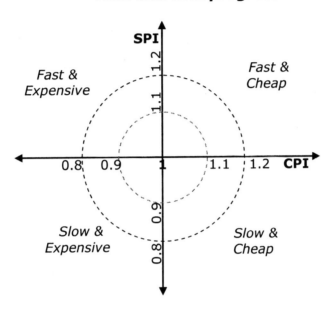

📖 Exercise 10.4 – Performance report

Complete the blank cells of Project SUDOKU in the following table.

WBS	PLAN	ACTUAL		COSTS			SCHEDULE		
	PV	EV	AC	CV	CV/EV	CPI	SV	SV/PV	SPI
Planning		30	25	5			0		
Construction	100		100			0.80			
Tests	20	10			0%				0.5
Total									

✋ Take 15 minutes to solve this exercise. Review the formulas for earned value management and interpret the results.

Answers to Exercise 10.4

WBS	PLAN	ACTUAL		COSTS			SCHEDULE		
	PV	EV	AC	CV	CV/EV	CPI	SV	SV/PV	SPI
Planning	30	30	25	5	17%	1.20	0	0%	1
Construction	100	80	100	-20	-25%	0.80	-20	-20%	0.8
Tests	20	10	10	0	0%	1.00	-10	-50%	0.5
Total	**150**	**120**	**135**	**-15**	**-13%**	**0.89**	**-30**	**-20%**	**0.8**

If we analyze the project in general, we can conclude the following:

Cost analysis: we have spent $15 more than we were supposed to spend in relation to the work performed, which represents a 13% overpayment.

Schedule analysis: we have worked $30 less than it was planned, which represents a 20% delay.

Summarizing communications management

In the following figure we summarize the main inputs, outputs, and interrelations for the communications management processes.

Integrating communications management

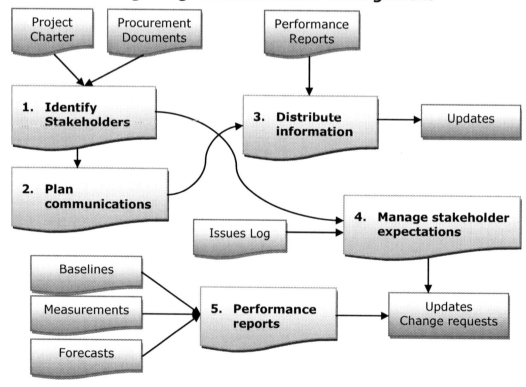

Exam 10 – Communications

Number of questions: 15
Time to respond: 18 minutes
Pass score: 80% (12 correct answers)

1. You are the project manager for a huge mining project from a Canadian multinational company with various worldwide projects. There have been various communication problems in the opening of a new mine, mainly because of bad interpretations by the stakeholders. You need to grab the attention of the company's members. What type of communication could help solve these problems?
   A. Informal verbal
   B. Vertical
   C. Formal
   D. Formal written

2. You have just been assigned as the project manager in a project dealing with the manufacturing of wireless keyboards for computers. While reviewing the current project status, you discover that one member of the team is not respecting the quality standards established by the company. What is the best way to communicate with this person in order to solve the problem?
   A. Formal written
   B. Informal verbal
   C. Formal verbal
   D. Informal written

3. Phrases such as: *"are you crazy, we haven't done that before"*, or *"that's going to be expensive"*, or *"don't even think about it, that's impossible to do"*, are examples of:
   A. Effective communication
   B. Feedback
   C. Conflict generators
   D. Communication blockers

4. You are the project manager for the refurnishing of a rural school. To achieve a successful project, it will be important to have a fluid communication with the Client, the school's Principal. Why is so important having good communication between these stakeholders?
   A. The Principal will fill out a satisfaction survey about the project manager's work performance
   B. The Principal does not understand the modern project management terminology, which is why she has to be educated
   C. Although the scope of the project is detailed in the contract, communication between stakeholders will facilitate the understanding of the objectives
   D. Communication noises between the receiver and the transmitter will be avoided

5. The PM for Project XYZ is communicating the stakeholders, internal and external, about the project's performance. The report shows the actual status in relation to the following constraints: scope, time and costs. What type of report is this?
   A. Status
   B. Time series
   C. Earned value
   D. Progress

6. The planning phase for the project "Highway" has finalized and the execution phase for the road is now underway. During the process of distributing information, all the guidelines in the communications plan were followed. The original plan established the use of elaborated concrete for the whole road. However, it was decided to use other materials for a small portion of the road. All stakeholders were informed of this change. However, a contractor informed the project manager that he was never told of the need to use new materials. Therefore, he continued using the same concrete established in the original plan. What should the project manager do?
   A. Identify the noises between the transmitter and the receiver that affected the communication
   B. Analyze the communications management plan and make the necessary revisions
   C. Determine why the contractor did not receive the information
   D. Ask the sponsor why the contractor did not understand his responsibility

7. Between the transmitter and the receiver exists verbal and non-verbal communications (facial expressions, hand gestures, and corporal movements). Approximately, what percentage of communication is non-verbal?
   A. Less than 10%
   B. Close to 20%
   C. Between 20% and 40%
   D. Greater than 50%

8. The following actions from the project manager, in its role of the transmitter of a message, are part of an effective communication, EXCEPT for:
   A. Encode the message in a careful and correct manner
   B. Select the most appropriate method to send the information
   C. Decode the message in a careful and correct manner
   D. Confirm that the message was understood

9. The project manager is responsible for the performance reports. In a pisciculture project to develop a new variety of fish, the following are examples of performance reports, EXCEPT for:
   A. Actual state of the risks
   B. Summary of approved changes
   C. Forecasted project conclusion
   D. Lessons learned

10. You are working as the project manager in a telecommunications company. During the last days you have been dedicated to identify what are the communication needs of the project stakeholders. What would you have completed when you finish with this planning phase?
    A. Communications infrastructure requirements
    B. Communications management plan
    C. Stakeholder analysis
    D. Information distribution system

11. During the planning of a project to install a circus for kids in a city, four circus employees are discussing about which activities must be completed before erecting the columns. As the project manager you want to understand what is going on, so you need to pay close attention to:
    A. What is being said
    B. The tone of the voices and the corporal gestures
    C. Who is saying each thing
    D. The corporal gestures and what is being said

12. Based on the following project performance report, with blank cells that you must complete; what is the earned value for Activity B?

ACTIVITY	PLAN	ACTUAL		COST			SCHEDULE		
	PV	EV	AC	CV	CV/EV	CPI	SV	SV/PV	SPI
A		20	25	15			0		
B	100		100			0.80			
C	20	10			0%				0.5

    A. 80
    B. 100
    C. 80%
    D. 0

13. We are conducting a market study for a project to launch a new foodstuff for senior citizens. Which of the following communication tools allows keeping participant anonymity?
    A. Delphi technique
    B. Brainstorming
    C. Distances
    D. Active listening

14. During the process of distributing information, it is important to review the lessons learned from previous projects. Lessons learned should be completed by:
    A. The sponsors
    B. The project manager
    C. The team
    D. The stakeholders

15. You are working as the project manager for project "Dissected Strawberries" and you have 5 people in charge. By express request from the sponsor, you have been added nine persons to your work team. How many communication channels have been incorporated?
   A. 3
   B. 36
   C. 18
   D. 21

Lessons Learned

- ✓ Communication channels
- ✓ Encoding
- ✓ Effective communication
- ✓ Formal and informal communication
- ✓ Verbal and written communication
- ✓ Non-verbal communication
- ✓ Decoding
- ✓ Communication types
- ✓ Distribute information
- ✓ Active listening
- ✓ Effective listening
- ✓ Stakeholder expectations
- ✓ Distribution methods
- ✓ Para-linguistic
- ✓ Communications management plan
- ✓ Recommendations for effective meetings
- ✓ Noise

CHAPTER #11

RISK

Chapter 11 - RISK

Who searches for the truth runs the risk of finding it.
Manuel Vicent (1936-?); Spanish writer.

We should not start the project execution without a risk analysis. Risk planning is an integration area for the rest of the knowledge areas. For example, we cannot state that we have a realistic schedule and budget if we have not completed the risk management plan. With the risk analysis, the duration and cost contingency reserves that should be included in the project management plan will be determined.

When you finish this chapter you will have learned the following concepts:

- ✓ Risk management basic concepts
- ✓ Plan risk management
- ✓ Identify risks
- ✓ Perform qualitative risk analysis
- ✓ Perform quantitative risk analysis
- ✓ Plan risk responses
- ✓ Monitor and control risks

Risk management basic concepts

Every project is risky. This is valid for small projects, like the organization of a birthday party, as well as for multi millionaire projects, such as the launching of a space rocket.

We could say that risk is something unknown that, if produced, affects in a negative or positive way the project objectives. Therefore, a risk event could be good or bad.

> ✎ *Risk represents the potential impact of all the threats or opportunities that could affect the achievement of the project objectives.*

▪ *Uncertainty and risk*

Uncertainty occurs when we don't know the probability of an event occurrence. While in a risk situation, we could estimate the probability of occurrence. For example, uncertainty would be if we don't have a clue if a weather catastrophe will occur in a project. But if we could estimate the

probability of bad weather based on weather reports, then we would be in a risk situation.

- ### *Probability*

Each risk event has a chance to occur. For example, the probability of having earthquakes in a particular city is 2%. This means that on the long term, the earth will shake 2 of every 100 days. If the probability were 4% the event has doubled the possibilities of occurrence, in relation to the 2% probability.

An improbable event has a probability close to zero. While, an event that is almost certain has a probability close to 100%. Therefore, mathematically, the probability is usually represented on a scale that goes from 0 to 1.

Sometimes we do not know exactly the probability of a risk event and the only thing we have is a perception based in an opinion or research that maybe is not correct. On these cases, an estimated probability range can be used, and a sensitivity analysis can be made of the potential impact of each of the scenarios on the project objectives.

- ### *Impact*

Risk is not only quantified by its probability, but also by its impact on the project objectives (scope, time, cost, quality). For example, if the probability of bad weather is very high, but its damages on the project are very low, we should not be too concerned about that risk.

A project will be riskier if it presents a 10% probability of causing damages worth $500,000, than in the case when it presents a 10% probability of causing damages worth $100,000.

> ✍ *If an event causes important impact on a project and, in addition, the probability is unknown, we will surely be unable to make good decisions for this project.*

- ### *Expected monetary value*

A good estimate for the expected benefits or costs of a risk event can be obtained if its probability is multiplied by its impact.

> ✍ *Expected monetary value = Probability x Impact*

For example, a 10% probability of losing $100,000 is $10,000, while a 20% probability of earning $200,000 represents an expected profit of $40,000.

Another way of analyzing the expected monetary value is comparing it with the premium that is paid to an insurance company. If I want to insure my company such that I don't lose $100,000 in case of fire, for which the probability is 10%, I should pay an insurance premium of $10,000 (without including administrative costs and insurance profit margin). This is because if the insurance covers a great number of companies with the same risk, the sum of all the premiums will be equal to the amount that would have to be paid for the claims of those events that occur.

- **Unknown risks or unforeseen events**

Unforeseen events are those unknown risks that may occur without having anticipated its occurrence. These events depend in the unusual combination of factors that were not able to be thought proactively.

For example, an unforeseen event during the construction of a building could be a change in regulation that forces the original planned project scope to change.

Experience says that unforeseen events are the most dangerous risks for the project feasibility. Given that these unforeseen events are unknown, it is very easy to omit them. Therefore, one of the most important tasks during the risk management process is the identification of the maximum possible number of risk events, regardless of the undoubted difficulty that this task presents.

- **Contingency reserves**

A monetary reserve for contingencies can be estimated for the risks that are known, identified, and quantified.

On the other hand, unknown risks cannot be managed proactively and could be considered by assigning a general management reserve to the project, that is not part of the cost baseline, but it is included in the total project budget.

Contingency reserves

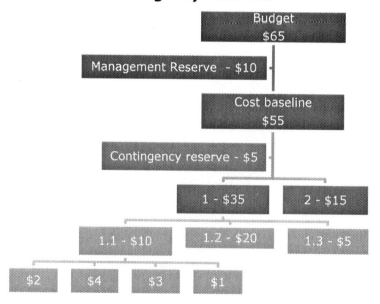

Risk management processes *

Risk management is the systematic process of planning, identifying, analyzing, responding, and controlling project risks. This process tries to maximize the probability of positive events and minimize the probability of adverse events.

> ✎ *Book: PING; Author: STUART AVERY GOLD*
> *The wise Owl advises the young Frog before jumping the river:*
>
> *When you analyze a risk correctly, the probability of failure will be much less. Define that risk with precision. Determine which obstacles and difficulties you should overcome to succeed. Prepare for the unforeseen. What is the worst that could happen? What is your plan B if plan A fails? In other words, look closely before jumping.*

In the following sections we will develop the risk management processes that are distributed amongst the planning and, monitoring and controlling processes as presented in the following table.

Risk management processes

	Initiating	Planning	Executing	Controlling	Closing
Integration	1	1	1	2	1
Scope		3		2	
Time		5		1	
Cost		2		1	
Quality		1	1	1	
HR		1	3		
Communications	1	1	2	1	
Risks		. Plan Risk Management . Identify Risks . Perform Qualitative Analysis . Perform Quantitative Analysis . Plan Risk Response		Monitor and Control Risk	
Procurements		1	1	1	1
TOTAL	**2**	**20**	**8**	**10**	**2**

The six risk management processes are:

1. **Plan risk management:** how the activities for identification, analysis, response, and monitoring of risks will be planned and executed.

2. **Identify risks:** what risks affect the project.

3. **Perform qualitative risk analysis:** estimate qualitatively (e.g. high, medium, low) the probability and impact of each risk to be able to prioritize them.

4. **Perform quantitative risk analysis:** estimate numerically the probability (e.g. 5%) and impact (e.g. $10,000) to prioritize the risks with more precision.

5. **Plan risk response:** plan the actions that will take place to improve the opportunities and reduce the threats.

6. **Monitor and control risks:** monitor and execute the risk response plans.

Plan risk management

During the risk planning process we should answer the following questions:

- Who will identify the risks?

- When will the risks be identified?

- What scale will be used for the qualitative risk analysis?

- How will risks be prioritized?

- What tools will be used for the quantitative analysis?

- Which will be the strategies to implement each risk?

- How often will risk follow up be done?

What do I need to start?

↓ Plans: Scope, Schedule, Budget and Communications

What tools can I use?

✂ **Planning and analysis meetings**

What do I get at the end of the process?

↗ **Risk management plan:** the components of this plan, among others, are:

✓ Methodology
✓ Roles and responsibilities of the risk management team
✓ Risk management budget
✓ Risk categories
✓ Frequency to perform the risk processes during the project life cycle
✓ Scales of probability and impact, and the risk matrix
✓ Format of the reports

Risk Management Plan (Example)

Methodology: the risk project management processes recommended in the PMBOK® Guide will be applied. For the identification of risks work sessions will be integrating multifunctional teams with different internal and external areas of the project. The qualitative risk analysis and the risk register will be completed using Word and Excel templates. Qualitative risk scores will be calculated multiplying the probability by the impact of each identified risk. For the quantitative risk analysis, we will use software already owned by the company, such as: Excel, @Risk for Excel, Ms Project y @Risk for Project.

Risk management team: will be composed of Mary, Joanne and Joseph. The custodians of each identified risk that requires mitigation actions will be specified in the risk register.

Definition of probabilities: the probability was defined as: 1 (Very Low), 2 (Low), 3 (Medium), 4 (High), 5 (Very High).

Definition of impact:

IMPACT	Very Low 1	Low 2	Medium 3	High 5	Very High 10
COST Millions of $	< 3	3 - 9	9 - 30	30 - 60	> 60
SCHEDULE Months delay	< 1	1 - 4	4 - 6	6 - 8	> 8
SECURITY Injuries	Laws	Minor	Major	Disability	Death
ENVIRONMENT Spread through Media	Local	Provincial	National	South America	International

Risk Matrix:

Probability \ Impact	1	2	3	5	10
1	1	2	3	5	10
2	2	4	6	10	20
3	3	6	9	15	30
4	4	8	12	20	40
5	5	10	15	25	50

Risk categorization:

Score	Priority	Strategy	Meaning of each strategy
1 - 2	Very Low	Passive Acceptance	Don't do anything
3 - 4	Low	Active Acceptance	Leave in writing what will be done when the risk occurs
5 - 10	Medium	Mitigate	Actions to decrease the probability and/or the impact
11 - 24	High	Transfer	Transfer the risk to a third party. Example: insurance
25 - 30	Very High	Avoid	Do not advance the project until the score diminishes

<u>Note</u>: If a risk cannot be transferred, the mitigation strategy will be used.

Risk categories: a risk breakdown structure will be used with the categories that are presented in the following figure.

Risk breakdown structure

Format and content of the risk register: an Excel template will be updated with the contents presented as follows:

Content	Explanation
Update	Last date updated
Numbering	1, 2, 3, ... n (numbering of the identified risks)
Risk	Name of each identified risk
Consequences	Schedule, Cost, Quality, Security
Probability	Scale 1 to 5
Categorization	Technical, External, Organizational, Project Management
Impact	Scale 1 to 10
Score	Probability x Impact = 1 to 50
Changes	New, ↑ (increased), ↔ (stayed the same), ↓ (decreased)
Strategy	Passive acceptance, active acceptance, Mitigate, Transfer, Avoid
Action	What will be done to implement the strategy
Custodian	Person responsible of reporting status of the risk
Cost	Estimated cost of the mitigation actions

Monitor and control: During the monitor and control process, the same information system defined for the project will be used to concentrate all updated risk information in one place. The risk management plan will be updated on a monthly basis, incorporating the subject in the project status meetings.

Identify the risks

Once the risk management plan is complete, it is necessary to start identifying risky events that would affect the project result, for better or for worse. Special attention should be paid to the identification of events that could seriously affect the project, even when its probability is very low.

> ✎ *The work team should participate in the identification of risks to improve the ownership of the project and the responsibility towards the risky events.*

What do I need to start?

⬇ Risk management plan

⬇ Plans and baselines: scope, schedule, budget, quality

⬇ Stakeholder register

⬇ Project documents

> ✎ *The identification of risks is an iterative process that is updated in each of the risk management processes.*

What tools can I use?

✂ **Document revisions**

✂ **Gathering of information:** brainstorming, interviews, panel of experts, Delphi technique, etc.

> ✎ *Delphi Technique: the group members are physically separated and a general coordinator contacts all the members to comment on potential risks, maintaining the anonymity of the participants. The coordinator then informs the participants for each opinion on the identified risks and requests a reevaluation of their response to dig into their analysis. This iterative feedback process continues until there are no more changes to make.*

✂ **Checklist:** elaborated lists based on historic information from similar projects.

The following table presents an example of a risk identification checklist:

Checklist

Potential Risk	✓
Fire	
Storm	
Strike	
Non-compliance with quality	
Non-compliance with schedule	
Going over budget	
Lack of required raw material	
Lack of plan forecasted financing	
Lack of leadership to coordinate teams	
Change in regulations	
The contractor does not finish work on time	
The initial agenda is unreal	
Lack of resource training	
Lack of communication between the work team	
Inadequate quality controls	
Lack of technical support	

> ✎ *It is practically impossible to have a checklist that covers all project risks.*

✕ **Assumption analysis:** review the assumptions used in the project plans to analyze if they are complete and consistent. Those cases of discrepancy or inconsistency in the hypothesis or assumptions are usually a focus for potential risks.

✕ **Diagramming techniques:** cause and effect diagrams, flowcharts, influence diagrams, etc.

✕ **SWOT Analysis:** identification of strengths, weaknesses, opportunities, and threats.

What do I get at the end of the process?

↗ **Risk register:** document that includes the identified risks, the possible answers, the risk causes, and the risk categories.

> ✎ *The risk register starts like an output to the indentify risks process and then is updated and completed throughout the rest of the risk processes.*

Perform qualitative risk analysis

The qualitative analysis consists of evaluating what is the impact and probability of each one of the risks identified. In this process, the risks are ordered according to their relative importance in regards to the project objectives.

What do I need to start?

- ↓ Risk management plan
- ↓ Risk register

What tools can I use?

✂ **Probability and impact evaluation:** the impact and probability of each risk is estimated by performing interviews with experts.

For example, the probability of occurrence of an event can be classified as low, medium, or high. Also, it could be classified with a numeric score: "1" (low), "2" (medium), or "3" (high).

The risk analyst can define the risk scale. For example, a risk with high probability is that event that has occurred more than 5 times per year and it is expected the same frequency for next year. A very low probability is for those events that have occurred not more than one time.

On the other hand, the impact of a risk on the project objectives could also be classified in a qualitative scale. For example, from very low to very high (or a numeric scale from 0 to 1).

If a numeric score is applied to impact, the scale leveled with cardinal numbers do not have to be lineal. For example, in the following table a score of .10 is applied to very low impacts, and .90 to the very high ones. This slant on the high impacts indicates that the analyst is averse to risk and wishes to avoid those risks with a high or a very high impact.

Impact evaluation

Impact / Risk	Very low 0.10	Low 0.20	Medium 0.30	High 0.50	Very high 0.90
Cost excess ($)	< 1%	1%-9%	10%-20%	21%-50%	> 50%
Schedule delay (days in excess)	< 1	2 – 4	5 – 8	9 – 12	> 12
Bad quality (failures in every 1,000)	< 2	3 – 5	6 – 10	11 – 20	> 20

✂ **Probability and impact matrix:** it is usually represented with a double entry table where the probability and impact are combined to be able to prioritize risk.

After obtaining the impact and probability score of a risk, a score is assigned to that risk, multiplying the impact by the probability.

The risk matrix presented below shows an example with the scores that a specific risk could have. For example, if we estimate that a risk has a medium probability and a high impact, its score could be 30 (3 x 10).

Impact Probability matrix

Impact ⟍ Probability	Very low 1	Low 2	Medium 3	High 5	Very high 10
Very low 1	1	2	3	5	10
Low 2	2	4	6	10	20
Medium 3	3	6	9	15	30
High 4	4	8	12	20	40
Very high 5	5	10	16	25	50

The risk analyst could set a scale to categorize and prioritize risks. For example, using the scores from the example, the analyst could define that those risks, which scores are between 0-9 are low priority, those between 10-19 are medium priority, and those over 19 are very high priority.

There is no unique way to establish the scores for probability and impact, and the risk prioritization scales. The qualitative score in this matrix could be established with the company before starting the project depending on the project type, the company's risk policies, the context, the financial backup, the policy for risk diversification, the capacity to confront risks, etc.

> ✍ *Although the scores given to probability and impact are usually subjective, the probability impact matrix achieves its objective to help ordering and prioritizing the identified risks.*

📖 Exercise 11.1 – Risk matrix

A company that is evaluating an agricultural project assigns a .05 score to the very low impacts, going up to .08 for the very high impacts. Also, the company has defined the risk categorization according to the following table:

Impact Risk	Very low 0.05	Low 0.10	Medium 0.20	High 0.40	Very High 0.80
Cost excess ($)	< 1%	1%-5%	5% - 10%	10% - 20%	> 20%
Schedule delay (days in excess)	< 2	3 – 5	6 – 15	16 – 30	> 30
Bad quality (failure in every 10,000)	< 5	6-10	11-20	21-40	> 40

The estimated costs for the project can be affected by the variations in the currency exchange rate. In case of an increase in the exchange rate, the price of the imported items will increase and the estimated budget could increase in approximately 3%. A very high probability of occurrence is estimated for this risk.

On the other hand, it was detected that adverse weather conditions could cause delays. In case of unfavorable weather, the project would be delayed approximately 20 days. There is a high probability for bad weather during the time the project is planned to be executed.

Lastly, it was detected that some employees might not commit to the project and produce goods with defects. If this occurred, which has a medium probability, the company could discard approximately 2 of every 10,000 products.

The company has established a scale to categorize and prioritize risks. Those risks with a score between 0 – 0.49 are low priority, those between .5 – 1 are medium priority, and those over 1 are high priority.

Risk matrix					
Impact Probability	0.05 (Very low)	0.10 (Low)	0.20 (Medium)	0.40 (High)	0.80 (Very high)
1 (Very low)					
2 (Low)					
3 (Medium)					
4 (High)					
5 (Very high)					

What priority would the identified risks have?

🖐 Take 10 minutes to solve this exercise

Answer to Exercise 11.1

What follows presents first the localization of each of the identified risks and then the score of each risk is calculated.

		Impact				
		Very low	Low	Medium	High	Very high
Probability		0.05	0.1	0.2	0.4	0.8
Very low	1					
Low	2					
Medium	3	employees				
High	4				weather	
Very high	5		exchange			

		Impact				
		Very low	Low	Medium	High	Very high
Probability		0.05	0.1	0.2	0.4	0.8
Very low	1					
Low	2					
Medium	3	0.15				
High	4				1.60	
Very high	5		0.50			

The risk with score .15 (employees) is low priority.

The risk with score .50 (currency exchange) is medium priority.

The risk with score 1.60 (weather) is high priority; therefore, a prompt action should be planned. In this particular case, the plan could be changed to try not to construct in bad weather season or to make some type of investment (i.e. retaining walls) to mitigate the impact of damages to the project.

- ✂ **Data quality evaluation:** examine the accuracy, quality, reliability, and consistency of the information used for the project's estimation. If the data is not of good quality, the qualitative risk analysis will not be of useful.

- ✂ **Risk categorization:** group the risks based on common causes. For example, use a risk breakdown structure (RBS), identify risks within the WBS, group them by project lifecycle, etc.

The following are different risk categorization examples.

Risk categories by type

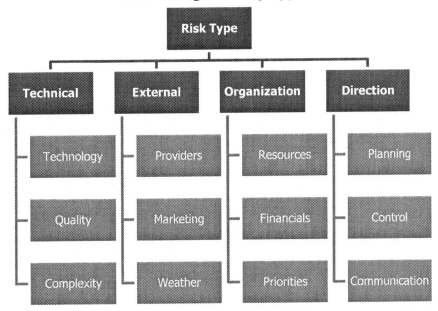

Risk categories by causes

Political Cause				Economic Cause				Internal Cause (or by Project)				Natural Cause			Financial Cause		
Weak government	Public opinion	Legislation change	Wars	Decrease in demand	Competition	Inflation	Currency exchange	Bad planning	Lack of leadership	Lack of training	Lack of control	Bad weather	Fire	Earthquake	Lack of financing	Low margin	Low rotation

Risk categorization in the project lifecycle

Initiating	Planning	Executing	Closing
• Experts bias • Lack of consensus to correctly define the problem • Lack of time to correctly evaluate feasibility	• Design failure • Discrepancies between quality and resources • Unrealistic timeline • Lack of communicat. • User do not participate	• Taste changes • Lack of quality control • Cost duplication • Unskilled contractor • Lack of technical support • Weather accident • Delays in construction	• Time is not allocated for project closure

> ✎ *Another risk categorization usually is:*
> *Internal: time, cost, scope, people*
> *External: regulations, government, weather*
> *Technical: change in technology*
> *Unforeseen events: only a 10%*

> ✎ *There are business risks like loss of time and money; and pure risks like injuries or death.*

✂ **Urgency evaluation:** evaluate what risks require a quick response.

In the following figure, an example of how risk prioritization could be determined is presented considering the time of response and the score of each risk.

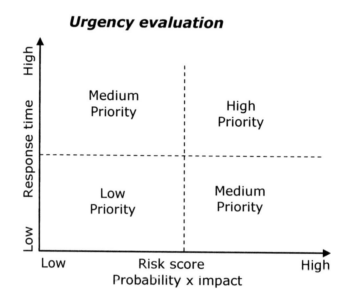

According to this figure, the events located in the upper right hand are the risks that have a high score and require an immediate response. These events should be treated with urgency.

On the other extreme, in the lower left hand corner are the low priority risks and can be put into an observation list in case the score changes in the future.

What do I get at the end of the process?

↗ **Updated risk register:** priorities of each risk, categories, causes and urgency.

Perform quantitative risk analysis

In the quantitative risk analysis the probability (%) and the impact ($) of each risk is quantified to prioritize risks according to their relative importance.

📖 Exercise 11.2 – Qualitative vs. quantitative analysis

In a factory of textiles the main problems that have occurred in the past 10 years have been analyzed:

Year	Problem	Code	Damage
1	Broken machine A	1	$ 2,000
1	Loss of oil in machine B	2	$ 100
2	Lack of gas supply	3	$ 1,000
3	Power outage	4	$ 400
3	Lack of gas supply	3	$ 900
4	Lack of gas supply	3	$ 1,200
4	Broken machine A	1	$ 2,200
4	Power outage	4	$ 460
5	Lack of gas supply	3	$ 1,100
5	Power outage	4	$ 500
6	Loss of oil in machine B	2	$ 80
6	Broken machine A	1	$ 1,960
7	Lack of gas supply	3	$ 960
8	Lack of gas supply	3	$ 1,180
9	Broken machine A	1	$ 1,840
10	Broken machine A	1	$ 1,800
10	Lack of gas supply	3	$ 980

a) Distinguish between the qualitative and quantitative data in the table.

b) Perform a quantitative risk analysis.

Problem	Probability	Impact	Expected value

c) Prioritize the risks according to the qualitative analysis.

Problem	Probability	Impact	Priority

✋ Take 15 minutes to solve this exercise

Answer to exercise 11.2

a) *Qualitative data*: year, problem and code.

Year and code, regardless of being numbers, are not quantitative data. Quantitative data is that which can be added, subtracted, divided, multiplied, and a result with economic meaning is obtained.

The year could also be classified as a time series, which does not respond to a qualitative or quantitative category.

The code variable is indicating the type of problem. For example, 3 means "lack of gas supply".

Quantitative data: damage to the company

b) Quantitative risk analysis

Problem	Quantity	Probability	Impact	Expected Value
Broken machine A	5	50%	$1,960	$980
Loss of oil in machine B	2	20%	$90	$18
Lack of gas supply	7	70%	$1,046	$732
Power outage	3	30%	$453	$136

In this case, the expected monetary value means the average annual cost caused by each identified risk. For example, the power outage happens 3 out of every 10 years, every time this happens causes approximately $453 in damages. This negative event is generating an average cost of $136 per year. The higher the expected value, the higher priority we should assign to the identified risk.

☹ *Error 1*:

Problem	Probability
Broken machine A	5 / 17 =29.41%
Loss of oil in machine B	2 / 17 =11.76%
Lack of gas supply	7 / 17 = 41.18%
Power outage	3 / 17 = 17.65%
TOTAL	100%

Being independent events, the probability of each event does not have to add 100%. For example, if only two risky events existed in the factory, like fire and accidents, the sum of these probabilities could be 1.5% or any other number. There is no economic sense in adding up the probabilities of independent events.

To estimate the probability that the next year a risk event will occur, under the assumption that the future will be the same as the past, we could divide the number of times that the event occurred in the past by the 10 years of samples.

☹ _Error 2_:

Problem	Impact
Broken machine A	$9,800
Loss of oil in machine B	$180
Lack of gas supply	$7,320
Power outage	$1,360

When you add all the damages of one event, you would be overestimating the impact. For example, it would not be very probable to pay $9,800 if the next year machine A is broken. The most rational thing to do would be to estimate a simple average, under the assumption that damages are not increasing, nor decreasing throughout time.

> ☺ _Double Nelson: if you calculate wrong the probability and the impact._

c) Qualitative risk analysis

If we did not have historical information, it would be very costly and even inefficient, to perform quantitative analysis for all the problems. In this situation, we should first perform a qualitative risk analysis.

For example, through interviews, the risk analyst could ask experts what probability they estimate for each event (high, medium, low) and which would be the impact in case the risk occurs (high, medium, low). If the expert that responds is not lying, we could obtain a qualitative result similar to the one shown in the following table:

Problem	Probability	Impact	Priority
Broken machine A	H	H	High
Loss of oil in machine B	L	L	Low
Lack of gas supply	H	H	High
Power outage	M	M	Medium

As you can see, the priorities of these risks are similar to the results obtained with the quantitative analysis. It would be inefficient to dedicate resources to a quantitative analysis to low priority risks, while high priority risks should be detailed with a quantitative analysis.

> ✎ _A qualitative risk analysis should be performed first, and then continue with the quantitative risk analysis for medium and high priority risks._

What do I need to start the quantitative analysis?

- ⬇ Plans: schedule, budget, and risk plans.
- ⬇ Risk register

What tools can I use?

✂ **Interviews**: expert information is obtained to estimate the probability (%) and the impact ($) of each identified risk. For example, an interview with automation process experts can determine the probability of a broken machine and the monetary impact that the event will cause in the project costs.

✂ **Probability distributions:** there are various types of probability distribution that can be used in the risk analysis, such as: uniform, triangular, beta, normal, log normal, poison, hyper geometric, Chi-squared, etc.

It is not the intention of this book to provide a detailed statistical analysis; therefore, in this section we will only superficially analyze three types of probabilities: uniform, triangular, and normal.

- *Uniform probability distribution:* it is used in those cases where we only have information about two extremes future estimated values.

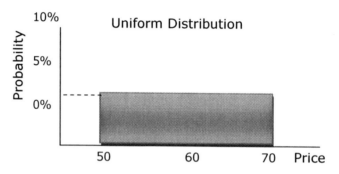

Based on the previous figure, you could say that the estimated price for a product could have a value between $50 and $70. Any price within this range has the same probability.

- *Triangular probability distribution:* it is used in those cases where we have information about three scenarios: pessimistic, more probable, and optimistic.

For example, if we are evaluating the impact that could be caused by a power outage in the costs of the project, the interviewed expert could respond in the following manner: $80 optimistic, $90 most probable, and $120 pessimistic.

If the risk analyst used the middle value, $90, to estimate the impact on the project, an error could be made in the estimation. It would also be incorrect to use the simple average between the 3 scenarios ($96.7) as the most probable value.

A triangular distribution could be use to estimate with more precision the impact of these scenarios on the project. In the figure you may observe an example measuring the impact (cost) in the x-axis and the probability in the y-axis.

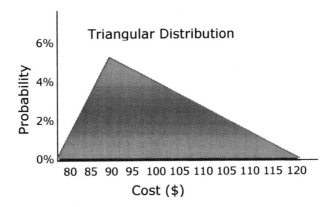

As we can see, in this particular case there is an inclination towards the pessimistic scenario given that the interval (90;120) has more probability of occurrence than the interval (80;90).

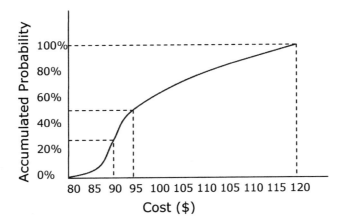

With this data we could evaluate what is the probability that the impact is less than $90. For this, we could graph the function of the accumulated probability, where there is a 27.5% probability that the impact is less than $90. This example demonstrates why it is not appropriate to use a value of $90 as the medium impact.

We could take as an example a $95 value to estimate the risk impact, given that there is a 50% probability that the impact is less than that value and a 50% that it is higher.

- **Standard normal distribution:** is based on the gathering of historical data. As a result of that sample, we get the median (or arithmetic average) and the standard deviation.

It is usually used in the evaluation of projects such as to estimate the age of a person, rain for a region, sales by hour, etc.

The form of the normal distribution is a symmetrical bell shape and it is also known as the Gauss bell.

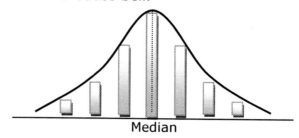

Median

Some of the characteristics of the normal standard distribution are:

- The highest point of the curve is at the median and it is the value with the highest probability.
- The normal distribution is symmetrical, with the shape of the curve identical to the left and to the right of the median.
- The ends of the curve extend to infinity in both directions and are asymptotic in the horizontal axis.
- The total area under the normal distribution is equal to one.
- The standard deviation is a measure of the spread of the data in respect to the median. It determines the width of the curve. The bigger the standard deviation, the wider the curve, which indicates a higher spread of the data.

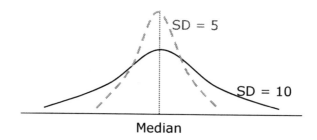

Median

- The probability that a variable be in the range of:

    Median +/- 1SD, is 68.26%

    Median +/- 2SD, is 95.44%

    Median +/- 3SD, is 99.72%

✂ **Expected monetary value:** is obtained by multiplying the probability by the impact. For example, a risk which probability is 30% and its impact is $50,000, has an estimated cost of $15,000.

Let us analyze an example for the construction of a factory where we do not know what will be the future demand and we need to make a decision on the size of the plant to build. The net benefits of this project depend on the level of demand that the company faces and on the size of the plant that was built.

In the following table are the net project benefits for different sizes of the plant and future demand.

Size	High Demand	Medium Demand	Low Demand
Small	$ 50	$ 30	$ 20
Medium	$ 70	$ 50	$ 10
Large	$ 100	$ 40	$ -20

Let us suppose we have estimated with an acceptable precision the probability of the demand at 30% (high), 50% (medium) and 20% (low). With this information the calculation of the expected monetary value for each construction alternative would be as follows:

Expected Value (small) = 0.3 x $50 + 0.5 x $30 + 0.2 x $20 = $34

Expected Value (medium) = 0.3 x $70 + 0.5 x $50 + 0.2 x $10 = $48

Expected Value (large) = 0.3 x $100 + 0.5 x $40 – 0.2 x $20 = $46

Using the expected monetary value approach, if only the maximization of earnings is under analysis, the recommended decision is to build a medium plant because it represents the maximum expected net benefit ($48).

📖 Exercise 11.3 – Expected monetary value

A company has to select between 4 agricultural projects which net income depending on weather conditions. Three future scenarios have been estimated: optimistic, normal, and pessimistic. Each one of these scenarios will influence the profitability of each project.

Based on the meteorological statistics we could estimate the probability of each scenario in the future. In the following table, the probability of each scenario and the net income of each project are summarized:

Scenario	Probability	P1	P2	P3	P4
Optimistic	35%	720	1,280	640	800
Normal	45%	440	240	400	240
Pessimistic	20%	0	-280	-40	-40

➤ *Calculate and interpret the expected monetary value of each alternative.*

🖐 Take 5 minutes to solve this exercise

Answer to Exercise 11.3

Scenario	Probability	P1	P2	P3	P4
Optimistic	35%	720	1,280	640	800
Normal	45%	440	240	400	240
Pessimistic	20%	0	-280	-40	-40
Expected value		**450**	**500**	**396**	**380**

The best project should be P2 because it has the highest expected monetary value: 35% x $1,280 + 45% x $240 – 20% x $280 = $500

A $500 expected monetary value means that an average earning of $500 per year is expected. It should be taken into account that some years a lot more will be earned ($1,280) and some years there will be losses ($ -280), but after various years of operation, the average will be $500 per year.

✂ **Decision tree:** diagram that describes the implications of selecting one alternative versus another, among all the possibilities. A problem can be divided in smaller segments, tree branches, with the intention of facilitating the decision-making.

This technique incorporates the probability and impact of each event's logical step and future decisions. The decision tree resolution indicates what other alternatives produce the best expected value for the decision maker when all implications, costs, and benefits are quantified.

By focusing on the expected value and the decision tree, the best decision strategy can be determined. Having all the probabilities and impacts assigned to each tree branch, it is possible to calculate the expected value of each alternative.

The possible impacts and probabilities are weighted for each decision alternative. Assuming that it is about a benefit maximization problem, the decision maker will select as the best alternative the tree branch that has the highest benefit expected value.

📖 Exercise 11.4 – Decision tree

In a construction project we have to decide the best project size. We face three size alternatives: small (S1), medium (S2) and large (S3). The main risks the project faces are that we do not know with precision what will be the project's demand and what will be the taxes applied by the government for this type of venture.

According to data from economists that performed the market study, it is estimated that the demand can be low (D1) with a 30% probability, or can be high (D2) with a probability of 70%. Also, the experts estimated that the taxes billed by the government will be low (T1) with an 80% probability, or can be high (T2) with a 20% probability.

The project economic results can be summarized in the following table.

	Demand		Taxes	
Probability	30%	70%	80%	20%
Size	D1 (low)	D2 (high)	T1 (low)	T2 (high)
Small (S1)	$ 10,000	$ 25,000	-$ 5,000	-$ 15,000
Medium (S2)	$ 5,000	$ 35,000	-$ 10,000	-$ 25,000
Large (S3)	$ 0	$ 50,000	-$ 15,000	-$ 30,000

For example, if a medium project is performed (S2) and in the future a high demand is faced (D2), the benefits will be $35.000. For that project size, if the government decides to charge a low tax (T1), we will have to pay $10,000. Therefore, on this scenario (S2, D2, T1) the net project result will be $25,000 ($35.000 - $10.000).

The analysis could be made to the rest of the 11 alternatives, after calculating the probability of each scenario and finally estimating the expected value of each alternative to select the best size.

➢ *Build a decision tree to select the best size.*

🖐 Take 5 minutes to pose the exercise. Do not dedicate time to its resolution, because something this complicated will not be presented in the exam.

Answer to Exercise 11.4

A tree like the one presented in the following page can be drawn. In this particular case the software "Precision Tree" of Palisade has been utilized.

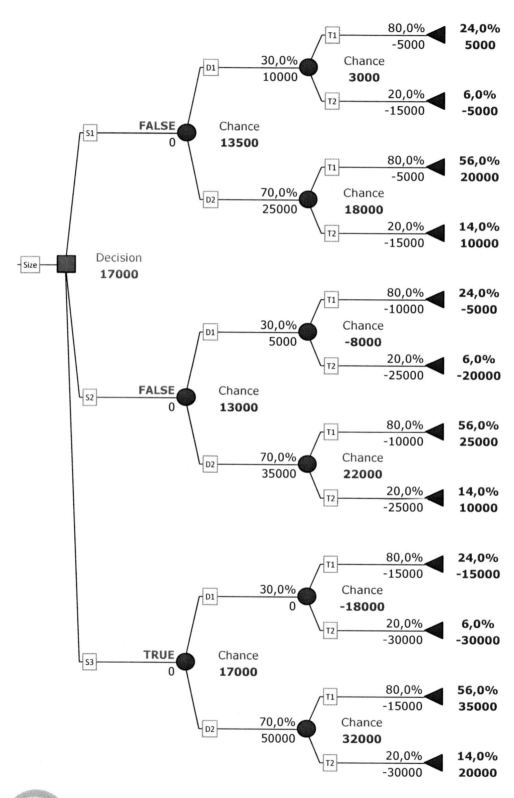

As we can see, there are 12 possible scenarios that combine size, demand and taxes.

The interpretation of the decision tree is, for example, the following:

- The probability of the alternative S3–D2–T1 is 56% (70% x 80%)
- The impact of the scenario S2–D1–T2 goes up to –$20,000 ($5,000–$25,000)
- The expected value of the scenario S1–D2–T2 is $1,400 (10,000 x 14%)

Each project size presents 4 scenarios (D1–T1; D1–T2; D2–T1; D2–T2). The sum of the probabilities of each scenario should be 100%

The sum of the expected values of each scenario of a size alternative indicates the expected value for that decision. For example, the expected value for a big size goes up to $17,000 (–$3,600 – $1,800 + $19,600 + $2,800). Being this value higher than the other alternatives (S1 = $13,500 and S2 = $13,000), the decision for best size based on the expected value would be to build a big project (S3).

📖 Exercise 11.5 – Decision tree II

? Based on the following figure, is it convenient to invest in a prevention tool to decrease the costs of non-conformance to quality?

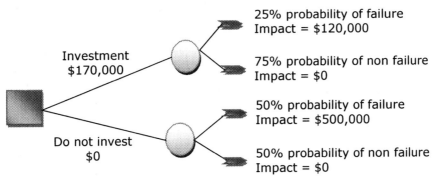

? Based on the following figure, which airline is more convenient?

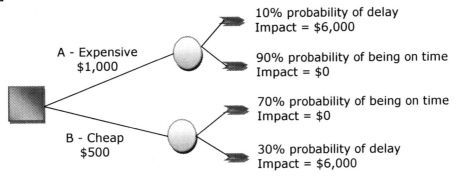

✋ Take 10 minutes to solve both questions

Answer to Exercise 11.5

Conformance Costs: make investment

Invest= $170,000 + 25% x $120,000 + 75% x $0 = $200,000

Do not invest = $0   + 50% x $500,000 + 50% x $0 = $250,000

Airlines: Select A

A = $1,000 + 90% x $0 + 10% x $6,000 = $1,600

B = $500 + 70% x $0 + 30% x $6,000 = $2,300

> ☺ You get what you pay for!

✂ **Sensitivity analysis:** consists of asking which would be the impact in the project objectives if a variable changes. A sensitivity for only one variable could be made (point of equilibrium) or for various variables simultaneously (scenarios analysis).

📖 Exercise 11.6 – Sensitivity analysis

A short-term project is being evaluated that consists of a $30,000 investment in the purchase of bananas to sell them in 3 months during the next season. With this investment you can buy the minimum purchase of 60,000 Kg. of bananas and you have the funds to make this investment.

The estimated average sale is 10,000 kilograms of bananas per month during the next three months. The bananas that are not sold at the end of the project must be discarded.

Based on historical data, it is observed that the price of bananas fluctuates through time.

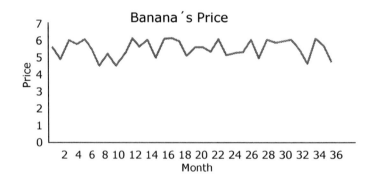

Based on historical information, the bananas´ price has a distribution similar to the standard normal which a median of $5.5 and a standard deviation of $0.5.

Price per kg.

Month / Year	1	2	3
Jan	5.59	6.04	5.28
Feb	4.88	4.94	5.99
Mar	5.91	6.03	4.92
Apr	5.80	6.07	5.96
May	6.00	5.97	5.88
Jun	5.46	5.12	5.92
Jul	4.52	5.53	6.02
Aug	5.23	5.56	5.49
Sep	4.51	5.33	4.60
Oct	5.10	6.05	6.03
Nov	6.09	5.11	5.62
Dec	5.56	5.23	4.69
Median	5.50		
Std. dev.	0.50		

The opportunity cost of the $30,000 to be invested is very low because the best alternative is to put the money in the bank at an insignificant interest rate, and the project duration is very short. On the other hand, on this informal economy, taxes are not paid.

The only thing that is known with certainty on this project is the investment because a contract has been made with the provider.

The exact value of the fixed costs is unknown. They are estimated to be between $19,000 and $21,000 monthly, once the project starts.

The sales (Kg.) and the variable costs can also vary once the project starts. Based on expert interviews, there are 3 possible scenarios (pessimistic, most probable, and optimistic). The estimated sales could be 9,000, 10,000, or 10,500 Kg. monthly and the variable costs 44%, 40%, or 38% of the total sales.

a) What will be the profitability in the most probable scenario? You may assume a discount rate equal to zero.

b) What will be the profitability in the pessimistic and the optimistic scenarios?

c) How could you calculate the risk level of losing money?

✋ Take 15 minutes to solve this exercise

Answer to exercise 11.6

a) Most probable scenario

	M0	M1	M2	M3	Total
Sales		10,000	10,000	10,000	
Price		5.5	5.5	5.5	
Income		55,000	55,000	55,000	165,000
Fixed Costs		-20,000	-20,000	-20,000	-60,000
Var. Costs		-22,000	-22,000	-22,000	-66,000
Investment	-30,000				-30,000
				Profitability	9,000

b) Scenarios

Assumption: we will work with a price range of +/- 2 standard deviations.

Pessimistic

	M0	M1	M2	M3	Total
Sales		9,000	9,000	9,000	
Price		4.5	4.5	4.5	
Income		40,500	40,500	40,500	121,500
Fixed Costs		-21,000	-21,000	-21,000	-63,000
Var. Costs		-17,820	-17,820	-17,820	-53,460
Investment	-30,000				-30,000
				Profitability	-24,960

Optimist

	M0	M1	M2	M3	Total
Sales		10,500	10,500	10,500	
Price		6.5	6.5	6.5	
Income		68,250	68,250	68,250	204,750
Fixed Costs		-19,000	-19,000	-19,000	-57,000
Var. Costs		-25,935	-25,935	-25,935	-77,805
Investment	-30,000				-30,000
				Profitability	39,945

c) To calculate the probability of losing money we could use the Monte Carlo simulation explained as follows.

× **Modeling and simulation**: simulates the expected value results of a project variable through the random assignment of a value to each critical variable that influences upon it.

For example, we will apply the **Monte Carlo simulation** to exercise 11.6. The profitability of this project will be measured by its net result. The variables that influence on the result are: investment, sales, price, fixed price and variable cost.

In first place we define the probability distribution of each variable as presented in the following table.

Variable	Probability distribution
Investment	Not applicable (known at $30,000)
Sales (kg.)	Triangular (9,000; 10,000; 10,500)
Price	Normal (median 5.5 and Standard Deviation 0.5)
Fixed price	Uniform (between 19,000 and 21,000)
Variable cost	Triangular (38%; 40%; 44%)

Once the variables that affect the project result, their interrelations and probability distributions have been defined, a random value is assigned to each variable.

This process of assigning random variables to each variable is performed with the help of some simulation software such as @Risk, Crystal Ball, Oracle Primavera, etc. The software will assign simultaneously random values to all variables that affect the result of the project. This way, thousands of scenarios can be run.

Once all scenarios are run you get, let's say, 10,000 project results. If these values are graphed, given the statistical law of large numbers, surely the distribution will be similar to a standard normal function.

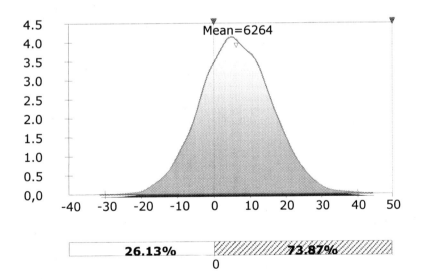

For example, when changing all the project variables simultaneously, a $6,264 median was obtained. The probability of having a positive result goes up to 74% and there is a 26% probability of losing money.

The conclusion of this analysis is that although on average the project is profitable, there is a 26% probability that it will not be, indicating the level of risk of the project.

The Monte Carlo Simulation provides much more complete information in regards to using only the average expected value.

☺ *Given the Monte Carlo simulation, each day there are more sighted people without work.*

📖 Exercise 11.7 –Monte Carlo Simulation

We are evaluating, the implied risk on the completion dates of a software development project that has 4 activities and two parallel paths as summarized in the following Gantt chart.

Id	Task	Jan Feb Mar Apr May Jun Jul Aug Sep Oct Nov Dec
1	Market research	
2	Software development	
3	Labor procurement	
4	Handbooks development	

The duration estimate for each activity has been done based on three possible scenarios.

Id	Task	Optimistic	Most probable	Pessimistic	PERT
1	Market research	20	30	60	33.33
2	Software development	50	60	150	73.33
3	Labor procurement	20	30	60	33.33
4	Handbooks development	50	60	150	73.33

a) What is the critical path for this project?

b) What is the estimated project duration?

c) What would be the estimated duration if only activities 2-3 are included?

d) Estimate project duration of the 4 activities using Monte Carlo

🖐 Take 5 minutes to solve this exercise. Do not solve part d.

Answer to exercise 11.7

a) There are two critical paths:
  ➢ Path 1 – 2
  ➢ Path 3 – 4

b) To estimate the project duration you have to add the durations of the activities in the critical path. The duration using PERT would be 106.66 days. If PERT was not used, the most probable duration would be 90 days, but this would not be a good schedule estimate.

c) If there were only two activities, the estimated duration would stay at 106.66 days.

Reflection: it is not rational to estimate the same duration for a project with 2 activities than for a project with 4 activities. Or is it? If the project had 20 critical paths and 40 activities, all with parallel paths, we would have also estimated 106.66 days duration. A schedule of 106.66 days in all these cases, does not consider the implied risk that an activity will go wrong. The higher the number of activities, the higher the project-estimated duration.

> ✎ *Estimating the project duration using PERT leads you to a good estimate when there is only one critical path and the almost critical paths have enough slack. However, Monte Carlo simulation should be used when there are parallel paths or the slack between almost critical paths is small.*

d) Monte Carlo Simulation

Variable	Probability distribution
1. Market study	Triangular (20; 30; 60)
2. Develop software	Triangular (50; 60; 150)
3. Contract technician	Triangular (20; 30; 60)
4. Develop manuals	Triangular (50; 60; 150)

The simulation results using the @Risk for Project software are the following:

- The most probable duration of the project goes up to 137 days (simple average of 10,000 simulations)
- The probability that the project takes 90 days (duration without PERT) or less is 0.25%.
- The probability that the project takes 106.66 days (PERT duration) or less is 7.8%.
- If we work with a 174 days schedule, the probability of being on schedule is 95%.

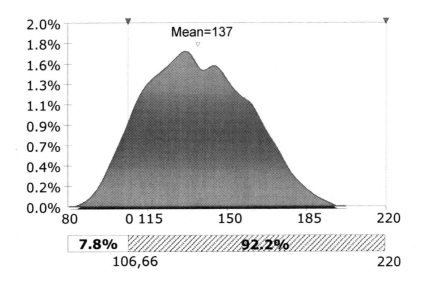

> *Criticality index: number of times that a project path was in the critical path during the Monte Carlo simulation.*

What do I get at the end of the process?

➚ **Updated risk register:** prioritization of quantified risks, probability of reach the schedule and costs objectives, and trend estimates.

Plan risk response

The risk response planning consists of developing procedures and techniques that allow improving the opportunities and decreasing the threats on the project objectives. This is usually the most important process in risk management since the decision to responds to each identified risk is made.

What do I need to start?

⬇ Risk register

⬇ Risk management plan

What tools can I use?

The following tools are usually used for the **negative risks**: avoid, transfer, mitigate, or accept.

✂ **Avoid:** change the original conditions of performing the project to eliminate the identified risk. For example, if bringing an imported technology will bring serious problems in the post-sale services, avoid would be to not contemplate the use of that technology and replace it for another one. This strategy many times implies cancelling the project.

✂ **Transfer:** move the risk's negative impact to a third party. For example, contract insurance or put a penalty in the provider's contract.

✂ **Mitigate:** decrease the probability and/or impact. For example, install an alarm system in case of fire.

✂ **Accept:** do not change the original plan. An active acceptance consists of establishing a policy of how to react in case the negative event occurs. For example, instructions on how to continue to bill in a manual way in case there is a power outage. While a passive acceptance consists of not doing absolutely anything with an identified risk.

Based on probability and impact of each identified risk, we could work on a risk response strategy matrix, as presented in the following table.

Risk response strategy matrix (example)

Impact / Probability	Very low 1	Low 2	Medium 3	High 5	Very high 10
Very low 1	Accept	Accept	Accept	Accept	Transfer or Mitigate
Low 2	Accept	Accept	Accept	Transfer or Mitigate	Avoid
Medium 3	Accept	Accept	Accept	Transfer or Mitigate	Avoid
High 4	Accept	Accept	Transfer or Mitigate	Avoid	Avoid
Very high 5	Accept	Transfer or Mitigate	Transfer or Mitigate	Avoid	Avoid

On the other hand, the following strategies or tools are usually used for the **positive risks**: exploit, share, improve, or accept.

  ✂ **Exploit:** perform actions to concrete the opportunity for the project´s benefits.

  ✂ **Share:** take advantage of the synergies of another person or organization with better abilities to capture the market opportunity. For example, a joint venture.

  ✂ **Improve:** perform actions to increase the probability and/or impact.

  ✂ **Accept:** do not change the original plan.

Lastly, strategies could be designed that will be used only in case of contingencies. For example, if the CPI is less than 0.7, perform a team meeting to analyze the root cause of the problem and evaluate the need for a scope change.

> ✍ *Always include a risk custodian or owner of each action that is decided to be implemented as a risk response.*

📖 Exercise 11.8 – Risk response strategies

Mark in the following table the risk response that was implemented for each case.

Description	Strategy
Eliminate a project work package	
Put a security alarm in the factory in case of burglary	
Assign a subject matter expert to the project to decrease duration	
Change the start date of the crop to take advantage of the elevated costs of pre-season	
Joint venture to leverage on synergies and specialization	
Put in writing how to react if a worker is absent	
Outsource a risk activity to another company	
Implement a quality policy to have all workers use a helmet	
Select a certified facilitator to increase the chance of passing the PMP® Exam	

🖐 Take 5 minutes to solve this exercise.

Answer to exercise 11.8

Eliminate a project work package	Avoid
Put a security alarm in the factory in case of burglary	Mitigate probability
Assign a subject matter expert to the project to decrease duration	Exploit
Change the start date of the crop to take advantage of the elevated costs of pre-season	Improve impact
Joint venture to leverage on synergies and specialization	Share
Put in writing how to react if a worker is absent	Active Acceptance
Outsource a risk activity to another company	Transfer
Implement a quality policy to have all workers use a helmet	Mitigate impact
Select a certified facilitator to increase the chance of passing the PMP® Exam	Improve probability

What do I get at the end of the process?

↗ **Updated risk register:** strategies and actions for each risk, risk custodians, symptoms, triggers, alarm signals, residual risks, secondary risks, and contingency reserves.

> ✎ *Symptoms: event that indicates some difficulty in the project. Example: delays.*

> ✎ *Triggers: when the variables overcome the acceptable level (threshold), risk response plans are implemented to alleviate the impact. For example, if the schedule performance index is less than .8 you decide to fast tracking.*

> ✎ *Residual risk: stays after having implemented the risk response. It should be accepted and managed to verify that it stays within the project acceptable limits.*

> ✎ *Secondary risk: is the one that originates as a direct consequence of the implementation of risk responses.*

↗ **Contract agreements** related to the risks. Example, guarantee insurance.

↗ **Updates**

📖 Exercise 11.9 – Risk response plan

Our team is currently working in a housing construction and sale project. The project estimated cost is $20 millions. This project involves important risks given that it is necessary to coordinate a great number of individuals and material resources. We have identified 9 risks to which we need to provide the most appropriate answer. The risk scoring criteria for the probability and impact are the following: Very low (1), Low (2), Medium (3), High (4), Very high (5).

Identified risks	Probability	....	Impact	....	Score
Insufficient time for the work	Low		Medium		
Work accident	Medium		Very high		
Storms	Low		Very high		
Insufficient sales	Medium		Medium		
Materials not delivered on time	High		Medium		
Lack of design consensus	High		Low		
Construction failures	Very low		High		
Lack of financing	High		Very high		

The company has defined the following policy to select strategies:

Score	Strategy
16-25	Avoid
11-15	Transfer (if possible)
6-10	Mitigate
3-5	Actively accept
1-2	Passively accept

a) Prioritize risks according to their probability and impact.

b) Complete the following table to develop a risk response plan:

Risk	Strategy	Required Action	Responsible
Construction failures			
Insufficient time for the work			
Lack of design consensus			
Insufficient sales			
Barrages			
Materials not delivered on time			
Work accident			
Lack of financing			

c) The time comes to create a risk response plan for residual risk. What activities would you plan to prevent the delayed delivery of materials?

d) If even with this prevention plan there are delays with the delivery of materials, it will be necessary to put in place a response plan to mitigate the risk. What actions could you take to implement the risk response plan?

🖐 Take 20 minutes to solve the exercise.

Answer to exercise 11.9

a) Prioritization of risks

Identified risk	Probability	....	Impact	....	Score
Lack of financing	High	4	Very high	5	20
Work accident	Medium	3	Very high	5	15
Materials not delivered on time	High	4	Medium	3	12
Storms	Low	2	Very high	5	10
Insufficient sales	Medium	3	Medium	3	9
Lack of design consensus	High	4	Low	2	8
Insufficient time for the work	Low	2	Medium	3	6
Construction failures	Very low	1	High	4	4

b) Risk response plan

Risk	Strategy	Required action	Responsible
Construction failures	Accept		
Insufficient time for the work	Mitigate		
Lack of design consensus	Mitigate		
Insufficient sales	Mitigate	Modify commercial strategy	Sales manager
Storms	Mitigate	Construct defenses	Project manager
Materials not delivered on time	Transfer	Contract with fines to vendor	Procurements manager
Work accident	Transfer	Purchase insurance	Procurements manager
Lack of financing	Avoid	Look for other sources / change scope	Project manager

> ☞ First you should complete the actions for the priority risks. On this table we should start with lack of financing, then work accidents, and so forth. I did not have time to complete the three less important risks, that's why they are left blank.

c) Additional prevention actions
   1. Select two or more supplier per item.
   2. Fluent communications with providers and periodic follow up.
   3. Supplier contracts with on-compliance fines.
   4. Create a contingency reserve for costs (additional stock).

d) Response plan execution
   1. Request to another supplier from the preferred list of vendors
   2. Temporary resignation of tasks to non-compliant vendors
   3. Use the reserved deposits stocks for contingencies

Monitor and control risks

During the risks **monitoring** phase information is gathered and progress and evolution through time is documented. This monitoring brings updated information about the state of each identified risk and allows indentifying new risks, watch the residual and secondary risks, and monitor the changes in the risk profile due to internal and external factors. We should start following up on priority risks. For example, monitor periodically the schedule delays and watch that the costs stay within acceptable limits.

On the other hand, risk **control** requires implementing the response plans, perform corrective actions, redefine response plans, or modify the project objectives. The risks control is an activity that goes beyond monitoring, it means making decisions in regards to it. For example, if during the risks monitoring we observe that there is a delay outside of the acceptable limits, during control we should implement a response plan and corrective actions.

What do I need to start?

↗ Plan and Risk register

↗ Performance reports

What tools can I use?

✂ **Reevaluation:** identify new risks and perform again a qualitative and quantitative analysis of the ones that were identified.

✂ **Audits:** document the effectiveness of the implemented response for each risk.

✂ **Variation and trend analysis:** compare the project results with the baseline. For example, risks of delay and cost excess can be evaluated with earned value management.

✂ **Technical performance measurements:** compare the project deliverables with the pre-established quality metrics. For example, each door's height.

✂ **Reserve analysis:** to compare the reserve that is left for the outstanding risks. Is the pending reserve enough?

✂ **Status meetings:** include risk management items in the project's status meetings' agenda.

What do I get at the end of the process?

↗ Updates

↗ Change requests

? What needs to get done with non-priority or non-critical risks?

Non-priority risks need to be included in a watch list and reviewed in a periodic basis.

? *What is the most important thing in a project meeting?*

The most important thing is to identify and analyze risks.

Summarizing risk management

On the following figure the main inputs, outputs, and dependencies between processes are summarized.

Integrating risk management

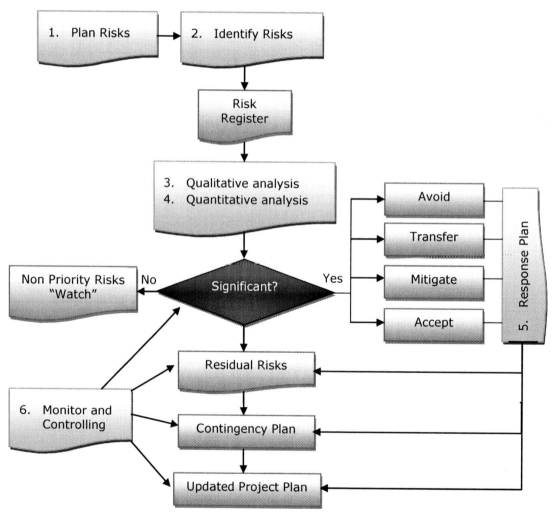

Exam 11 – Risks

> **Number of questions**: 15
> **Time to respond**: 18 minutes
> **Pass score**: 80% (12 correct answers)

1. In a housing construction project, Monte Carlo simulation is applied to estimate the most probable project duration. After performing 1,000 iterations, the criticality index is calculated. What information does the criticality index adds to the project?
   A. The most probable project duration in a range of two standard deviations
   B. The percentage of times that a path is over the critical path
   C. The percentage of times an activity is delayed
   D. The expected project value

2. In the planning processes group, you and your project team are finishing the risk response planning. This process' output would be:
   A. Secondary risks
   B. Identified risks
   C. Prioritized list of risks
   D. Reserve analysis

3. Your company is evaluating three mutually exclusive investment projects. Project A has a 50% probability of earning $50,000 and 50% probability of losing $10,000. Project B has a 30% probability of earning $40,000 and a 70% probability of earning $10,000. Project C has a 60% probability of earning $50,000 and a 40% probability of losing $15,000. Based on the expected monetary value, what project should be selected?
   A. Project A
   B. Project B
   C. Project C
   D. None

4. The project management team is planning the risk response plans. The following different strategies could be implemented according to the particularity of each risk. The following items are risk response strategies, EXCEPT:
   A. Contingency reserves
   B. Exploit
   C. Share
   D. Accept

5. You are tossing a dice with numbers 1 to 6. If you toss the dice twice, what probability exists for obtaining number 3?
   A. 1/6
   B. 2/6
   C. 11/36
   D. 1/36

6. You are working as the project manager for the construction of a diamond mine of magnitude never seen before. The estimated project cost is $2,300 million and you will use 5 contractors. The internal annual rate of return is 45% with a payback period of 6 years. Once the project starts, it cannot be cancelled because the sunk costs represent 85% of the initial investment. What should you do first in this project?
   A. Carefully analyze all of the contractor proposals
   B. Identify all risks
   C. Calculate the net present value in terms of feasibility
   D. Establish a risk response plan

7. The system that generates credit cards for a financial company generates 500 plastics per days. Today the system failed and the cards requested by clients could not be generated as usual. The alarm signal was detected and the inconvenience exceeded the level of critical action. The risk response plan was executed, but the implemented solution did not solve the problem. What is the first thing you should do in this situation?
   A. Fix the alarm signal to report sooner
   B. Determine why the problem occurred
   C. Fix the problem
   D. Adjust the risk response plan

8. During the quantitative risk analysis for a project to open a greenhouse for flowers, the following tools are being used, EXCEPT:
   A. Interviews
   B. Decision trees
   C. Data quality evaluation
   D. Expected monetary value

9. In the risk identification process for a project that builds chips for digital television, the project team has determined that there are risks that will probably occur and have not been identified. However, based on lessons learned of similar projects performed by the company in the past, history says that there are always unforeseen risks. Therefore, the project manager decided to add a _____ on the project baseline to determine the final budget.
   A. Control account
   B. Activity
   C. Alert signal for the cost excess
   D. Management reserve

10. The project manager and his team just finished the risk response plan for a $120 million telecommunications project. What is the next thing that will most probably occur for this project?
   A. Determine the risks that require urgent attention
   B. Modify the work packages in the work breakdown structure
   C. Estimate the probability of the project meeting schedule on time
   D. Analyze the control list

11. The construction project for the river contention dam is scheduled to be completed in 5 months. The subcontracted company reports that they will most probably stop some of the efforts during the next months to give their workers a rest. In case this occurs, the sponsor will contract another company to work during that month in some secondary tasks to minimize the project delay. These secondary tasks were planned for the last month, but could be performed at any time starting now. On the other hand, the buyer does not have control over the subcontracted company that pretends to stop the work. What risk response has the Sponsor planned?
    A. Mitigate the probability
    B. Transfer the risk to a new company
    C. Actively accept the risk
    D. Mitigate the impact

12. The project manager is using a decision tree to determine the best tractor to buy for an agriculture project. Tractor A costs $10,000 and has a 30% probability of failure. In case of failure the repair for Tractor A costs $4,000. On the other hand, Tractor B has a value of $12,000 and a 5% probability of failure. In case Tractor B breaks, its repair cost is $1,000. What tractor is more convenient purchase?
    A. Tractor A
    B. Tractor B
    C. Is the same to buy A or B
    D. There is not enough information to complete the decision tree

13. In a project to design a sports car, the project team identified a risk in relation to the airbag. It is estimated that the place where they want to install the airbag is not appropriate because when the airbag goes off in an accident the bag pressure could hurts the driver. Therefore, the project team decides to modify the automobile design to put the airbag in a more secure place that will not hurt the driver. This change implies various additional costs to the project that cannot be added to the to the product's retail price. The technique used to manage some of this project risk is called:
    A. Avoid
    B. Active acceptance
    C. Mitigate
    D. Transfer

14. In a gas station that sells bio-fuel, the list of risks is obtained principally during the following risk management processes:
    A. Quantitative analysis and identification
    B. Identification, qualitative analysis and quantitative analysis
    C. Qualitative analysis and control
    D. Identification, monitor and control

15. You are the project manager for the manufacturing of a pistons pump custom made for the client. Along with the project team, you have determined what will be done when uncertain events occur and who will be the person responsible for monitoring and controlling the risks? What has just been completed for this project?
   A. Quantitative risk analysis
   B. Risk responses planning
   C. Risk identification
   D. Qualitative risk analysis

Lessons Learned

- ✓ Accept
- ✓ Avoid
- ✓ Contingency reserves
- ✓ Decision tree
- ✓ Expected monetary value
- ✓ Exploit
- ✓ Impact probability matrix
- ✓ Improve
- ✓ Mitigate
- ✓ Monte Carlo
- ✓ Non-priority risks
- ✓ Probability and impact
- ✓ Reserve analysis
- ✓ Residual risk
- ✓ Response strategies
- ✓ Risk categories
- ✓ Risk owner
- ✓ Risk register
- ✓ Secondary risks
- ✓ Share
- ✓ Tolerance
- ✓ Transfer
- ✓ Triggers
- ✓ Uncertainty

PROCUREMENT

Chapter 12 - PROCUREMENT

> *Sometimes, it costs more to eliminate one defect than to purchase one hundred virtues.*
> Jean de la Bruyere (1645-1696); French writer.

The PM should not be an expert in contracting and procurement, but if it does not manage the basic concepts in this field, it will jeopardize the project's success. Signing a good contract with the vendors is an excellent proactive action in order to reduce risks, before starting the project's execution.

When you finish this chapter, you will have learned the following concepts:
- ✓ PM's role in procurement
- ✓ Procurement processes
- ✓ Plan procurements
- ✓ Make or buy analysis
- ✓ Types of contracts
- ✓ Administer procurements
- ✓ Close procurements

*Procurements management processes ***

Before moving on with the processes, let us look at some generalizations relating to procurement management:
- ✓ Project = buyer (client, customer, requester, purchaser, etc.)
- ✓ Provider = seller (contractor, sub-contractor, vendor, supplier, etc.)
- ✓ <u>All</u> project requirements must be in the contract
- ✓ What is not in the contract, can only be changed through the integrated change control
- ✓ Any change must be in writing and must be signed by both parties

> ☝ *Sellers are the ones who sell inputs to the project, in other words providers or contractors. Do not confuse with people who sell products to the company.*

* Project Management Institute, Ibidem.

The PM's main roles in procurement management are the following:

- ✓ Collaborate in reviewing how adequate is the fulfillment of the project's needs by the contract
- ✓ Ensure that the contract includes all project requirements
- ✓ Include in the project schedule time for contracting
- ✓ Incorporate risk mitigation actions in the contract
- ✓ Understand all contract terms
- ✓ Participate in the contract negotiation to take care of the relation with the seller
- ✓ Administer the contract and its changes

> ✎ *The PM should be assigned before the contract is signed in order to reduce the risks.*

In the following sections we will develop the procurement management processes, which are distributed among the "Planning", "Executing", "Monitoring and Controlling", and "Closing" process groups, as presented in the following table.

Procurement management processes

	Initiating	Planning	Executing	Controlling	Closing
Integration	1	1	1	2	1
Scope		3		2	
Time		5		1	
Cost		2		1	
Quality		1	1	1	
Human Resources		1	3		
Communications	1	1	2	1	
Risks		5		1	
Procurement		Plan procurements	Conduct procurements	Administer procurements	Close procurements
TOTAL	2	20	8	10	2

The four procurement management processes are:

1. **Plan procurements**: What to buy? When? How? Document the product requirements and identify the sellers.

2. **Conduct procurements**: contact sellers to obtain proposals and budgets, review proposals, select sellers, negotiate and award contracts.

3. **Administer procurements**: evaluate seller performance, monitor and manage changes to the contract.

4. **Close procurements**: approve and close each contract when finalizing the project or a phase.

Plan procurements

During plan procurements, you determine which goods and services must be acquired outside of the organization, and which could be provisioned internally by the project team. Moreover, you should analyze which type of contract is more convenient for each case; prepare all the documentation necessary to conduct requests for proposals and budgets; and establish the criteria that will be used to select vendors.

What do I need to start?

➚ Requirements documentation

➚ Activity resource requirements

➚ Plans: scope, schedule, budget

➚ Risk register and risk-related contract decisions

➚ Teaming agreements (if applies): contracts between buyer and seller to jointly manage the project. For example, corporate joint ventures, partnerships, etc.

What tools can I use?

✂ **Make or buy analysis**: determine if it is convenient whether to produce a project input within the organization or to buy it outside of the project.

Influencing factors to:	
Make	Buy
• Lack of quality or trust in providers • Know-how or experience to produce the input • Maintain the plant's minimum utilization level • Maintain control over the production process • Take care of confidentiality topics	• Specialization • Economies of scale • The vendor is the license owner

? A computer's leasing is $240 per month, including maintenance. A new computer costs $2,000 and requires monthly maintenance for $40. How many months do you need in order to be indifferent to buy, instead of leasing?

    A. 5
    B. 10
    C. 15
    D. 20

> <u>Answer</u>: B
> ($2,000 / **?**) + $40 per month = $240 per month
> **?** = 10 months

✂ **Types of contracts**: the three most used contracts are:

- **Fixed-price or lump-sum**
  Fixed-price (FP)
  Fixed-price-incentive-fee (FPIF)
  Fixed-price economic price adjustment (FP-EPA)

- **Cost-reimbursement** (CR)
  Cost-plus-fixed-fee (CPFF)
  Cost-plus-incentive-fee (CPIF)
  Cost-plus-award-fee (CPAF)
  Cost-plus-percentage of cost (CPPC)

- **Time and materials** (T&M)
  They have a variable component (e.g.: amount of hours), plus a fixed component (e.g.: hourly rate)

> ✎ *The contract type that is selected will determine the risks for both the buyer and the seller.*

In the following table, we present advantages (+) and disadvantages (-) of different items to consider in contracts.

Turnkey	Material's administration
+ Few contracts	- Many contracts
+ Less administrative load	- More administrative load
+ Responsibility over one contractor	- Responsibility shared over various
- Greater cost	contractors
- Less control	+ Lower cost
	+ Greater control
Fixed-price	**Cost-reimbursement**
+ Less risk for the buyer	- More risk for the buyer
- Needs complete project	+ It can be contracted with
information	incomplete project information
Final payment over deliverable	**Payment with advances**
+ Greater vendor commitment	- Less vendor commitment
+ Less risk for the buyer	- More risk for the buyer

? What is the riskier contract?

- A. Cost-plus-percentage of cost
- B. Cost-plus-fixed-fee
- C. Time and materials
- D. Fixed-price

Answer: A
From the buyer's point of view, the contract with the greatest financial risk is the cost-plus-percentage of cost. This type of contract is not recommended because it neglects the buyer's interests.

Buyer's financial risk

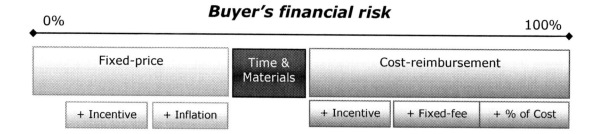

✍ If the buyer has a lower risk because of a contract type, that risk is passed to the seller and it could be detrimental to the project. For example, in a negative event, the seller could not fulfill the contract and be forced to make adjustments in the scope, delivery dates, add costs, etc.

✍ In order for a contract to be legally valid, it must have: object, offer, and the parties' agreement.

📖 Exercise 12.1 – Type of contracts

In the following table, select the most convenient type of contract.

Options: Fixed-price, Cost-reimbursement, Time and materials

Situation	Contract
Work should start as soon as possible and the definite project scope is not finished	
Buying 10,000 kilograms of soy	
Contract the services of a consultant to reduce project risks	
In a project, there are changes in the scope and market prices are transparent and easily accessed	
The scope is defined and you do not have time to control vendor's expenses	

✋ Take 2 minutes to solve the exercise.

Answers to Exercise 12.1

Situation	Contract
Work should start as soon as possible and the definite project scope is not finished	Time and materials
Buying 10,000 lbs of soy	Fixed-price
Contract the services of a consultant to reduce project risks	Time and materials
In a project, there are changes in the scope and market prices are transparent and easily accessed	Cost-reimbursement
The scope is defined and you do not have time to control vendor's expenses	Fixed-price

? In a cost-reimbursement contract, you estimate a cost of $200,000 and a fee of $30,000. If the vendor spends less, the savings will be split in 50% for each one. If the final cost is $160,000, how much will the buyer end up paying?

A. $160,000
B. $190,000
C. $200.000
D. $210.000

Answer: D
$160,000 + $30,000 + 50% x $40,000 = $210,000
This would be an example of cost-reimbursement plus an incentive contract.

? What type of contract (Fixed-price, Cost-reimbursement, time and materials) is better for the following types of documentation?

A. Invitation for bid (IFB)
B. Request for quotation (RFQ)
C. Request for proposal (RFP)

Answer
IFB = Fixed-price
RFQ = Time and materials
RFP = Cost-reimbursement

> ✎ Letter of intent: *It is not a contract. It indicates the buyer's intention of acquiring a good or service from a seller.*

What do I get at the end of the process?

↗ **Procurement management plan**: it defines how the next three procurement processes will be managed. In this plan, you should be able to respond the following questions:

- What is produced inside the project and what will be bought?
- What contract type is the most appropriate?
- Who will develop the seller evaluation criteria?
- How will we do vendor management and tracking?
- What constraints and assumptions will affect procurements?
- What is the schedule for each contract deliverable?
- What warranties exist if the contract is not fulfilled?
- Which are the pre-qualified sellers?
- What are the metrics to evaluate sellers?

↗ **Procurement statements of work (SOW)**: it includes the detailed scope of the products that will be acquired with the contract. The objective for the seller is to evaluate if it will be able to do the provisioning.

↗ **Make-or-buy decision**: documentation that defines which project inputs will be produced internally and which will be acquired through third parties.

↗ **Procurement documents**

- Request for **information** (RFI): request for information about the sellers and the products they offer.

- Invitation for **bid** (IFB): a general price for the whole proposal is presented.

- Request for **proposal** (RFP): not only the price is analyzed, but the technical proposal and the abilities of the sellers are usually more important.

- Request for **quotation** (RFQ): itemized prices for the project are presented.

> ✎ *A preliminary contract model is usually included in the procurement documents.*

↗ **Source selection criteria**: price, operational and maintenance costs, technical capability, management capability, financial background, similar project references, etc.

↗ **Change requests**

Conduct procurements

Once the project enters its execution phase, it is necessary to contact the sellers of complementary goods and services for the project and apply the evaluation criteria in order to choose who will be the project's sellers.

The evaluation criteria will depend on each particular project, and could include items such as: price, post-sale services, delivery time, technical proposal, financial background, etc.

> *Selecting a single seller could be good to take advantage of economies of scale and lower costs. However, in the case that the seller backs out, the risk to the project to have just one seller could be high.*
>
> *Working with multiple sellers for the same task has the effect of diversifying the risks. If one seller backs out, it can be replaced with the other that is complying.*

What do I need to start?

- ⤢ Procurement management plan
- ⤢ Risk register and related contracts
- ⤢ Procurement documents
- ⤢ Source selection criteria
- ⤢ Qualified seller list (pre-selected providers)
- ⤢ Seller proposals
- ⤢ Make-or-buy decisions
- ⤢ Teaming agreements

What tools can I use?

✂ **Bidder conferences**: make the documentation available to all the sellers and answer any questions that may arise.

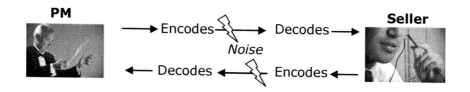

> ✎ *During the bidder conferences, questions and answers should be made public to the rest of the sellers, so everyone has the same project information.*

✂ **Proposal evaluation techniques**: follow a formal process for seller selection.

For example, with a weighted system, qualitative information is used for the selection between providers. Each evaluation criteria can have a different relative weight. An example to select between two sellers is given below.

Criteria	Weight	Seller 1		Seller 2	
		Rating	Score	Rating	Score
Warranties	50%	7	3.5	9	4.5
Post-sale	30%	7	2.1	6	1.8
Price	20%	7	1.4	5	1
TOTAL	**100%**	21	**7**	20	**7.3**

In this example, you should select Seller 2 because it has the greater weighted score.

> ✎ *Technical proposals tend to be evaluated separately from economic proposals (price).*

📖 Exercise 12.2 – Weighted system

A company has to select the furniture between 3 different providers for one of its new offices.

For the selection of the provider they are evaluating different characteristics of the furnishing: cost, delivery, functionality, maintenance, compatibility, and warranty.

Not all of these criteria have the same importance for the company.

The proposals delivered by each provider were reviewed by three company officials with the know-how to decide over office furnishing. These people qualified each one of the characteristics of the materials with a scale of 1 (bad) to 10 (excellent).

Based on the responses from each official, a simple average of the scores was calculated in order to assign a unique value to each criterion.

Complete the proposal selection matrix presented below in order to decide who the most convenient provider is.

CRITERIA	Weight	Provider 1		Provider 2		Provider 3	
		Rating	Score	Rating	Score	Rating	Score
1. Cost	20%	4		5		7	
2. Delivery time	15%	8		7		4	
3. Functionality	25%	4		5		9	
4. Maintenance	10%	6		6		4	
5. Compatibility	10%	8		6		4	
6. Warranty	20%	6		6		6	
TOTAL	100%						

✋ Take 5 minutes to solve this exercise

Answer to Exercise 12.2

CRITERIA	Weight	Provider 1		Provider 2		Provider 3	
		Rating	Score	Rating	Score	Rating	Score
1. Cost	20%	4	0.8	5	1	7	1.4
2. Delivery time	15%	8	1.2	7	1.05	4	0.6
3. Functionality	25%	4	1	5	1.25	9	2.25
4. Maintenance	10%	6	0.6	6	0.6	4	0.4
5. Compatibility	10%	8	0.8	6	0.6	4	0.4
6. Warranty	20%	6	1.2	6	1.2	6	1.2
TOTAL	100%		5.6		5.7		**6.25**

You should select Provider 3 because it has the greatest weighted score.

✂ **Independent estimates**: the buyer prepares his own cost estimates to compare against the proposals sent by the sellers. It obtains approximate values to what the good or service should cost. This is very useful to validate if prices are commensurate to the requested scope.

> ✎ *If your own estimates are far superior to the ones sent by a seller, you should suspect that you are buying risk for a possible breach of scope, quality, deadlines, or costs.*

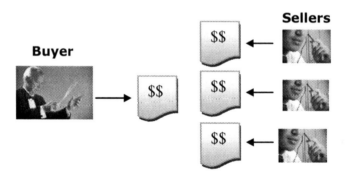

✂ **Advertising**: communicate bids in newspapers, magazines, government official bulletins, etc.

✂ **Internet search**: investigate about the providers, and the needed goods and services through the Internet.

✂ **Procurement negotiation**: it should pursue the objective of getting a reasonable price to develop good relations with the seller. Negotiations should end up with a win-win contract. If a win-lose contract is signed, the seller will be more worried with recuperating what has been lost, than finishing the job. In turn, the buyer must check for risks of extra costs, quality, and time.

What do I get at the end of the process?

↗ **Selected sellers**

↗ Procurement **contract** award: it is a legal agreement between buyer and seller. Some of the contract's components usually are:

- Work statement and deliverables
- Schedule
- Performance reports
- Roles and responsibilities for each party
- Price and payment method
- Acceptance criteria and quality metrics
- Warranties
- Post-sale support
- Rewards and penalties
- Change requests management
- Etc.

> ✑ *Contract breach: when a contract obligation is not met.*

↗ **Resource calendars**: dates are documented with the availability of each contracted resource.

↗ **Change requests**

↗ **Updates**

Administer procurements

While the project is in execution, it is necessary to monitor and control the different contracts. You must evaluate if the deliverables are in accordance with the contract terms and make the corresponding payments. In addition, you evaluate the seller's performance to analyze if it has enough competencies to continue being a provider of goods and services for the project.

? *Company A gets in a contract with Company B for a tunnel construction. Afterwards, Company B sub-contracts Company C to perform the tasks. If Company A requests Company C that they stop the tunnel's progress, what should Company C do?*

    A. Stop all progress activities, as requested by A
    B. Continue with the activities until B informs them otherwise
    C. Request A that they put the request in writing
    D. Change their contractual relation with B

Answer: B.
Generally, there is no contractual relation between A and C. A should inform B and then could inform C.

What do I need to start?

    ↗ Procurement plan and procurement documents

    ↗ Contracts

    ↗ Performance reports

    ↗ Approved change requests

What tools can I use?

    ✂ **Contract change control system**: document including in which cases, how, when, and who can modify the contract.

> ✍ *If it is not clarified in any other way, the contract administrator is the only one who can make changes to it.*

    ✂ **Procurement performance reviews**: evaluate if the seller complied with the scope, quality, costs, and the schedule of the contract. This can be done through **inspections and audits**, provided it is allowed in the contract. Moreover, **seller performance reports** should be produced.

✂ **Payment systems**: revisions and approvals of payments to providers.

✂ **Claims administration**: manage incidents, claims, disputes, and appeals when both parties do not agree with a contractual item and its respective payment. All these claims are documented, and if there is no agreement between the parties, an arbitrator should look for a conflict resolution.

✂ **Records management system**: keep an index of all the documentation related to the contract to archive and retrieve all the documents in an efficient manner. This system is part of the project management system and tends to use the support of information technologies.

What do I get at the end of the process?

↗ **Procurement documentation**: contracts, schedule of deliverables, changes, technical documents, work and seller's performance, warranties, payments, inspection logs, etc.

↗ **Change requests**

↗ **Updates**

Close Procurements

During the Close Procurements process, you verify that the goods and services delivered by the sellers comply with the contract terms. This process complements the project closing (Integration) and tends to include some administrative closing activities, such as records archive. In the following table, we present a comparison between Close Procurements and Close Project or Phase.

	Close Procurements	Close Project or Phase
When it occurs	At the end of the contract	At the end of each phase
How to document improvements	Contract audits	Lessons learned
Formality	High	Medium
Main beneficiary	Buyer and seller	Project (Buyer)

During Close Procurements (or external closure), the following is done:
- ✓ Verify deliverables with the client
- ✓ Closing of signed legal agreements
- ✓ Closing of individual contracts
- ✓ Letter of contract termination (debt free)
- ✓ Formal acceptance or certificate of receipt of goods
- ✓ Cancellation of warranties
- ✓ Client satisfaction evaluations

What do I need to start?

↗ **Procurement documentation**

What tools can I use?

✂ **Procurement audits**: formal and systematic revision of all procurement processes, where improvements and lessons learned are identified for future contract processes.

✂ **Negotiated settlements**: negotiation tends to be used for the definite contract closure and incident resolution.

✂ **Records management system**: archive in an indexed and ordered manner all the contractual documentation to facilitate its retrieval in the future.

What do I get at the end of the process?

↗ **Closed procurements**

↗ **Updates**

> ✎ *You could find approximately 5 questions in the exam relating to the contract closure.*

External closure survey

Client: Eli Corp. Project Manager: Paul Leido		Start date: 06-15-13 End date: 12-20-13			
Project	Bad	Poor	Good	Very Good	Excellent
Objectives					
Dead-lines					
Report					
Presentation					
Usefulness					
Team	Bad	Poor	Good	Very Good	Excellent
Marcel Pim					
Jerry Guire					
General Opinion Positive: Negative:					

Close procurements also includes activities from the administrative closure such as: final report on scope, costs, and time; contract records updates, etc.

Summarizing procurements management

In the following figure, we summarize the main inputs, outputs, and interrelations of the procurements management processes.

Integrating procurements management

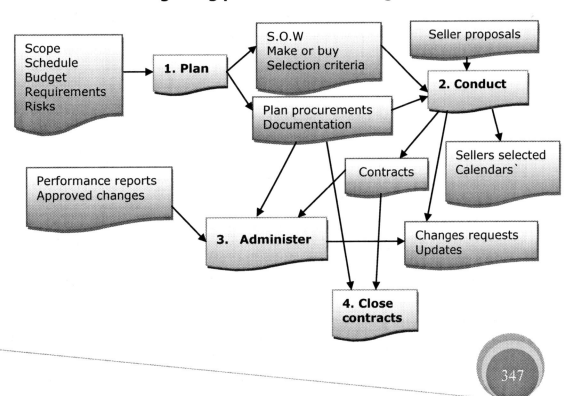

Exam 12 – Procurements

Number of questions: 15
Time to respond: 18 minutes
Pass score: 80% (12 correct answers)

1. A government department sends a formal invitation to sellers. In the bid terms it is clarified that the seller must include, in a detailed manner, the activities to perform, the work methodology, and the deliverables. This is called:
   A. Invitation for Bid
   B. Notice of Offer
   C. Request for Budget
   D. Request for Proposal

2. The following statements are part of the project manager's role in the procurements management process, EXCEPT for:
   A. Ensure that the contract includes all of the project's requirements
   B. Write the contract, in conjunction with the contract administrator
   C. Give support for the incorporation of risk mitigation actions to the contract
   D. Administer the contract and its changes

3. You are the owner of a cabin, rented to tourists in a temporary manner. The floor polisher is broken and it needs to be replaced immediately. You are evaluating the option of buying a new polisher or lease it. A new polisher costs $1,200, with maintenance of $20 per day. In turn, you could lease one for $80 per day, with maintenance included. How many days would you need to use the polisher to be reasonable buying it, instead of leasing it?
   A. 12
   B. 20
   C. 60
   D. There is not enough information to answer

4. In a cost-plus-incentive-fee contract, you estimate a cost of work of $100,000 and a fixed-fee of $20,000. The incentive is a variable amount that consists of granting 20% of the cost savings to the seller. In addition, in the event of the final cost exceeding $100,000, the fixed-fee will be reduced in the same amount as the excess. If the final cost is 20% less than the estimate; what amount will the seller get?
   A. 104,000
   B. 80,000
   C. 120,000
   D. 24,000

5. A project is reaching its closure and the project manager is making a list of the activities that he should perform to definitely close the project. The following actions are part of the contract closure, with the EXCEPTION of _____, which is part of the administrative closure.
   A. Structured revision of the procurement process with audits
   B. Send a formal written note to the seller notifying of the end of the project
   C. Update records and archive the information
   D. Gather lessons learned at the end of a project phase

6. During the procurements management process for an international program, a bidder conference is conducted. This is part of the process of:
   A. Plan procurements
   B. Negotiated settlements
   C. Administer procurements
   D. Conduct procurements

7. The project for the manufacturing and selling of ready to drink citric juices is starting the initial phases of provisioning. The project manager is evaluating the best type of contract for the upcoming work. The country's laws prohibit the use of cost-plus-percentage of costs contracts, in order to protect the buyer's interests. Why would this type of law be in effect? Because with the cost-plus-percentage of costs contract _____
   A. There is no incentives for the buyer to control the costs
   B. It is necessary the use of a detailed purchase order
   C. The seller has incentives to not control costs
   D. The percentage of the costs requires audits from the buyer

8. The project manager and his team are working during the risk management phase of planning for a project of mass consumption. Which of the following items is a tool of risk mitigation?
   A. Contract
   B. Purchase order
   C. Seller's proposal
   D. Project assumptions

9. A project involves the manufacturing of mother boards. The contract administrator is elaborating the terms and conditions for the contract in order to buy electronic circuits. These inputs are common in the market, and the company can buy them from ten qualified sellers. Surely, the contract administrator is writing a contract of the following type:
   A. Fixed-price-incentive-fee for immediate delivery
   B. Cost-plus-fixed-fee
   C. Cost-plus-incentive for immediate delivery
   D. Cost-plus-percentage of costs

10. A gastronomic company has signed a cost-plus-fixed-fee contract with its main food provider. During an invoice audit, the project manager detects that costs in one of the invoices are excessively high, in relation to market prices. However, the contract does not clarify what to do in these cases. In this solution, the buyer should:
    A. Not pay the fixed fee
    B. Interrupt the payments until the seller clarifies the extra cost in that invoice
    C. Nullify the contract and start legal actions to recuperate the excessive payments
    D. Continue with the payments for the invoices

11. The Company MDZ has contracted an Actuarial Consulting firm to build a retirement fund in direct relation to the seniority of the company's personnel. The consulting firm has established fees for $180 per hour, throughout the project. What type of contract have they signed?
    A. Cost-plus-percentage of costs
    B. Time and materials
    C. Fixed-price-plus-incentive
    D. Cost-plus-fixed-fee

12. You are the project manager of the departmental party that is celebrated every year in your city. You have created a cost-reimbursement contract for your client. What elements must this type of contract always have?
    A. Offer
    B. Certified by an attorney
    C. Monetary value of the acquired item
    D. Start and acceptance date

13. A project has sub-contracted part of the work to an external seller. The work implies the socio-economic evaluation of a road infrastructure project. The first delivery of the preliminary report has been already done and it has been detected that this report does not comply with the minimum requirements established in the contract terms. The seller affirms that he cannot do what the contract says, thus it cannot make changes to the report. What should the project manager do?
    A. Cancel the contract and find another, more efficient seller
    B. Offer the seller an additional incentive to adjust the report per the contract specifications
    C. Maintain additional meetings with the vendor to analyze the problem and find a solution
    D. Seek legal advice from the contract administrator

14. In a project for cattle commercialization, the project manager is requesting the sponsor that an incentive is included in the contract with the seller. The main objective of these incentives will be to:
    A. Facilitate the control of invoice from the seller
    B. Synchronize objectives between the buyer and the seller
    C. Transfer the cost risk to the buyer
    D. Incentivize the use of purchase orders

15. During the planning phase of procurements in a project of energy distribution, you are evaluating the possibility of buying some inputs, instead of manufacturing them yourself. What type of contract will have more cost risk for the buyer of these inputs?
    A. Fixed-price economic price adjustment
    B. Cost-plus-incentive
    C. Fixed-price
    D. Time and materials

- ✓ Bidder conferences
- ✓ Close procurements
- ✓ Contract breach
- ✓ Cost-plus-fixed-fee
- ✓ Cost-plus-incentive
- ✓ Cost-plus-percentage of costs
- ✓ Cost-reimbursement
- ✓ Evaluation criteria
- ✓ Fixed-price
- ✓ Fixed-price economic price adjustment
- ✓ Fixed-price- incentive-fee
- ✓ Invitation for bid (IFB)
- ✓ Make-or-buy
- ✓ Objectives of negotiation
- ✓ PM's role in procurements
- ✓ Purchase order
- ✓ Request for proposal (RFP)
- ✓ Request for quotation (RFQ)
- ✓ Time and materials

✍ *Now that you have finalized studying all the knowledge areas, it is important that you go back and review Integration Management (Chapter 4).*

CHAPTER # 13

PROFESSIONAL CONDUCT

Chapter 13 – PROFESSIONAL CONDUCT

> *The integrity of men is to be measured by their conduct, not by their professions.*
> Juvenal (67-127); Roman poet.

A good PM works with integrity and respect. To become a member of PMI®, you must agree with their code of ethics and professional conduct.

When you finish this chapter, you will have learned the following concepts:

- ✓ Code of Professional Conduct
- ✓ Responsibilities with the profession
- ✓ Comply with PMI's policies
- ✓ Professional practice
- ✓ Development of the profession
- ✓ Responsibilities with the client
- ✓ Development of professional services
- ✓ Conflict of interests

Project Manager Conduct

The PM must:
- ✓ Act with integrity and professional ethics
- ✓ Be within the law and ethical standards
- ✓ Contribute to the development of the profession
- ✓ Improve its professional competencies
- ✓ Promote interaction between project stakeholders
- ✓ Do things correctly
- ✓ Follow the correct processes

> ✎ *Since September 2011 the PMP® exam does not include a separate topic with professional ethics, instead the professional conduct is linked with al the other knowledge areas.*

? The PM has not promoted the utilization of a project charter and has started the schedule without doing a WBS. In other words, she has not followed the correct project management processes. Is the PM complying with its professional ethics?

Answer: NO. It is failing with her professional ethic because not using the correct processes implies problems for the client and for the project such as re-planning, cost excess, delays, poor quality, etc.

> ✎ *Before being a PMP®, maybe you did not know the correct processes. When you become a PMP®, if you do not use the correct processes that you already know, you will be violating your professional responsibility because that will cause problems to the project and/or the client.*

PMI's code of ethics and professional conduct

Next, we make a summarized translation of PMI's code of ethics and professional conduct, valid up to July 2009. It is worth clarifying that it is very important to read the complete document before becoming a PMI member.

Code of ethics and professional conduct *
Source Project Management Institute

CHAPTER 1 – Vision and applicability

1.1 Vision and purpose

As practitioners of project management, we are committed to doing what is right and honorable. We set high standards for ourselves and we aspire to meet these standards in all aspects of our lives—at work, at home, and in service to our profession.

This Code of Ethics and Professional Conduct describes the expectations that we have of ourselves and our fellow practitioners in the global project management community. It articulates the ideals to which we aspire as well as the behaviors that are mandatory in our professional and volunteer roles.

The purpose of this Code is to instill confidence in the project management profession and to help an individual become a better practitioner. We do this by establishing a profession-wide understanding of appropriate behavior. We believe that the credibility and reputation of the project management profession is shaped by the collective conduct of individual practitioners.

We believe that we can advance our profession, both individually and collectively, by embracing this Code of Ethics and Professional Conduct. We also believe that this Code will assist us in making wise decisions, particularly when faced with difficult situations where we may be asked to compromise our integrity or our values.

Our hope that this Code of Ethics and Professional Conduct will serve as a catalyst for others to study, deliberate, and write about ethics and values. Further, we hope that this Code will ultimately be used to build upon and evolve our profession.

1.2 Persons to Whom the Code Applies

1.2.1 All PMI members

1.2.2 Individuals who are not members of PMI but meet one or more of the following criteria:

1.2.2.1 Non-members who hold a PMI certification

1.2.2.2 Non-members who apply to commence a PMI certification process

1.2.2.3 Non-members who serve PMI in a volunteer capacity.

1.3 Structure of the Code

The Code of Ethics and Professional Conduct is divided into sections that contain standards of conduct which are aligned with the four values that were identified as most important to the project management community.

1.4 Values that Support this Code

Practitioners from the global project management community were asked to identify the values that formed the basis of their decision making and guided their actions. The values that the global project management community defined as most important were: responsibility, respect, fairness, and honesty. This Code affirms these four values as its foundation.

1.5 Aspirational and Mandatory Conduct

Each section of the Code of Ethics and Professional Conduct includes both aspirational standards and mandatory standards. The aspirational standards describe the conduct that we strive to uphold as practitioners. Although adherence to the aspirational standards is not easily measured, conducting ourselves in accordance with these is an expectation that we have of ourselves as professionals—it is not optional.

The mandatory standards establish firm requirements, and in some cases, limit or prohibit practitioner behavior.

CHAPTER 2 - Responsibility

2.1 Description of Responsibility

Responsibility is our duty to take ownership for the decisions we make or fail to make, the actions we take or fail to take, and the consequences that result.

2.2 Responsibility: Aspirational Standards

As practitioners in the global project management community:

2.2.1 We make decisions and take actions based on the best interests of society, public safety, and the environment.

2.2.2 We accept only those assignments that are consistent with our background, experience, skills, and qualifications.

2.2.3 We fulfill the commitments that we undertake – we do what we say we will do.

2.2.4 When we make errors or omissions, we take ownership and make corrections promptly. When we discover errors or omissions caused by others, we communicate them to the appropriate body as soon they are discovered. We accept accountability for any issues resulting from our errors or omissions and any resulting consequences.

2.2.5 We protect proprietary or confidential information that has been entrusted to us.

2.2.6 We uphold this Code and hold each other accountable to it.

2.3 Responsibility: Mandatory Standards

As practitioners in the global project management community, we require the following of ourselves and our fellow practitioners:

Regulations and Legal Requirements

2.3.1 We inform ourselves and uphold the policies, rules, regulations and laws that govern our work, professional, and volunteer activities.

2.3.2 We report unethical or illegal conduct to appropriate management and, if necessary, to those affected by the conduct.

Ethics Complaints

2.3.3 We bring violations of this Code to the attention of the appropriate body for resolution.

2.3.4 We only file ethics complaints when they are substantiated by facts.

2.3.5 We pursue disciplinary action against an individual who retaliates against a person raising ethics concerns.

CHAPTER 3 - Respect

3.1 Description of Respect

Respect is our duty to show a high regard for ourselves, others, and the resources entrusted to us. Resources entrusted to us may include people, money, reputation, the safety of others, and natural or environmental resources.

3.2 Respect: Aspirational Standards

As practitioners in the global project management community:

3.2.1 We inform ourselves about the norms and customs of others and avoid engaging in behaviors they might consider disrespectful.

3.2.2 We listen to others' points of view, seeking to understand them.

3.2.3 We approach directly those persons with whom we have a conflict or disagreement.

3.2.4 We conduct ourselves in a professional manner, even when it is not reciprocated.

3.3 Respect: Mandatory Standards

As practitioners in the global project management community, we require the following of ourselves and our fellow practitioners:

3.3.1 We negotiate in good faith.

3.3.2 We do not exercise the power of our expertise or position to influence the decisions or actions of others in order to benefit personally at their expense.

3.3.3 We do not act in an abusive manner toward others.

3.3.4 We respect the property rights of others.

CHAPTER 4 - Fairness

4.1 Description of Fairness

Fairness is our duty to make decisions and act impartially and objectively. Our conduct must be free from competing self interest, prejudice, and favoritism.

4.2 Fairness: Aspirational Standards

As practitioners in the global project management community:

4.2.1 We demonstrate transparency in our decision-making process.

4.2.2 We constantly reexamine our impartiality and objectivity, taking corrective action as appropriate.

4.2.3 We provide equal access to information to those who are authorized to have that information.

4.2.4 We make opportunities equally available to qualified candidates.

4.3 Fairness: Mandatory Standards

As practitioners in the global project management community, we require the following of ourselves and our fellow practitioners:

Conflict of Interest Situations

4.3.1 We proactively and fully disclose any real or potential conflicts of interest to the appropriate stakeholders.

4.3.2 When we realize that we have a real or potential conflict of interest, we refrain from engaging in the decision-making process or otherwise attempting to influence outcomes, unless or until: we have made full disclosure to the affected stakeholders; we have an approved mitigation plan; and we have obtained the consent of the stakeholders to proceed.

Favoritism and Discrimination

4.3.3 We do not hire or fire, reward or punish, or award or deny contracts based on personal considerations, including but not limited to, favoritism, nepotism, or bribery.

4.3.4 We do not discriminate against others based on, but not limited to, gender, race, age, religion, disability, nationality, or sexual orientation.

4.3.5 We apply the rules of the organization (employer, Project Management Institute, or other group) without favoritism or prejudice.

CHAPTER 5 - Honesty

5.1 Description of Honesty

Honesty is our duty to understand the truth and act in a truthful manner both in our communications and in our conduct.

5.2 Honesty: Aspirational Standards

As practitioners in the global project management community:

5.2.1 We earnestly seek to understand the truth.

5.2.2 We are truthful in our communications and in our conduct.

5.2.3 We provide accurate information in a timely manner.

5.2.4 We make commitments and promises, implied or explicit, in good faith.

5.2.5 We strive to create an environment in which others feel safe to tell the truth.

5.3 Honesty: Mandatory Standards

As practitioners in the global project management community, we require the following of ourselves and our fellow practitioners:

5.3.1 We do not engage in or condone behavior that is designed to deceive others, including but not limited to, making misleading or false statements, stating half-truths, providing information out of context or withholding information that, if known, would render our statements as misleading or incomplete.

5.3.2 We do not engage in dishonest behavior with the intention of personal gain or at the expense of another.

Responsibilities with the profession and the client

Once you become a PMI member and accept their code of ethics and professional conduct, you will have the following **responsibilities with the project management profession**:

A. Comply with PMI's policies:
✓ Provide information to PMI® requests in a precise and truthful manner
✓ Inform PMI® about any violation to the code of professional conduct
✓ Cooperate with PMI® regarding violations to the code of professional conduct

? *You have discovered that one of your colleagues in your work team is not following a company policy. You asked him why is he not complying with the policy and his answer was: because I don't feel like it! What should you do?*

Answer: Report him with the authority that wrote the policy.

B. Professional Practice:
✓ Provide precise and truthful information about your professional background
✓ Comply with your region's laws and ethical standards when providing project management services
✓ Keep the confidentiality about the questions in the PMP® Exam

? *A fixed-price contract has been signed, with an incentive of $100,000 to the project manager for finishing ahead of schedule. During the verification process the team informs that the product meets what was specified in the contract, but it does not meet the minimal functionality that the client needs. If that functionality is added to the project, it will not be delivered on time in order to obtain the incentive. What should the project manager do?*

Answer: Revise the situation with the client.

C. Development of the Profession:
✓ Recognize and respect the intellectual property rights developed by others
✓ Support and spread this code of professional conduct
✓ Share lessons learned

? You are working in a tags design company. The sponsor asks you to download a photo from the Internet that he liked. You discover that the photo has an explanatory note with the copyrights. What should you do?

Answer: Ask the author's permission.

On the other hand, the PM also has the following **responsibilities with the client**:

A. Development of professional services:
✓ Provide precise and truthful information to the client about cost estimations, services, and expected results
✓ Respect the scope and objective of the professional services offered

? *You and your work team finalized the WBS and estimate that the most probable project duration is 6 months. The Sponsor is not comfortable with that estimate and asks the project manager to shorten duration to 2 months. What should you do?*

Answer: Look for alternatives. For example: fast tracking, compression, re-estimating, or change the scope.

B. Conflict of Interests:
✓ Ensure that the conflict of interests does not damage the client or the project
✓ Put the project's interests ahead of personal interests
✓ Avoid conflict of interests. If it is not possible, inform the stakeholders
✓ Do not accept bribes or gifts for personal gain, unless it is permitted by the country's laws

? *Your company has presented a $300 million bid to build an oil platform in another country. Your project has been selected, but you have been informed of a $1 million fee that you must pay to that country's Environmental Minister in order to start the work. What is the best thing to do?*

Answer: *Find out if that type of payment is illegal in that country.*

? *Pedro is an employee of White Company and has been temporarily assigned as a project manager to Black Company, located in a different country. White Company does not allow its workers to accept any type of gifts from their clients. However, in the country where Black Company is located gifts are permitted in that company's policies and are covered by*

that country's laws. Pedro is offered a gift because his good performance. Can he accept the gift?

<u>Answer</u>: NO. He can only accept it if he is authorized by his company.

Lessons Learned

- ✓ Code of conduct
- ✓ Collaborate with the profession
- ✓ Confidentiality
- ✓ Conflict of interests
- ✓ Do the correct thing
- ✓ Follow the correct processes
- ✓ Honesty
- ✓ Integrity and Professionalism
- ✓ Justice
- ✓ Professional ethics
- ✓ Put the project's interest ahead of individuals
- ✓ Respect
- ✓ Responsibility
- ✓ Share lessons learned

CHAPTER #**14**

FINAL EXAM

Chapter 14 – FINAL EXAM

Number of questions: 200
Time to respond: 4 hours
Pass score: 80% (160 correct answers)

1. In the management for the construction of a hotel for high income tourists, it will be necessary to hire various external contractors. During the contract planning process the statement of work is included in one of the contracts with a vendor. The MAIN reason to include this in the contract is:
   A. Communicate how the process relating to the provisioning of inputs will be managed
   B. Define which type of contract is the most convenient
   C. Establish who will take control of vendor responses
   D. Include the necessary items so the provider clearly understands what is the organization asking for

2. In a project with a strong matrix organization, the main characteristics are that the project manager will have:
   A. Total authority, high resource availability, and full dedication
   B. High authority, low resource availability, and partial dedication
   C. High authority, moderate resource availability, and full dedication
   D. Total authority, high resource availability, and partial dedication

3. Suppose that a project has 2 critical activities with the following duration estimates (in days): Activity A: optimistic (12), most likely (16), pessimistic (32); Activity B: optimistic (2), most likely (4), and pessimistic (12). What will be the project duration in a range of 95.44%?
   A. 8.00 – 16.00
   B. 15.54 – 30.46
   C. 18.84 – 29.16
   D. 22.84 – 33.16

4. You have the option of leasing scaffolding for a construction project with a cost of $120 per day, with maintenance and surveillance costs included. The alternative is to buy them for $3,000 and pay the surveillance cost of $90 per day. How many days should you use the scaffolding in the project for the cost of buying to be equivalent to the cost of leasing?
   A. 25
   B. 33
   C. 100
   D. 120

5. You are evaluating a big project where quality is very important. During the quality planning process you will obtain the following results, EXCEPT:
   A. Quality metrics
   B. Quality checklists
   C. Process improvement plan
   D. Corrective actions

6. In a project for the construction and commercialization of wooden furniture, which of the following items do you need to control the project scope?
   A. Performance reports
   B. Inspection
   C. Requested changes
   D. Expert judgment

7. You are working as the project manager for the construction and startup of 30 new public schools. After the bidder conference to clarify the questions of the sellers, five sellers respond to the request for proposal. Two of them send fixed-price proposals, one sends a cost-reimbursement proposal, another sends a fixed-price economic price adjustment proposal, and the last one sends a time and materials proposal. Which one of these proposals will have the least amount of cost risk for the buyer?
   A. Fixed-price
   B. Cost-reimbursement
   C. Fixed-price economic price adjustment
   D. Time and materials

8. On the following diagram, the letters indicate an activity and the numbers indicate duration in days. What is the slack in path F-G-H-I?

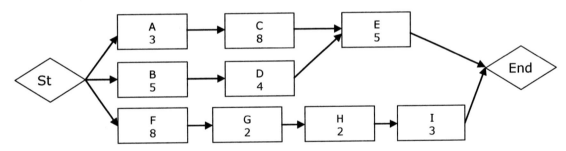

   A. 0
   B. 1
   C. 2
   D. 15

9. After various iterations, the project team has finally finished project planning with a level of detail good enough to start with the executing phase. What will be an output while the project is being managed?
   A.   Change requests
   B.   Forecasts
   C.   Approved change requests
   D.   Project management plan

10. The sponsor has signed the project charter during the initiating processes group. What is the MAIN characteristic of this document?
    A.   Identifies the project and its importance to the organization
    B.   It is written by the stakeholders to authorize the use of company resources
    C.   The project could start without this document
    D.   It must be a written memo

11. The project manager and his work team have finished the project schedule. However, when reviewing the resource histogram they discover that they do not have enough workers to be able to complete the scope as planned. The sponsor informs them that they cannot cut the project scope and they must level the schedule as good as possible. What is the best they could do?
    A.   Delay the start of the activities with a positive slack
    B.   Compress the project
    C.   Delay the end of the project
    D.   Use a project management software to solve the problem

12. You and your team finalized the risk management plan and will start with the process of risk identification. You are working in a software development project. Which of the following elements would be the MOST important in the phase you are about to start?
    A.   Network diagrams
    B.   Enterprise environmental factors
    C.   Organizational process assets
    D.   Work breakdown structure

13. You are preparing the cost budget, as presented in the following table. What will be the cost baseline at the end of the fifth month?

Activity	Months					
	M1	M2	M3	M4	M5	M6
A1	50	60	80	60	50	40
A2	150	170	190	200	220	180
A3	120	150	150	150	120	100
A4	200	200	200	200	200	200

   A.   590
   B.   2,330
   C.   2,920
   D.   3,440

14. A project to install electrical towers involves 75 stakeholders. It has been a few months since internal and external project communications are being poorly managed. Therefore, a project coordinator has been hired to collaborate in the solution for this problem. What is the difference between a project coordinator and a project expeditor?
   A.   None, both terms are equal
   B.   The coordinator can make some decisions
   C.   The expeditor has the same power as the project manager
   D.   The coordinator cannot make decisions without the project manager's authorization

15. You have to perform the project's cost estimates as soon as possible. Therefore, you communicate to the sponsor that you will use an analogous estimation technique, which is less precise, but it will satisfy the deadline restriction. This estimation technique is equivalent to what other type of estimation?
   A.   Parametric
   B.   Bottom-up
   C.   Top-down
   D.   Order of magnitude

16. An enterprise works with a total quality management (TQM) approach. In addition, it uses systems to manage raw materials with a just in time (JIT) approach. To perform quality control in their projects, the enterprise uses what is called "the seven basic tools". Which of the following items is NOT part of the seven basic tools for quality control?
   A.   Statistical sampling
   B.   Fishbone diagram
   C.   Histogram
   D.   Run Chart

17. The project sponsor is looking for the best profile of a person to name it as a project manager in a high-tech food company. This is a company with a functional structure and the majority of its employees are engineers using a technical jargon. What is the most important thing to look for when selecting the project manager?
   A.   A technical specialization, specific to food technology
   B.   That the candidate is an engineer with an MBA
   C.   Experience in the industry and the high-tech food business
   D.   Communication and integration abilities

18. You are planning the resource needs for a new project that will need 46 workers. Each one of them must be clear about what is their responsibility for each project work package right from the start. Once the work breakdown structure is finalized, you decide to develop a roles and responsibilities matrix. What is the difference between role and responsibility?
   A.   Responsibility is the work that a person is expected to perform in order to complete the activities.
   B.   Responsibilities describe the work package for which a person is accountable
   C.   They are synonymous
   D.   The assignment of roles refer to who decides what

19. Members of the work team have just finalized the work breakdown structure (WBS). Now they want to develop the WBS dictionary. What is the MAIN characteristic of the WBS?
    A.   Indicates a hierarchical project organization in a symmetrical form
    B.   Divides the project into smaller parts in order to continue with the planning processes
    C.   Indicates a sequence of tasks
    D.   The project is decomposed into the most number of parts possible

20. A financial company is expanding its portfolio of mortgage credit to low income customers. This will be a new project with a business concept different to what the company usually does. The project manager has created a series of processes to ensure that each approved credit complies with current laws. Once the project starts execution, which tool can be used to validate that those processes are being followed?
    A.   Flowchart
    B.   Cause-and-effect diagram
    C.   Checklist
    D.   Control chart

21. A project for the manufacturing and marketing of dairy products will involve 320 stakeholders. In order to proactively deal with the conflicts that this project will face, it will be very important to plan the communications. In which project management process group you will have to manage stakeholders?
    A.   Planning
    B.   Monitoring and Controlling
    C.   Executing
    D.   Initiating

22. To successfully close a project it is fundamental to document the following items, EXCEPT for:
    A.   Lessons learned
    B.   Final project scope and its compliance with quality metrics
    C.   Project selection method
    D.   Formal acceptance of the product

23. You are the project manager in a telecommunications company. The project's performance reports use earned value management to inform the progress to stakeholders. One of the team members does not understand the meaning of having a negative schedule variance. You explain that the project is behind, in relation to the original plan, and that that indicator is obtained in the following manner:
    A.   The difference between the earned value and the actual cost
    B.   The difference between the earned value and the planned value
    C.   The difference between the planned value and the actual cost
    D.   The ratio obtained when dividing the earned value by the planned value

24. You have been assigned as the project manager for the launch of the next space shuttle. Along with your project team, you are identifying the possible risks that the launch could face. What would be the BEST technique to use in this situation?
    A.   Delphi
    B.   Monte Carlo simulation
    C.   PERT
    D.   Risk matrix

25. In a project that has just entered its third execution year the project manager feels that employees are not motivated. Therefore, he needs to constantly tell them what to do. In addition, he needs to control and validate that they really do what they were told to do. Which motivational theory explains this?
    A.   Theory X
    B.   Theory Y
    C.   Theory Z
    D.   Herzberg Theory

26. A project has an estimated duration of 9 months. In the second month of execution, one of the activities in the critical path has a delay of 10 days due to bad weather. This has exceeded the project costs, but is within the acceptable limits. What is the BEST course of action?
    A.   Not to worry, everything is under control
    B.   Inform the client and the sponsor about the real status of the project
    C.   Compress the project to recover the lost time
    D.   Quickly inform the boss that the project is out of control

27. You are working on a project for the construction of a $430,000 pre-fabricated house with an estimated duration of 3 months. You are doing the project by materials administration and you need to select the team of painters. You will be able to do the vendor selection based on the following techniques, EXCEPT for:
    A.   Independent estimates
    B.   Bidder conference
    C.   Weighted system
    D.   Vendor rating system

28. Throughout the life cycle of a $23 million project, with a deadline of 3 years, the integrated change control is followed to ensure that any change in the project is beneficial. Which of the following items is not a result of the integrated change control?
    A.   Change requests
    B.   Approved change requests
    C.   Preventive actions
    D.   Validated defect repairs

29. The project has come to its closing phase. The project total cost was $26 million, with a total duration of 32 months. What is the MAIN characteristic of this project phase?
    A.   It generally consumes few resources, in relation to the executing phase
    B.   It is an unimportant phase in the project life cycle
    C.   It is generally more extensive than its previous phase
    D.   It ends when the production of the good or service is finished

30. In a project you have found a group of sellers under a fixed-price-incentive-fee contract. When the project has a 75% progress, the client requests a change in the scope, which requires a contract modification. Who has the authority to change the contracts?
   A.   The project manager
   B.   The sponsor
   C.   The contract administrator
   D.   The client

31. You have been assigned as the project manager for the design of an industrial park. You have great experience in the world of projects, but have never done before projects related to industrial parks. What is the first thing you should do?
   A.   Identify all of the project stakeholders
   B.   Collect historical information about similar projects performed by the sponsor
   C.   Contact a friend that has been the project manager for a similar project
   D.   Search the OMP3 database for similar projects

32. During the executing phase of a project for the closing of a nuclear plant, the project manager submits to the stakeholders, including the sponsor, a progress report informing about the project performance. Which report would that be?
   A.   Milestone diagram
   B.   GANTT chart
   C.   Network diagram
   D.   Earned value report

33. Once the project manager and his team have finished with the human resources planning, they should keep working with other human resources management processes during the project execution. Which of the following items is not part of these processes?
   A.   Acquire project team
   B.   Develop project team leadership styles
   C.   Manage project team
   D.   Develop project team

34. You have to select one of the projects presented in the following table, where IRR is the internal rate of return. The discount rate to use in these projects is 8%. Which project would you choose?

Project	IRR
A	6%
B	8%
C	12%
D	7%

   A.   Project A
   B.   Project B
   C.   Project C
   D.   Project D

35. Along with your team, you are trying to estimate your company's operating costs for next year. First, you collect the historical records for those costs during the last 36 months. Then you use a Run Chart to see the historical behavior of those costs. You apply some statistical tests to corroborate that the data is statistically significant. Finally, you make estimates of the future operating costs based on that historical data. What type of estimating are you doing?
   A. Bottom-up
   B. Parametric
   C. Analogous
   D. Order of magnitude

36. Your last project about writing a book is finishing. The book cover design was sub-contracted to a graphic designer studio. What is the last thing you should do in this project?
   A. Close procurements
   B. Release resources
   C. Close project
   D. Verify deliverables with the client

37. Based on Maslow's hierarchy of needs, which of the following items is at the base?
   A. Safety or Survival
   B. Hygiene agents
   C. Physiological needs
   D. Self-actualization

38. Which one of the following items represents the top hierarchical level in the work breakdown structure?
   A. Control account
   B. Planning package
   C. Activities
   D. Work package

39. You have been working as the project manager in the construction of a skyscraper in a foreign country. Your client, a millionaire entrepreneur from the oil industry, wants to give you a very luxurious diamond ring in appreciation for the majestic building that you have finished six months ahead of schedule. What should you do?
   A. Accept the ring because it is part of the business culture in that country and consider it a compensation for all the extra hours you worked
   B. Not accept the ring because it could be considered an act of bribery
   C. Accept the ring and then sell it to divide the money with your team members
   D. Not accept the ring because its value exceeds the gifts limit that your company policy allows

40. During which phase of the project life cycle you do the administrative closure?
   A. When the client accepts the final product
   B. When you finish each deliverable
   C. When you finish the executing phase
   D. When you finish each phase of the project

41. You are using project management software for the monitoring and controlling phase of your project. The project manager gives you a report with the following information. How is the project doing?

#	Task	SPI	CPI	PV	EV	AC	SV	CV
0	**Project**	**0.84**	**1.05**	**$5,000**	**$4,200**	**$4,000**	**-$800**	**$200**
1	Construction	1	1.5	$3,000	$3,000	$2,000	$0	$1,000
2	Design	0.6	0.6	$2,000	$1,200	$2,000	-$800	-$800
3	Testing	0	0	$ 0	$ 0	$ 0	$ 0	$ 0

    A.   Slow, but spending less than planned
    B.   Fast and spending less than planned
    C.   Slow and spending more than planned
    D.   Fast, but spending more than planned

42. A project is entering its final phase. What is the most important thing to do to close the project?
    A.   Plan the reassignment of the team members to other projects
    B.   Evaluate the performance of the team members to add it to the lessons learned register
    C.   Perform a closing event to celebrate with the team that is working with the culmination of the project
    D.   Obtain the formal finish approval from the client

43. A project that consists of the development of a project management plan for the opening of a new bank is almost finished. The procurement manager is performing an audit to determine the compliance level of the contract with the vendor. To which process group does this activity belong?
    A.   Planning
    B.   Executing
    C.   Monitoring and Controlling
    D.   Closing

44. How do you know that the decomposition of the project has reached an adequate partition level?
    A.   When the work breakdown structure has a minimum of 5 hierarchical levels
    B.   When you cannot keep breaking down the work packages
    C.   When the time and cost estimates can be done for each work package
    D.   When each work package is defined in the WBS dictionary

45. In a balanced matrix organization, the majority of the communications between stakeholders are:
    A.   Vertical
    B.   Horizontal
    C.   Vertical and horizontal
    D.   Formal written

46. In a project to develop juice concentrate for the manufacturing of exporting juices, the sponsor wants to start the project without errors. Before finalizing the project charter, the sponsor would need to know the following items, EXCEPT for:
    A. Organizational culture, organizational systems, and abilities of the available human resources
    B. Organizational policies and processes
    C. Project charter
    D. Historical information and lessons learned of similar projects

47. In a project for the mass production of women perfumes, the person responsible for the quality of the project is:
    A. Quality inspector
    B. Quality assurance manager
    C. Project manager
    D. Operations manager

48. The buyer and the seller have signed a formal written agreement. In order for this document to be considered a legal contract, it must include the following elements, EXCEPT for:
    A. Ability or willingness of both parts
    B. Consideration or Purpose
    C. Negotiation
    D. Lawful purpose

49. You are working as the project manager in an open-sky mine that produces diamonds. In this project, there are hundreds of stakeholders with conflicting interests and the efficiency with which you manage them will be the key for a successful project. Which of the following items is NOT necessary for the stakeholder management?
    A. Identify all stakeholders as soon as possible
    B. Give each interest group what they want
    C. Determine the expectations and needs of the different interest groups, and convert these into requirements
    D. Fluid communication with the stakeholders in order to manage their influence

50. Based on the following risk-probability-impact matrix, which has blank cells that you have to fill out, choose the CORRECT answer:

		Impact				
		VH	H	M	L	VL
Probability	VH	25	20	15	10	5
	H	20	16			4
	M	15	12			3
	L	10	8			2
	VL	5	4	3	2	1
Notes: VH: Very High; H: High; M: Medium; L: Low; VL: Very Low Risk of HIGH priority: score 15 to 25 Risk of MEDIUM priority: score 6 to 14 Risk of LOW priority: score 1 to 5						

A. The risk of impact and probability "M" will have a score of 3
B. The risk of probability "H" and impact "M" will have a MEDIUM priority
C. The risk of probability "H" and impact "L" will have a LOW priority
D. The risk of probability "L" and impact "M" will have a score of 5

51. You are negotiating a fixed-price contract with one of the sellers. The following items are negotiation strategies, with the EXCEPTION of:
A. Attack
B. Deadline
C. Focus on interests
D. Effective listening

52. A multinational company with a projectized approach has a project management office (PMO). At the same time, its project portfolio is ordered by programs, projects, and sub-projects. Which one of the following is NOT a role of the PMO?
A. Provide project management methodologies
B. Assign project managers
C. Assign funds to start with strategic projects
D. Provide support to manage projects for the organization

53. During the execution of a project, the client requests a change to the scope. The project manager evaluates the change's impact and looks for alternatives for its implementation. He later sends a report to the client informing about the change's impacts to project´s constraint. Which are the main constraints of the project?
A. Scope, time, and cost
B. Scope, time, cost, and quality
C. Scope, quality, and cost
D. Scope, time, cost, quality, resources and risks

54. During the human resources planning phase a resource histogram is incorporated to the resource management plan. What does this diagram indicate?
   A. Roles and responsibilities of the project team
   B. Organizational chart for the human resources
   C. Resource assignments by activities
   D. Resource utilization across time

55. You are the project manager for the construction of a shopping mall. The SV indicates a value of -$50,000. After a meeting with your project team, you all decide to work extra hours to accelerate the execution of some tasks. This way the project will go back to a schedule performance index of 1 in 15 days. Tomorrow you are having the project status meeting with the sponsor and the client. What should you inform in that meeting?
   A. The project is exceeding costs, but it will be back in its place after implementing fast tracking.
   B. The project is in line with the budget, but behind schedule
   C. The project is behind schedule, but you and your team will implement corrective actions to go back to the budgeted values
   D. The project is exceeding budget

56. What tools are used to examine the effectiveness of the risk response strategies during the monitoring and controlling phase?
   A. Risk urgency evaluation
   B. Risk audits
   C. Contingency response strategy
   D. Variance and trends analysis

57. You are evaluating a fruit export project. There are three types of fruits. In the following table there is a summary of the net cash flow for each type. If the capital cost of money is 10% annually, which type is the most convenient?

Type	Investment	Year 1	Year 2
A	-500	200	400
B	-500	80	530
C	-500	40	570

   A. Type A
   B. Type B
   C. Type C
   D. None, they all have a negative profitability

58. Your client does not agree with the project progress and it is complaining because one of the deliverables defined in the contract was not completed. On the other hand, your company affirms that that deliverable was not defined in the contract; therefore it is not part of the project. It is probable that both parts use arbitration and mediation techniques to reach an agreement. What type of techniques are these?
   A. Compromise
   B. Negotiation
   C. Communication
   D. Parametric

59. You are working in a project for the demolition of an old building. Among the activities in this project are "demolish walls" and "collect debris". What type of sequence do these activities have?
   A. Hard logic
   B. Discretional
   C. External
   D. Soft logic

60. In an industrial design project, the project manager decides to implement fast tracking for some activities. What can happen in this project?
   A. Sequence activities start-finish
   B. People work less extra hours
   C. An increment of the risk level
   D. Prolong the project's duration

61. You are working on a project for the planning of the layout of a frozen gourmet products factory. To be able to perform some of the project's activities, it is necessary for the client to provide the technical specifications for the imported machinery. However, this information will not be available in the next 20 days. This is an example of:
   A. Assumption
   B. Enterprise environmental factors
   C. Restriction
   D. Organizational process assets

62. You are the project manager for a new software development. This project must go live in 30 days, or the competition will beat you with a similar product in the market. The project is progressing according to plan until a team member discovers an error that must be repaired. This repair implies a change in the project and company policy establishes that it requires the approval of the Change Control Committee. To initiate this process and obtaining a response from the committee requires a minimum of 15 days, which jeopardizes the project schedule. What should you do?
   A. Perform the change without consulting the committee, since it is only a minor change
   B. Not change the scope of the project until it is approved by the committee. In the meantime keep working on the project according to plan
   C. Inform the team to repair the error, since you have enough authority to implement emergency changes, without having to wait for the committee's approval
   D. Inform the work team that all work is suspended until the change is approved by the committee

63. Upper management is evaluating different investment projects. Among the selection tools, they are using the benefits measurement method. Which one of the following items is NOT an example of this method?
   A. Scoring models
   B. Lineal programming
   C. Benefit contributions
   D. Economic models

64. Based on the following statements, what is the MOST useful tool to organize resources, estimate costs, and develop network diagrams?
    A. Project management software
    B. Expert judgment
    C. Spreadsheets
    D. Historical templates

65. The project management information system is very useful to integrate and spread the results of the project management processes. Which one of the following sub-systems is not part of the general project management system?
    A. WBS System
    B. Configuration management system
    C. Change control system
    D. Work authorization system

66. You are the project manager for the expansion of a hub airport. One of the project activities consists of changing the current flooring to a modern style. This activity will be subcontracted to a vendor, but you need to know how they will perform this activity without disrupting the airport's normal functions. What type of documentation will be the most appropriate for the procurement manager to prepare?
    A. Invitation for Bidding (IFB)
    B. Request for Quotation (RFQ)
    C. Request for Proposal (RFP)
    D. Time and materials contract

67. You are the project manager and you are working with 7 stakeholders in the planning phase. During project execution, 5 new stakeholders were incorporated. How many communication channels were added to the project?
    A. 45
    B. 50
    C. 66
    D. 78

68. You are working as the project manager for a forestation project that will require a great number of workers. During the human resource planning process you obtain the responsibility assignment matrix (RAM). What is the main purpose of the RAM?
    A. Know the distribution of the workers and their connections with the job across time
    B. Ensure that all team members understand their roles within the project
    C. Establish the availability of team members
    D. Provide a graphical hierarchical representation of the project's organizational structure

69. You are studying with a friend to take the PMP® certification. Each one bought a different book, with copyrights, to prepare for the exam. Later on, each one makes copies of the books and both exchange them in order to have more material and improve their chances of passing the exam. Choose the CORRECT answer:
    A. Since none of them is a PMP®, it is not necessary to apply the professional conduct code yet, therefore they can make the copies
    B. Sharing photocopies will generate a conflict of interests with the publisher that has the copyrights
    C. They cannot share those photocopies without asking permission to PMI
    D. Books cannot be photocopied

70. Your company decides to invite sellers to bid for the provisioning of one of the project deliverables. What type of contract is generally used for this type of documentation?
    A. Fixed-price
    B. Cost-reimbursement
    C. Time and materials
    D. Cost-plus-incentive

71. The project has entered its executing phase and everything is progressing perfectly, until the client requests a last minute change. This change will increase the scope and costs of the project. The client will pay for all the necessary additions. What is the next thing to do in your role as the project manager?
    A. Evaluate the change's impact to the other project constraints
    B. Request the change committee to approve the change requested by the client
    C. Include the new scope in the contract's terms and conditions
    D. Look for alternatives to implement the change

72. A project is in its executing phase and a group of stakeholders formally approve a change. If you are the project manager, what would you need to evaluate the change's impact on the project?
    A. The constraints
    B. The work breakdown structure
    C. The earned value
    D. The project performance

73. In relation to the project scope and the product scope, choose the item that is FALSE:
    A. The product scope includes the necessary processes to control its risks
    B. The project scope includes the necessary processes for the product to be provided with all the required functions and characteristics
    C. The product scope includes the functions and characteristics of the product or service
    D. The project scope is defined in the WBS and the WBS dictionary

74. Which of the following statements is NOT a main advantage of the work breakdown structure?
    A. Is the base for the estimation of resources, time, costs, roles and responsibilities assignments
    B. Details the work to be done in each work package and it mentions the responsible for that work
    C. Facilitates communication
    D. Facilitates the integrated change control

75. The following tools are used to develop the project schedule. Only one of them includes risk analysis in the estimates. Which one?
    A. Arrow diagramming method (ADM)
    B. Precedence diagramming method (PDM)
    C. Critical path method (CPM)
    D. Program evaluation and review technique (PERT)

76. What is the standard deviation of an activity whose most likely duration is estimated at 50 days, the optimistic scenario is 40 days, and the pessimistic scenario goes to 80 days?
    A. 6.67
    B. 40
    C. 44.44
    D. 53.33

77. The project manager is in the process of defining the project activities. This is a progressive process, so he decides to plan in detail the activities for the next 6 months and leave the rest at the planning component level. Which is NOT an example of a planning component?
    A. Work package
    B. Milestones
    C. Control account
    D. Planning package

78. In a project to open a messenger company, a risk management plan has been developed. This plan is part of the project management plan. Which of the following items is NOT part of the risk management plan? How to structure and develop _____
    A. The risk response plan
    B. The secondary and residual risks
    C. The risk identification
    D. The qualitative and quantitative risk analysis

79. A project has estimated spending most likely $100,000 to perform all the activities. If they want to work with a definitive precision level, what could be the total estimated cost for the project?
    A. 100,000
    B. Between 90,000 and 110,000
    C. Between 50,000 and 150,000
    D. 110,000

80. During the execution of a project for the construction of an energy distribution network, the subcontractor proposes to change some materials, included in the fixed-price contract, for more modern ones. This change will improve the quality of the deliverable without impacting the other project constraints. After the change is approved, in which document should this change be registered?
    A.   Procurement management plan
    B.   Baseline
    C.   Communications management plan
    D.   Organizational process assets

81. You hired a marketing company to perform the design of an advertising campaign for the launch of a new product. The advertising's design costs $50,000. You already paid 40% in cash, 30% with check at net 30 days, and 30% with check at net 60 days. The marketing department is not sure if the product will be in demand or not, so they are evaluating the possibility of not doing the advertisement campaign. Which cost from that study should they take into account to make the decision of launching the product to market?
    A. $0
    B. $20,000
    C. $35,000
    D. $50,000

82. In a multiple phase project, during each control phase there are two processes that are done in parallel to ensure the acceptance of the work performed and that it is well performed. Which are these two processes?
    A.   Perform quality assurance and perform quality control
    B.   Verify scope and perform quality control
    C.   Perform quality assurance and perform integrated change control
    D.   Verify scope and perform quality assurance

83. An earthquake damaged an international insurance company's databases. What should the project manager use to mitigate the damages caused by the earthquake?
    A.   Contingency reserve
    B.   Risk management plan
    C.   Reinsurance
    D.   Management reserve

84. The project is ending and the work team is very anxious and worried. They are surely working in what type of organization?
    A.   Weak matrix
    B.   Projectized
    C.   Strong matrix
    D.   Functional

85. Based on the information in the following table, answer the next 5 questions. How many weeks do the project lasts?

Activity	Duration (Weeks)	Predecessor
A	6	Start
B	8	Start
C	4	A
D	7	A
E	10	B
F	5	C, E
G	9	D, E, F
End	0	G

   A.   24
   B.   27
   C.   32
   D.   49

86. What is the critical path?
   A.   A-B-D-F-G
   B.   A-C-F-G
   C.   B-E-G
   D.   B-E-F-G

87. If activity C changes from 4 weeks to 11 weeks, what is the nearest critical path?
   A.   A-B-D-F-G
   B.   A-C-F-G
   C.   B-E-G
   D.   B-E-F-G

88. What is the free slack in weeks for activity D?
   A.   0
   B.   1
   C.   5
   D.   10

89. What happens with the project if activity D lasts 10 weeks more than it was planned?
   A.   Nothing, the project duration stays the same
   B.   The project will end 10 weeks later
   C.   The slack for path B-E-G decreases
   D.   The project risk increases

90. Your company has just hired Ruben Peuchene for the PMP® Exam preparation training. This facilitator did not meet the expectations of the participants. Therefore, the human resources manager implemented the risk response plan and decided to change this facilitator for another pre-qualified facilitator from the possible vendors list. The next training will be conducted by Lucile Leg in another company branch. Lucile is meeting expectations better than Ruben. However, there are still some key points in the contract that are not being adequately met by Lucile. What is this situation explaining?
    A.   Risk owner
    B.   Secondary risks
    C.   Defective risk response plan
    D.   Residual risks

91. In a project for the construction of a shipyard, the project team needs to shorten the critical path by 115 days. For this, they can do the following actions, EXCEPT for:
    A.   Compression
    B.   Perform activities in parallel
    C.   Re-planning
    D.   Eliminate slacks

92. The progress indicators, according to earned value management, inform that we are receiving $1.3 for each $ invested. However, we have progressed 60% when we supposed to be at 90%. What is the BEST thing to do in this project?
    A.   Fast tracking
    B.   Inform the client that the project will be delayed
    C.   Cut the scope
    D.   Compression

93. During the initiating process group, you are evaluating a series of investment projects. The opportunity cost for the company's is 12% annual. Project A has an IRR of 8%, project B has an IRR of 10%, and project C has an IRR of 6%. These are mutually exclusive projects and are not repeatable in time. Which one of these projects you should select?
    A.   None
    B.   Project A
    C.   Project B
    D.   Project C

94. You are working as the project manager in a hardware development company in an ever-changing environment. In the last 6 months, your competitors have designed 8 new hardware products similar to your company's. In addition, the client generally does not buy an old model, unless it is very cheap. In the next software development project, the key to success will be that the team has the flexibility of adapting the plan to the market's needs. What would be the BEST approach to develop the schedule for this project?
    A.   Network diagram
    B.   Milestone diagram
    C.   Fast tracking
    D.   Progressive elaboration

95. If you want to estimate with a good precision level the project costs, the most appropriate would be to use what kind of estimation technique?
   A.   Parametric
   B.   Analogous
   C.   Monte Carlo simulation
   D.   Bottom-up

96. The project manager is arguing with the quality manager in relation to the terms of precision and accuracy. In relation to these concepts, which of the following statements is FALSE?
   A.   Precision is achieved when the data has little standard deviation
   B.   Precision and accuracy are synonymous
   C.   Accuracy is achieved when the objective is met
   D.   You can have precision without accuracy

97. You are the project manager for the launching of a sea water treatment plant. You have finalized planning and everything is ready to start the execution. For this you will need to acquire specialized personnel to perform certain activities. However, you cannot contract whoever you want, because in the project charter there are team members already assigned to those activities. That would be an example of what?
   A.   Procurement
   B.   Previous assignment
   C.   Activity's resource requirement
   D.   Manage stakeholders

98. You were the project manager for the installation of 25 computers in a government agency. The project has finalized and the client formally accepted the deliverables according to the contract terms. Another company in charge of installing the software in those computers has included you in their schedule of activities to collaborate during the installation process. What should you do?
   A.   Ask the client if he needs you to keep collaborating during the process of installing the software on the computers you installed
   B.   Request an economic retribution to the vendor for your collaboration in those activities
   C.   Request the vendor to send you the work schedule details so you can accommodate your intervention in the project
   D.   Clarify the vendor that you have just closed the project based on the scope and that you cannot collaborate with that new project

99. On month 3, a project has a planned value of $300, an actual cost of $220, and an earned value of $250. The budget at completion on month 6 is $600. What would be the cost variance and the schedule performance index?
   A.   30 ; 0.83
   B.   -50 ; 1.2
   C.   -50 ; 1.14
   D.   30 ; 0.88

100. Based on the data of the previous question: What would be the estimate at completion (EAC) if the performance indexes until moth 3 are being affected by temporary problems that will not be repeated in the future?
   A.   528
   B.   570
   C.   600
   D.   720

101. Based on the data of question 99: What would be the estimate to complete (ETC), assuming that in the future the project will behave similar to what the performance indexes are indicating until month 3?
   A.   350
   B.   308
   C.   528
   D.   300

102. During a project's executing phase the project manager wants to verify that the scope is being fulfilled. What action should be done for this?
   A.   Variance analysis
   B.   Re-planning
   C.   Inspection
   D.   Stakeholder analysis

103. A project requires an initial investment of $500,000 and it will start generating positive net benefits starting on the next month. The first month the net benefits are $20,000, the second month the benefits are $30,000, and starting on the third month the benefits will be $30,000 per month. In how many months will we get the payback period for this project?
   A.   12
   B.   5
   C.   11
   D.   10

104. You are the project manager for the construction of a commercial store in your city's downtown. You have all the necessary inputs to estimate the duration of the activities. What tools could you use for this process?
   A.   Published estimated data, bottom-up estimating, expert judgment
   B.   Expert judgment, three-point estimates, precedence diagramming
   C.   Parametric estimating, reserve analysis, resource breakdown structure
   D.   Expert judgment, parametric estimating, variance analysis

105. You are working as the project manager in the process of planning the communications in an IT project. The main objective for creating a communications management plan is:
   A.   Define the amount of communication channels
   B.   Establish the communications technology to be used
   C.   Establish the frequency of communications
   D.   Communicate with all stakeholders

106. During the execution of a project for the construction of a food court in a shopping center, the progress indicators are doing very well. However, the work team members are complaining because they have to submit reports to two different areas within the organization and nobody is paying them extra for the duplicity of functions. In which type of organization is this project being done?
    A.   Projectized
    B.   Functional
    C.   Matrix
    D.   OPM3

107. The project has an estimated duration of six months, based on its critical path and not considering contingency reserves. The client asks you to deliver the project 30 days ahead of schedule, so the project now has a negative slack. What should you do?
    A.   Fast tracking
    B.   Consult with the sponsor
    C.   Inform the client about the impact of that change
    D.   Compression

108. You are executing a project that involves 23 internal stakeholders and 17 external stakeholders. Due to the high amount of communication channels, conflicts are arising within different stakeholder groups. What tool for conflict resolution should you use if you want long term solutions?
    A.   Confrontation
    B.   Compromise
    C.   Avoid
    D.   Smoothing

109. The quality control manager is using a control chart to evaluate deviations of one of the project deliverables. The maximum tolerance level for that deliverable is +/- 1 sigma over the mean. All products that fall beyond that range must be re-designed before client delivery. Until now all products have been within the control limits. However, in the last week she observes that there are seven consecutive data points over the mean, but below the control limit and maximum tolerance level. What does this mean?
    A.   The process is out of control and the special cause for the variation should be evaluated
    B.   The process is under control, because it has not gone beyond the tolerance limit
    C.   Pareto Principle 80/20
    D.   The process is under control, because it has not gone beyond the control limit

110. During scope management for a project to install fiber optic in an apartment building, the project manager should be involved in the following processes:
    A.   Collect requirements, define, estimate, develop, and control
    B.   Planning, create WBS, verify, and control
    C.   Planning, define, estimate, verify, and control
    D.   Collect requirements, define, create WBS, verify, and control

111. You have signed PMI's professional code of conduct in order to take the PMP® Exam. Once you sign that contract, you will have the following responsibilities, with the EXCEPTION of:
   A. Comply with your country's ethical standards
   B. Solve conflicts with a win-win approach
   C. Give precise and dependable information
   D. Implement the correct project management processes

112. A good project manager, instead of asking for the percentage of completion of activities without doing a review of a project's real progress, could use another type of rules to manage the project's progress. For example, she could assign a 50% progress when the activity starts and another 50% progress once it finishes. Which of the following items is NOT related with techniques of managing project progress?
   A. Assign only a 100% progress once the task is finished
   B. 20/80 Rule
   C. 80/20 Principle
   D. 50/50 Rule

113. In a $23 million real-estate development project with a schedule of 18 months, the project plan has already been developed and approved by the stakeholders. Later, the client requests to add a change to the project without delaying the estimated due date. The client is willing to pay more for this change. What is the first thing the project manager should do?
   A. Start a new project for the change the client is requesting
   B. Estimate contingency plans so the project is not delayed
   C. Start the integrated change control process
   D. Modify the scope per client's request and send an invoice for the additional costs

114. Deming is known for his 14 steps for total quality management. This approach is aligned with PMI's quality management processes. Which of the following items is NOT part of Deming's total quality management approach?
   A. Continuous improvement
   B. Use the quality control's statistical theory
   C. Teamwork
   D. Eliminate arbitrary numerical goals for the personnel

115. During a weekend, one of the biggest consulting firms in the world suffered a major fire to all its administrative offices. The company had 95% of its digital files backed up off site. The risk response plan was activated by a special crisis committee. The building reconstruction would take 45 days. The crisis committee decided to relocate in leased offices while the buildings were repaired. In only 48 hours all workers were back at work as usual. What type of risk response was implemented in relation to the office relocation?
   A. Avoid
   B. Exploit
   C. Transfer
   D. Accept

116. During the planning of a project, techniques for the evaluation of the costs of quality are being used. The project manager is worried because the company where the project is located has big failure costs due to the lack of applying proactive measures. The following examples are costs of non-conformance of quality, with the EXCEPTION of _____, which is a cost due to defects or poor quality.
    A.   Maintenance
    B.   Corrective actions
    C.   Training
    D.   Inspection

117. The scatter diagram and statistical sampling are tools used during the process of:
    A.   Perform quality assurance
    B.   Perform quality control
    C.   Verify scope
    D.   Monitor and control risks

118. You are a certified PMP® and you are the project manager for a huge project. This project has never been done in the past; therefore the project management processes will be very important. Among your professional responsibilities is applying the correct processes. You should make sure that the following items are part of the project, with the EXCEPTION of:
    A.   Project management plan
    B.   Project charter
    C.   Work breakdown structure
    D.   Situational leadership style

119. A structured and independent revision to determine if the project activities comply with project and organizational policies, processes, and procedures is called:
    A.   Quality audit
    B.   Comparative studies
    C.   Process analysis
    D.   Cost of quality

120. In a project, the transmitter sends a message to the receiver. However, the message is interpreted wrong. Who is responsible for this problem?
    A.   The transmitter
    B.   The receiver
    C.   Noise
    D.   The transmitter and the receiver

121. What are procurement documents and source selection criteria?
    A.   Tools for the Plan Procurements process
    B.   Outputs of the Conduct Procurements process
    C.   Outputs of the Plan Procurements process
    D.   Tools of the Administer Procurements process

122. You are the project manager and along with your team are almost finishing the activities. The project will finish ahead of schedule, so you will receive a $50,000 bonus for exceeding the objectives. Every agreement in the contract has been completed perfectly, but you discover that the deliverable could cause environmental damages within a few years. To solve this problem you have to make some modifications to the product, causing the project to be delayed and you not getting the bonus. What is the best thing to do?
   A. Fulfill the contract by delivering the product and get the bonus. In the future, fix the products to avoid environmental damages.
   B. Explain the situation to the client to look for solution alternatives
   C. Not delivering the product until the repairs have finalized, despite project delays
   D. Finish the project according to the contract and later inform the client about the possible contingency

123. The MAIN key for the success of a project is when:
   A. The sponsor creates the project charter
   B. There is a good connection between the business strategy and the project deliverables
   C. The project manager is a good leader
   D. The project manager has a high level of formal authority

124. When planning the appropriate technology for the communications of a project for the government's reform, the LEAST important thing to consider should be:
   A. Actual availability of the technology
   B. Revision meetings
   C. Personnel competencies
   D. Working environment

125. A $200 million project, whose deadline is in two years, is in its execution. Who would have the authority to accept or reject a requested change?
   A. The project manager
   B. The stakeholders
   C. The sponsor
   D. The change control committee

126. Along with your work team, you have finalized the WBS and you estimate a schedule of 8 months with an estimated cost of $150,000. The sponsor does not agree with that estimate and requests you to cut the budget by 10%. What is the BEST thing to do?
   A. Follow his suggestion and cut the budget, but explain the associated risks of that action
   B. Evaluate alternatives of fast tracking and/or compression
   C. Do not accept the budget cut that the sponsor is requesting
   D. Evaluate alternatives of scope reduction and/or re-estimate costs

127. In a big project with 120 workers, 25 direct contract companies, and 12 sub-contracted companies, it is very important to plan the work authorization system. What is the main advantage of this system?
    A.   Inform the roles and responsibilities for each stakeholder
    B.   Ensure that the work is performed in the right sequence
    C.   Inform what work will be done and who will do each task
    D.   Ensure compliance with quality metrics in each project phase

128. You have been working as the project manager in an energy company for the last 25 years. A project manager with a competitor sends you an email asking for help with a problem in his new project. You know this person from the international project management congress and you know that he is very honest and professional. What is the BEST thing to do in this case?
    A.   Lend him your project management books, which you know will help him with his problem
    B.   Do not collaborate with this person to avoid conflicts of interests with your company
    C.   Collaborate with him during off-hours, this way you will fulfill your professional role of developing the project management profession
    D.   Ask your superiors before contacting him

129. A company works under a weak matrix structure. The project manager is not getting full commitment to the project from the team members. What would be the best type of authority to improve this problem?
    A.   Referent
    B.   Expert
    C.   Penalty
    D.   Directive

130. You need to organize the project activities to develop the schedule. Which of the following statements is the MOST IMPORTANT to be able to do this?
    A.   Critical path
    B.   Network diagrams
    C.   Gantt chart
    D.   Work breakdown structure

131. Which of the following items is NOT a component of the risk management plan?
    A.   Assumption analysis
    B.   Methodologies
    C.   Periodicity
    D.   Tolerances

132. You are working as the program manager for the paving of 50 roads in a region. The project is in its execution and it is delayed by 30 days in relation to the plan. The main reason for the delay is the weather factors, which are beyond the program manager's reach. Unfortunately, snow storms in the mountains are taking longer than usual and the tasks in the mountain roads are on hold. Therefore, you re-plan the order of the roads to pave and start working with those roads that were not planned until 60 days from now. This is an example of:
A. External dependencies
B. Hard logic
C. Delay
D. Discretionary dependencies

133. You are the project manager for the startup of a plastic bottles factory. In general, what would be the leadership style that you should apply during the initial phases of this project?
A. Directive
B. Consultative
C. Participative
D. Autocratic

134. Based on the next figure, choose the CORRECT answer:

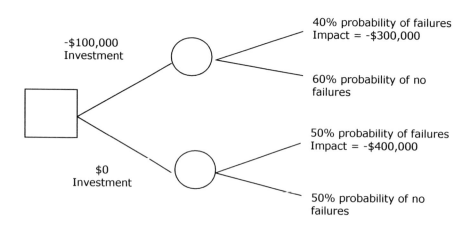

A. It is preferable not to invest because the expected monetary value is - $200,000
B. It is preferable to invest because the expected monetary value is - $220,000
C. It is preferable not to invest because the expected monetary value is - $400,000
D. It is preferable to invest because the expected monetary value is - $100,000

135. Mary works for INT Company, but has been temporarily assigned to EXT Company outside of her country. She has been assigned as the project manager for a great acquisitions and mergers project. The INT Company does not allow its employees to accept gifts from clients. However, in EXT Company's country gifts are allowed under company policies and are covered by that country's laws. In addition, it is part of the local culture to give presents for good performance. For her excellent job during the acquisitions and mergers project, they offer Mary a gift. What should Mary do?
   A. Accept the gift because it is permitted in EXT Company and it is part of the local culture in that country
   B. Not accept the gift because it is not permitted by INT Company
   C. Accept the gift because it does not have a high monetary value
   D. Not accept the gift because it could be considered bribery

136. In a balanced matrix organization, the project manager tells the human resource manager that the employees are convinced that their effort will get them an effective performance, thus being well rewarded. Which theory affirms this reasoning?
   A. X-Y
   B. Z
   C. The pyramid of needs
   D. Expectancy

137. Which of the following statements is NOT a result of the risk response plan?
   A. Risks grouped by categories
   B. Residual risks
   C. Secondary risks
   D. Symptoms and risk triggers

138. A project has a budget at completion (BAC) of $33 millions. Up to date, the project is 30% advanced, the cost performance index is 0.80, and the schedule performance index is 0.75. To mitigate these problems the sponsor requests the project manager to improve the risk response plan and to work in conjunction with the people in charge of implementing the strategies coming out of those response plans. Who are these people that execute the risk response plans?
   A. The project manager and his work team
   B. People who love risks
   C. Stakeholders
   D. Risk owners

139. The general manager of your software development company wants you to send him the progress report every month. What type of diagram should you send him?
   A. Detailed Gantt
   B. Milestones
   C. Network
   D. Histogram

140. A project indicates a cost performance index of 0.6. What can we say about this project?
   A.   We could accelerate the project if we make a compression
   B.   The project has budget problems
   C.   We could accelerate the project with fast tracking
   D.   The project has schedule risks

141. The project manager's main role is to integrate all project parts as a cohesive whole and to communicate. If the estimate to work is 1,500 hours in an aerospace project in a projectized organization, how many hours approximately will the project manager dedicate to stakeholder communications?
   A.   750
   B.   150
   C.   1,350
   D.   1,500

142. Based on the data from the previous question, how many hours approximately will the project manager dedicate to non-verbal communication, such as kinesis and paralinguistic?
   A.   500
   B.   750
   C.   250
   D.   1,400

143. You are the project manager for a tunnel drilling. You are in your weekly project management meeting with your work team. What is the MOST important thing to consider in that meeting?
   A.   Stakeholder expectations
   B.   The project's performance indexes
   C.   Risk identification
   D.   Team member's motivational level

144. Who is responsible for the quality in a mass production project?
   A.   The quality assurance manager
   B.   The quality control manager
   C.   The project manager
   D.   The project team

145. Based on the data in the following table, what is the expected monetary value?

Scenario	Probability	Impact
A	0.4	2,200
B	0.3	4,300
C	0.2	-2,500
D	0.1	-1,500

   A.   880
   B.   1,520
   C.   2,170
   D.   2,500

146. A project manager in a strong matrix structure is having great difficulty getting full cooperation from its team members. Why could this be happening? Because the team members _____
    A. Are not receiving a 360° feedback
    B. Do not have the capabilities to work in that project
    C. Did not participate in the creation of the work breakdown structure
    D. Do not acknowledge the limited authority of the project manager

147. The project manager is performing the risk monitoring and control during the executing phase of the project. Which of the following tools is the LEAST probable to use to perform these activities?
    A. Audits
    B. Earned value analysis
    C. Sensitivity analysis
    D. Reserve analysis

148. A project is 67% advanced. Last week, the project had to be stopped because the main contractor was suspended for violating a quality clause established in the contract. Recently, another vendor has been contracted to continue with the project activities. What is the most important thing that you should communicate to the new vendor in the initial meeting?
    A. Clarify the objectives of the project
    B. Define the authority levels
    C. Introduce the project team members
    D. Hand over the work breakdown structure dictionary

149. The S curve is a graphic used for:
    A. Justify project costs
    B. Report performance
    C. Level the financing limits
    D. Analyze the cost dispersion and correlation

150. You have been assigned as the project manager for a mutual guarantee society with the means to finance a productive cluster in your country. You are working in a strong matrix organization. One of your project team members has been giving you trouble since the beginning. He is not only wearing out your patience, but also has problems with the rest of the team members. This person wants to sabotage the project because it is not feeling comfortable with neither the project and peers. What should you do?
    A. Call up a meeting with all the team members to vote about the disciplinary actions to take with this person
    B. Suspend that team member until the project is finalized
    C. Inform upper management about the situation so they can solve the problem
    D. Request upper management to re-assign the team member to another project where it could feel more comfortable

151. You are in the process of verifying the scope of a deliverable with the client. What is the most important thing you should make sure of?
    A. The precision of the deliverable
    B. Meet the deadlines and not exceed the budget
    C. The client's formal acceptance
    D. Have the work breakdown structure dictionary on hand

152. Based on the data in the following table, select the budget at completion (BAC):

Activity	Progress	AC	EV
A	80%	500	500
B	75%	402	450
C	90%	600	900

A.   1,502
B.   1,850
C.   1,827.67
D.   2,225

153. Management wants to analyze how the project is evolving in relation to other similar projects done in the past. To make a valid judgment, management should compare the projects using the following tool:
A.   Flowchart
B.   Trend diagram
C.   Histogram
D.   Benchmarking

154. You are the project manager for a project with a cost performance index of 1.2 and a schedule performance index of 1.1. The project team has 5 members. The client has formally accepted 10 deliverables without any complaints. The roles and responsibilities matrix has not been changed since the beginning of the project. The project is being developed in a strong matrix organization. Although the client is very happy with the project, two team members are constantly complaining about the amount of effort that they are putting daily into the project activities. What is the BEST thing to do by the project manager?
A.   Improve the project's rewards system
B.   Try to improve the project schedule's performance
C.   Negotiate with the client an extension to the project schedule
D.   Use his formal power to put an end to the employees' complaints

155. A big and complex project for port expansion will be done in a foreign country. This requires some coordination to move equipment through the streets of that country. To ensure that the equipment is moved satisfactorily, your contact in that country informs you that you will have to pay the police to coordinate the traffic. What should you do?
A.   Not pay the police, because it is considered bribery
B.   Pay the police
C.   Don´t do the project
D.   Change the scope of the project

156. One of the project team members has requested more time to finish an activity. You, as the project manager, discovered that a delay in that activity will cause a delay in one of the paths with slack. The client will impose a penalty if the project misses the deadline. What is the BEST you can do?
A.   Send the information to the change control committee
B.   Implement the change because it will not change the project deadlines
C.   Implement the change because it will not change the project costs
D.   Wait for the response from the rest of the stakeholders to see if there is an objection to the change

157. The client requests to the project manager a substantial change to the technology that will be used in the project. The request is to replace the coaxial cable to fiber optics. What is the most important impact that the project manager should consider?
    A. Project's communications plan
    B. Project constraint components
    C. Sponsor opinion
    D. Activities' duration

158. Becky privately informs you that George, a customer support employee, is trying to boycott the project. Becky has repeatedly requested George to stop that type of behavior, but the problem persists. What is the best course of action in your role as the project manager?
    A. Meet in private with George and threaten him with legal actions if he does not change his behavior
    B. Facilitate a meeting between Becky and George so they both can work in a friendlier way
    C. Suggest to Becky to avoid contact with George
    D. Contact the functional manager in charge of George to setup a meeting to discuss this inconvenient

159. Your company is involved in a new project for the manufacturing of food for domestic animals, very similar to the one done last year. In order to define this project's activities, what is the first thing that should be considered?
    A. Establish a project team with the same abilities defined in last year's project
    B. Perform a brainstorming session with the project team members
    C. Organizational process assets
    D. Hire an external expert to avoid the same mistakes of other similar projects

160. A complex project to detect the potential demand of a new product is being developed in multiple countries simultaneously, with stakeholders physically located within the different countries. The work packages from the work breakdown structure need to be integrated with those defined and created by the client. What is the BEST thing to use by the project manager to control this situation?
    A. Change control committee
    B. Work authorization system
    C. Assumptions
    D. Historical information

161. A financial consulting employee has been doing illegal activities inside the company for the past couple of years. He is feeling guilty, so he tells you what happened to seek your advice. What should you do?
    A. Ask him about all the details of the illegal acts committed
    B. Confirm through other sources that the acts are truly illegal
    C. Recommend him to not say anything until someone verifies that they were illegal acts
    D. Inform management about the acts committed

162. The following stakeholders are part of a project in a balanced matrix organization. Which one of them do you think can influence the LEAST in the definition of project activities and deliverables?
A.   The project work team
B.   The functional manager
C.   The product's final user
D.   The project manager

163. A project manager is investigating the cause of some activities not being done when they were supposed to. The PM is based on a report delivered by his project team, which contained project tendencies. What could be the indicator that the project manager is using to investigate this situation?
A.   The cost performance index is 0.80
B.   The budget at completion will be 25% higher to what was originally planned
C.   The schedule performance index is 0.95
D.   The schedule variance of activity A is $5,000

164. The project scope verification finalizes when _____
A.   The project finishes
B.   The project starts
C.   Each project phase finishes
D.   The planning process finishes

165. You must finish the project 3 weeks ahead of schedule. Which one of the following options do you think is the best alternative?

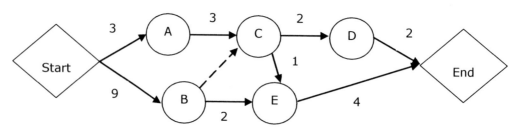

A.   Eliminate part of activity D-End to save $5,000 and shorten duration by 3 weeks
B.   Move work from activity A-C to activity B-E to save $2,000 and shorten duration of activity A-C by 3 weeks
C.   Assign a more experienced person to activity Start-B for an additional $7,000 in order to finish that activity in 6 weeks
D.   Intensify activities C-D and D-End, spending an additional $2,000, to shorten that path's duration by 3 weeks

166. You and your team have decided to do a compression of the project. What is the most probable thing that will happen in this project?
A.   The project will finish later than forecasted
B.   The costs will increase
C.   Activities will be done in parallel to shorten project duration
D.   The risk of finishing the project on time will increase

167. You are doing the monitoring and control for a livestock farm project. What will be the process LEAST used?
   A. Verify scope
   B. Manage stakeholders
   C. Report performance
   D. Control scope

168. You are doing a quantitative risk analysis using the Monte Carlo simulation as a complement of a project management software package. What results you will NOT get with this tool?
   A. Project risks caused by the incomplete nature of assumptions
   B. The probability of finishing the project before a determined date
   C. The probability of finishing the project after certain amount of days
   D. The most probable duration to finish the project

169. In relation to the project management process groups, select the CORRECT answer:
   A. In the planning process group is where the project is defined and authorized
   B. The processes described in the PMBOK® Guide must always be applied uniformly in every project
   C. The application of the project management processes to a project is done only once, without having to repeat or revise them
   D. The process groups are not project phases

170. What does the standard deviation tell us?
   A. The risk of the estimation
   B. The confidence level of the sample
   C. Whether the estimation is precise or not
   D. If contingency reserves were included in the estimation

171. In a project for the elaboration of bio-gas based on hen stools, the team is planning how many warehouses it should build and how the project will be integrated with the food production. What will be the LEAST used process?
   A. Create WBS
   B. Develop project team
   C. Perform quantitative risk analysis
   D. Collect requirements

172. In a complex project the variable "quality" has been defined as the most important project restriction. This project has never been done before anywhere. What is the BEST thing to do in your role as the project manager?
   A. Audit work as it is being completed to identify continuous improvement actions
   B. Improve the configuration management system
   C. Update periodically the human resources management plan
   D. Use flowcharts to detect the root cause of the problems

173.   You are almost done with your project's initiating processes. The two main results that you will obtain from this process are:
A.   Project charter and stakeholder register
B.   Project charter and scope statement
C.   Project charter and work breakdown structure
D.   Scope statement and work breakdown structure

174.   We have re-planned the project schedule so that we could use the same amount of resources every month. This is an example of _____
A.   Leveling
B.   Compression
C.   Slack
D.   Fast tracking

175.   You want to make sure that the project activities are done in their assigned time and with the correct sequence. What is the main tool that you should use?
A.   Earned value management
B.   Work authorization system
C.   Project management software
D.   Change control system

176.   One of the team members is working on 5 projects. He informs the project manager that she is not clear about which project should she assign the most importance. Who is responsible of prioritizing projects in the company?
A.   The project manager
B.   The project management office
C.   The project team
D.   The client

177.   One of the team members informs you that they made a mistake in one of the activities, so it will be impossible meeting the deadline of the next milestone. What is the BEST thing you could do as the project manager?
A.   Change the date of the milestone as soon as possible
B.   Apply the punishment system with those involved in the mistake
C.   Meet with your team to teach them not to make more mistakes
D.   Develop alternatives to meet the deadline of the milestone

178.   A process to control the factors that produce changes has been implemented in order to ensure that those changes are beneficial and to manage the approved changes. The following statements are inputs to this process, EXCEPT for:
A.   Change requests
B.   Work performance information
C.   Recommended defect repairs
D.   Approved corrective actions

179. Based on the projects in the following table, which one would you choose as the BEST?

Project	Net Present Value	Duration (Years)
1	50,000	8
2	20,000	4
3	30,000	2
4	25,000	1

A. Project 1
B. Project 2
C. Project 3
D. Project 4

180. The project "Sadface" that has been assigned to you does not look like any other project that has ever been worked on the company. The resources used in this project are in high demand by other company projects. The project deadline defined by the sponsor is very demanding. For the purpose of meeting the schedule and the costs, there were some deliverables that were sent to the client without doing quality inspections. After the complaints by the client for some defective products, there was some re-work done with high costs associated. Why did these problems happen?
A. Poor quality management
B. Poor performance reports
C. Poor risk identification
D. Poor human resources management

181. In a company, they have defined four main categories for costs: labor, supplies, materials, and equipment. The enumeration system used to monitor project costs by category is called:
A. Quality management plan
B. Cost management plan
C. Procurements management plan
D. Accounts plan

182. One of the tools when requesting vendor responses is the bidder conference. These conferences could have a detrimental effect to the project if the project manager does not ensure that _____
A. Each bidder receive answers just to their questions
B. The meetings are with each vendor separately, in order to keep information confidential
C. Every question and answers are put in writing and sent to all the bidders
D. All bidders are genuinely interested in the bid

183. The following tools are part of the quality control process, with the EXCEPTION of:
A. Quality audits
B. Flowcharts
C. Statistical sampling
D. Inspection

184. While the project is being planned, three colleagues of the project manager consult him about the new project management methodology being implemented in the organization. They do not agree with the methodology because it differs from the traditional way they have always managed their projects. What should the project manager do?
   A. Inform their colleagues that he will maintain fluid communication with them about the project
   B. Notify the project management office
   C. Make sure your friends understand that you are the authority in this project
   D. Explain them that this is the only way to do this project

185. You are the project manager for the manufacturing of innovative chemicals for the efficient extraction of oil. You have been hired by the company "Petrol" to manage this project. When the project is 80% advanced, the company "Gas", direct competitor of "Petrol", requests your professional services to manufacture similar products to the ones being done by "Petrol". What should you do?
   A. Not do the project with "Gas" due to the conflict of interests
   B. Do the project for "Gas" using the same resources being used at "Petrol"
   C. Review the intellectual property clause for the "Gas" project before making a decision
   D. Do the project for "Gas" using new resources

186. The process of reporting project performance implies to collect data from the baseline and distribute the stakeholders' performance information. When finishing this process, you will obtain the following results, EXCEPT for:
   A. The actual state of risks
   B. Change requests
   C. Approved changes
   D. The project's forecast (including time and cost)

187. In a status meeting for a forestation project, various topics are being brought up at the same time. In addition, some key team members are not participating in the meeting. What should have the project manager done to have an effective meeting?
   A. Control who has authorization to speak
   B. Schedule the meeting with more lead time
   C. Publish an agenda and a group of rules to control the meeting
   D. Make sure that the right people attend the meeting

188. You have just started managing a contract when the general management decides to rescind it. What is the first thing you should do?
   A. Close procurements
   B. Requests responses from contractors
   C. Improve the procurement plan
   D. The project's administrative closure

189. You are the program manager for a city's productive development. You have been managing this program for the past two months. Suddenly, a project manager makes an important discovery that could improve the way things are done for the rest of the projects. What is the first thing you should do?
    A.   Ensure the discovery is included in the program's lessons learned
    B.   Ensure the discovery is shown in the monthly progress report
    C.   Ensure you inform the discovery to the rest of the project managers in next week's meeting
    D.   Ensure you mention the discovery in the quarterly meeting with the sponsors

190. You are expecting 30 people to attend the next project status meeting to analyze the project's performance. Select the CORRECT answer:
    A.   There are 435 communication channels
    B.   The amount of participants of the meeting is reasonable for an effective meeting
    C.   There are 450 communication channels
    D.   There are few people in the meeting to make effective decisions

191. You are convinced that the project team members' efforts will drive effective performance and as a result, they will be rewarded. What human resources management theory would you be endorsing?
    A.   Expectancy Theory
    B.   Ouchi's Theory Z
    C.   Locke's Theory
    D.   McGregor's X-Y Theory

192. Your company has won a bid for the construction of a concrete lining work for an irrigation canal, whose value is $1,200,000. You are the project manager in another similar project being executed in your company. What is the first thing you should do?
    A.   Request information to management about how the resources will be used in the new project
    B.   Do resource leveling in your project
    C.   Request information to management about how the new project will impact your project
    D.   Compression of your project

193. You have finished the work breakdown structure (WBS) of the project for the startup of a recycling plant. The WBS will be useful for the following statements. Which of these statements tends to be the one who requires the LEAST support from the WBS?
    A.   Estimate costs
    B.   Plan human resources
    C.   Plan procurements
    D.   Develop schedule

194. You and your team are working at the processes group that is consuming most of the time and resources. Which processes group is this?
    A.   Executing
    B.   Planning
    C.   Closing
    D.   Monitoring and Controlling

195. You are the project manager for the children entertainment center "Happy Kid". The project has 50 video game machines and you are thinking of adding 30 more. The building where the children gathering will take place is under construction. You are finalizing the early finish date, late finish date, early start date, and late start date calculations for the project activities, without taking into consideration the resources restrictions. You have just obtained the estimated duration for each project activity. Select the FALSE statement:
    A.   You have used the critical path method
    B.   You have created the project schedule, but have not yet assign the resources
    C.   Your next step could be the schedule compression and the resource leveling in a heuristic form
    D.   You are working with the precedence diagramming method

196. The work breakdown structure tends to be used for what type of communications?
    A.   Internal with the project team
    B.   External with the client
    C.   Internal and external
    D.   Oral

197. You are the project manager for a project that involves a multi-disciplinary team with people from different nationalities. When you arrive to the weekly status meeting, you realize that a group of people is laughing at the clothes of a team member that have just being added to the project coming from a foreign country. What is the BEST you can do?
    A.   Since the company does not have a dress code, there is nothing you can do
    B.   Inform management about this incident
    C.   Start the meeting with a brief introduction to respecting different religions, fashions, and personal integrity
    D.   Continue with the meeting as if nothing happened

198. You need to shorten your project's duration. Based on the data in the following table, which activities would you select for fast tracking?

Activity	Slack
A	3
B	4
C	6
D	0
E	5
F	0

A. C, E
B. A, B
C. D, F
D. A, B, C, E

199. You are the project manager for the food provisioning of a school dinner. The project team members are afraid of you because they think of you as if you were the president of the company. The team members know that if you get a bad impression from them, their salary bonus at the end of the year will be impacted. This is an example of what kind of power?
A. Coercive
B. Formal
C. Referent
D. Expert

200. Michael is the project manager for the installation of an administrative office in the city center. He wants a provider to offer him a price for all the work he has just detailed. What type of document is Michael looking for?
A. Request for bidding
B. Request for proposal
C. Request for information
D. Invitation to negotiations

CHAPTER # 15

EXECUTIVE SUMMARY

Chapter 15 –SUMMARY AND TIPS

> *Success is not for geniuses, but for the ones who persevere.*
> Paul Leido, Project Manager from UK (1971 -)

Congratulations for reaching the end of this book without dying in the attempt. Now you only need the final step, deepen you studies and take the exam to obtain your PMP® certification.

When you finish this chapter, you should have learned the following concepts:

- ✓ Which topics I must study
- ✓ Some tips to take the exam

Book summary

The following is a summary of the most important topics in this book that you should dominate to perfection on the day of the exam. If you only learn these topics, you will not pass the exam. It is important to complement this book with the PMBOK® Guide and with more simulation questions.

Organizational Systems

Assume that you work in a matrix organization: strong, balanced or weak.

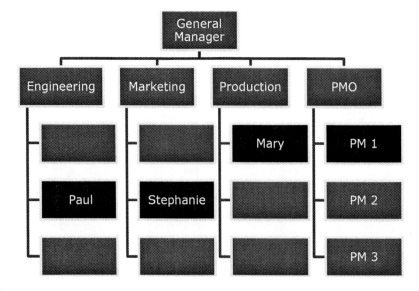

Processes *

	Initiating	Planning	Executing	Controlling	Closing
Integration	. Project Charter	. Project Management Plan	. Manage Project	. Control project work . Change Control	. Close Project
Scope		. Collect requirements . Define Scope . Create WBS		. Verify Scope . Control Scope	
Time		. Define Activities . Sequence Activities . Estimate Resources . Estimate Durations . Develop Schedule		. Control Schedule	
Cost		. Estimate Costs . Determine Budget		. Control Costs	
Quality		. Plan Quality	. Perform Quality Assurance	. Control Quality	
Human Resources		. Develop Human Resource Plan	. Acquire Project Team . Develop Project Team . Manage Project Team		
Communic.	. Identify Stakeholders	. Plan Communications	. Distribute Information . Manage stakeholder	. Report Performance	
Risks		. Plan Risk manag. . Identify Risks . Qualitative Risk Analysis . Quantitative Risk Analysis . Plan Risk Responses		. Control Risks	
Procure.		. Plan Procurements	. Conduct Procurements	. Administer Procurements	. Close Procurements
TOTAL	2	20	8	10	2

* Project Management Institute, Ibidem.

Initiating

Project: temporary effort to create a unique product.

Project selection criteria:

- Benefit measurements: NPV, IRR, Payback
- Mathematical models: linear, integer, and dynamic programming

Project charter: formal authorization to start the project. It designates the PM and its level of authority.

Identify the stakeholders and their expectations.

Scope

Scope statement: the base for every project decision.

Include <u>only</u> the work needed to complete the project.

Project scope: include all the processes necessary for a successful project.

Verify scope: at the end of each phase, confirm that the project meets the requirements. This takes it to the deliverable's formal acceptance.

WBS: the base to estimate activities, resources, schedule, costs and risks.

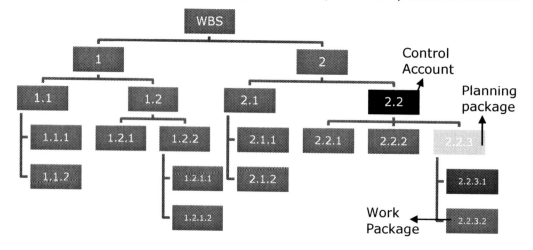

Schedule

Critical path: made of critical activities that form the longest path and determine the project duration.

Total slack: the amount of time an activity can be delayed without changing the project duration.

Free slack: the amount of time an activity can be delayed without causing slippage (delay) to the early start date of any of its successors.

Project slack: the amount of time the project can be delayed without delaying the published finish date imposed by the client. It can be negative.

Slack = LS – ES ; *Slack* = LF – EF

PERT

Standard Deviation = σ = (Worst – Best) / 6

Variance = σ^2

Estimated duration = (Best + 4 x Most Probable + Worst) / 6

Normal Standard Distribution

+/-   1σ = 68.26%
+/-   2σ = 95.46%
+/-   3σ = 99.73%
+/-   4σ = 99.99%

Cost

Analogous estimating

- Use estimates from previous projects
- Cheaper and less exact

Parametric estimating

- Cost = function (X1 , X2, ..., Xn)
- Examples: cost per hour, cost per meter

Bottom-up estimating

- Estimate each work package's cost and add them up
- More expensive, but the most exact

Earned Value

EV = Progress % x BAC

CV = EV – AC

SV = EV – PV

CPI = EV / AC

SPI = EV / PV

EAC = BAC / CPI

ETC = EAC – AC

VAC = BAC – EAC

Quality

Cost of Quality (COQ)

1. *Conformance costs*

    a. Prevent non-compliance
       ✓ Policies, <u>Processes</u>, Maintenance, Training

    b. Evaluate product's conformance
       ✓ Supervision, Surveillance, Control, Inspection

2. *Nonconformance costs or "Deficient quality"*

    a. Internal failures: repair defects before they occur
       ✓ Re-work, Repairs, ↑ Inventory, ↓ Productivity

    b. External failures: repair defects "after the fact"
       ✓ Fines, Warranties, Devolutions, Discounts, ↓ Sales

Quality control tools
1. Cause and effect diagram (Ishikawa, Fishbone)
2. Control chart - are there any variations?
3. Flowchart – what is done
4. Histogram – graphical look of the variations
5. Pareto chart – 80% problems / 20% causes
6. Run chart - historical
7. Scatter diagram – relation between variables
8. Statistical sampling

Kaizen technologies: small continuous improvements

Human Resources

Responsibility Assignment Matrix (RAM): output from the human resources plan.

Types of power: the expert power is the best.

Develop the team: forming, storming, norming, performing, and adjourning.

Maslow's Hierarchy of Needs: 1st physiological, 2nd security, 3rd social, 4th esteem, 5th self-esteem.

Mc Gregor's X and Y Theory
   ▪ Person X ☹: lazy, needs orders
   ▪ Person Y ☺: works without nobody asking

Mc Clelland's Needs Theory: each person needs to be motivated based on their need (achievement, affiliation, power).

Expectancy Theory: people work in relation to the rewards they receive.

pablolledó
projectManagement

Locke's Goal Setting Theory: reaching goals is the basic source of motivation.

Herzberg's Motivational Theory: agents do not motivate people, but are necessary (e.g.: job security, salary). The motivational agents are: responsibility, recognition, and education.

Ouchi's Theory Z: people are motivated by trust, close relationships, and personalized treatment.

Conflicts: well managed conflicts are positive for the project.

Communications

It is the PM's most important ability.

 # Channels = [n x (n-1)] / 2

Effective communication: observe corporal language (kinesis) and interpret the tones of the voice (paralinguistic).

Effective listening: ask questions to clarify concepts

Barriers, blockers, or noises in communication: negative phrases, hostility, cultural differences, distance.

Risks

Risk: could have negative or positive impacts.

Delphi: risk identification in an anonymous way

Risk types:

- Organizational, external, technical, etc.
- Business: loss of time and money
- Pure: theft, injuries, death

Risk response strategies:

- Avoid (Exploit) ⇒ change the scope
- Transfer (Share) ⇒ e.g.: insurance (joint venture)
- Mitigate (Improve) ⇒ change probability and/or impact
- Accept ⇒ active or passive

Procurements

Input: Statement of work (SOW)

Output:

- Invitation for Bidding (IFB),
- Request for Quotation (RFQ),
- Request for Proposal (RFP)

Bidder conferences: answer vendor's questions

Types of contracts:

- *Cost-reimbursement*: ↑ cost risk for the buyer
- *Fixed-price or Lump-sum*: ↑ cost risk for the seller
- *Time and materials*: combination of the other two
- *Purchase order*: unilateral contract

Code of professional conduct

1st Project's interests, 2nd individual interests

Maintain confidentiality about exam questions

Avoid and manage conflicts of interests

Report violations to the code of conduct

Continuous improvement: develop personal capabilities

Do the right thing and follow the correct <u>processes</u>

Tips to take the PMP® Exam

Recommendations for the exam

- ✓ Study thinking about big projects.
- ✓ Answer based on the PMBOK® Guide, not your experience.
- ✓ READ ALL THE OPTIONS before answering.
- ✓ Quickly eliminate the wrong answers.

The 6 tips - by Paul Leido

☹ Practice with simulation questions without rest during 4 hours.

☺ Plan the way to answer the test, then practice based on that plan. For example, 3 minute breaks after every 50 questions.

☹ Do not get frustrated with the impossible questions, select any option. Do not leave any question without choosing an answer. In addition, you can mark that question for revision, then you review it again before finishing the exam.

☺ If you study well, you will only have doubts about 20% of the questions. You can comeback at the end of the exam to review only those questions, since you will be more relaxed because you marked the other 80% without any doubt.

☹ Do not study anything else the night before the exam. You need to rest well in order to perform well during 4 hours. Your brain needs to process everything that has been learned and adding more concepts the night before could be detrimental.

☺ If you do not get a score of 80% in the simulation questions, do not worry. Remember that the second time you take the test will be cheaper.

☝ If you want to pass the PMP® Exam you will have to dominate the PMBOK® Guide processes, with their inputs, tools, and outputs.

The day of the exam

- ✓ Bring the authorization letter from PMI®.
- ✓ Bring 2 personal identifications (e.g.: driver's license and passport).
- ✓ Bring a simple calculator. Calculators that store information are prohibited. They will give you a pencil and paper.
- ✓ During the first minutes, write on the paper all the formulas that you have fresh on your mind.

If you take the exam on a PC

1st – You will have a 15 minute tutorial

2nd – You will have many instances to press finish

3rd – They will give you a printed report with your score

4th – YOU WILL BECOME A PMP® (Do not think otherwise)

5th – Send me an email to let me know we are colleagues: pmp@pablolledo.com.

6th - If we later cross paths in an airport, I invite you a drink.

How to interpret the results on the simulation exams

0-50%	**Study a lot**
50-70%	**Study**
70-80%	**Ready to take the exam**
80-100%	**Take the exam urgently!**

> ✎ *If your scores are above 60%, you should already be scheduling the exam. If you wait until being fully prepared, you will never schedule it because you will never feel you are ready.*

How to study?

> ✎ *The drop does not break the stone by its force, but its perseverance. (Ovidio)*

Frequently Asked Questions

1. What should I do to become a PMI® member?

Go to www.pmi.org and select "Individual Membership" where you will find all the information.

Any person that accepts the PMI® code of ethics and pays its membership can become a PMI® member. You do not need any type of experience or studies.

2. Where can I take the PMP® Exam?

Generally, you can take the exam in any institute that has the Prometric system for international exams (e.g.: TOEFL, GMAT, etc.). To locate an authorized center go to www.prometric.com/pmi.

3. How much is to take the PMP® Exam?

Exam type	Status with PMI	USD
Computer (CBT)	Member	$ 405
Computer (CBT)	Not member	$ 555
Reexamination CBT	Member	$ 275
Reexamination CBT	Not member	$ 375
Credential renewal every 3 years	Member	$ 60
Credential renewal every 3 years	Not member	$ 150

☞ *Prices @ 2011*

4. How do I certify the work experience hours in order to take the exam?

On the "Experience Verification Form", you must complete the information about your work experience. If you have a college degree, you must demonstrate 4,500 hours of work experience. If you do not have a college degree, you must demonstrate 7,500 hours of work experience.

This form is an affidavit and PMI® reserves the right of requesting records or references that corroborate what has been declared. The experience must be in the project phases: Initiating, Planning, Executing, Monitoring and Controlling, and Closing.

You can download from www.pablolledo.com (products) a free template that you can use as a guide to fill out the "Experience Verification Form".

5. What is the average time between sending an application and the approval to take the exam?

The candidates that send their applications on-line will receive the approval/rejection notification via email within 5 days.

6. How long it takes to receive the PMP® certificate once the exam has been passed?

If you take the exam on a PC, you will know your score on the same day and you will get a printed receipt. Whoever passes the exam will get the official certificate via postal mail in 6 to 8 weeks from the date of the exam.

7. How long does my certification last?

The PMP® certification lasts for 3 years. However, the certification could last a lifetime if every 3 years you earn and report 60 PDUs (Project Development Units). PDUs can be earned by attending PMI® events, performing voluntary work for PMI®, education, and many other alternatives for the profession's development and continuous improvement.

How do good project managers manage their projects?

In the following table, we present a summary of some characteristics of traditional project management, in comparison with the correct way of managing successful projects.

Area	Traditional management	To become a good PMP®
Integration	Improvisation	Strategies and processes
Scope	Omission of activities	Effective distribution
Schedule	Missed due-dates	Predictable due-dates
Cost	Out of budget	Efficiency and controls
Quality	Poor	Deliver what was requested
Human resources	Individualist / Authoritarian	Committed teams
Communication	Informal	Effective
Risks	High impact	Prevention
Procurements	Non-compliance	Win-win contracts
Integration	High wear and tear	Quality of life

CHAPTER # 16

**EXAM
ANSWERS**

Chapter 16 – EXAM ANSWERS

Answers to Exam 1 – Diagnostic

Quest. #	Correct	Explanation
1	D	A, B, and C are true. Generally, in the PMP® Exam there are no items that mention "all of the above" or "none of the above". But it works for study purposes.
2	B	A, C, and D are true. B is not on the PMBOK® Guide.
3	C	"Collaborate" is false due to being a lose-lose solution. The worst answer would have been "force" or "withdraw". The correct answer is "Confront" because it is equivalent to conflict resolution and that is the best alternative to look for a win-win solution.
4	D	A, B, and C are true, but D is the most important.
5	A	The output of risk quantification is the risk register update. B is false. C is an output of risk identification. D will be done based on the updated risk register.
6	B	A, C, and D are false.
7	C	A is an output of Planning. B is an input of Initiating. D is an output of Monitoring and Controlling. C is true because is an output of Initiating.
8	A	B, C, and D are true, but A is first.
9	C	If the projects are mutually exclusive and cannot be repeated, the project with the greatest NPV should be selected, regardless of each project's duration.
10	B	A and D are false. Project North = 35% x -$800 + 65% x $2,400 = $1,280. Project South = 40% x -$1,400 + 60% x $3,000 = $1,240.
11	A	B, C, and D are false.
12	B	A, C, and D are false.
13	C	A and B are false. D could be true, but generally is used to evaluate impact over cost and schedule. C is more correct than D.
14	B	The levels on Maslow's pyramid are: 1st Physiological Needs, 2nd Safety, 3rd Social Needs, 4th Esteem, and 5th Self-actualization. You cannot advance to the next level until the previous level has been satisfied.
15	D	CPI = EV / AC = 800 / 1,200 = 0.67
16	B	B is false. The cost-benefit analysis is done during the planning process group, not on closing.
17	A	A is false. The development of the plan should be done with the input from the main project stakeholders. For example, maybe the sponsor is not part of the work team, but it should participate in the development of the plan.
18	B	A, C, and D are true. But the most important aspect of project closure is B.

19	D	The PM is responsible for the project management plan, whether he created it or not.
20	D	Paths: BGHL = 18, ADFKL = 18, BCEKL = 12, BCDFKL = 21. The critical path is the longest, BCDFKL = 21.
21	B	Base durations: BGHL = 18, ADFKL = 18, BCEKL = 12, BCDFKL = 21. Duration when shortening D by 4 weeks: BGHL = 18, ADFKL = 14, BCEKL = 12, BCDFKL = 17. Duration is reduced from 21 to 18. In other words, it is reduced by 3 weeks.
22	D	Communication channels = (30 x 29)/2 = 435
23	C	A, B, and D are false.
24	A	The negative slack means that the project duration has to be shortened in order to meet the clients' requirements. A is true. B: if we free up resources, duration will surely increase. C: if the resources contracted do not work in the critical activities, duration will not be shortened. D: extend duration will not solve the problem. You could negotiate a deadline extension with the client.
25	C	Share is for positive risks. Transfer and Mitigate is for negative risks. Accept is a strategy for positive and negative risks.
26	D	A refers to planning quality. B is false. C is quality control.
27	A	A is true because is an output of the Develop Schedule process. B and D are inputs of that process. C is an output of the Monitoring and Controlling process.
28	B	A is false because it means that people work without anybody controlling them. B: these are people that need to be controlled to do the tasks. C is false. D refers to Ouchi's Theory Z.
29	A	BAC = 675,000. AC = 300,000. EV = 25% x BAC = 168,750. CPI = EV / AC = 0.5625. EAC = BAC / CPI = 1,200,000.
30	C	SV = EV – PV = 168,750 – 450,000 = - 281,250 PV = 16/24 x 675,000 = 450,000
31	C	A, B, and D are false. The conflict will be solved by the arbitrator specified in the contract.
32	C	A, B, and D are false. For an effective communication you need to know how to listen.
33	D	A, B, and C are tools for the collect requirements process. The requirements traceability matrix is an output of that process.
34	A	A does not require that much expert judgment, in comparison with B, C, and D.
35	D	A is false. B and C could be done after D.
36	D	A, B, and C are false.
37	A	On the initial phases, stakeholders can influence more in order to stop the project or authorize advancing to the next phases.
38	B	A, C, and D are false. Compression consists of adding resources (costs) to shorten the duration of the project.
39	B	A would no longer be applicable. B is the first thing that should be done. C and D are false.
40	A	A: the PM has more power than the functional manager. B: is false, refers to all team members being in the same work place. C: the PM shares the power with the functional manager. D: probably there is no PM with authority and control over the decision making.
41	D	A, B, and C are inputs of this process. D is false because is an output of this process.

42	A	B, C, and D are not the most important factors to take into account.
43	C	A and B are false. C: weighted milestones could be the 50/50 rule, 0/100, or any other weighting. D: report about the percentage completed tends to be too subjective.
44	A	A: is the most correct. B: adding resources not necessarily means shortening the duration. C is false. D: adding resources does not mean better quality.
45	D	A, B, and C are false. The first thing to do is to discuss the conflict of interests with the corresponding party.
46	D	Lessons learned can be used in any process group. However, in a new project they will be more useful during the initiating and planning process groups.
47	B	EV = % real progress x budget = 50% x $68,000 = $34,000
48	C	A, B, and D are false. The sender is responsible for the message arriving on time and in form.
49	C	A, B, and D are false.
50	C	A: requires time because historical information needs to be processed. B: is the most precise, but the slowest. C: is true, is less precise, but fast. D is false.

Answers to Exam 2 – Framework

Quest. #	Correct	Explanation
1	C	The importance of meeting the demand lies in the strategic plan. A and B could also be an option if C was not there. D is false.
2	B	Although identifying the stakeholders during the initial stages is very important, this is repeated during planning, executing, and monitoring and control. D could be considered if B was not there.
3	D	A, B, and C are not appropriate.
4	B	A, C, and D are false.
5	D	A, B, and C are related with matrix structures.
6	D	A, B, and C are false.
7	A	Uncertainty is greater at the beginning, stakeholders have greater power to make changes and the costs associated with those changes are lower.
8	C	A is false. B is done by the project manager and its team. D could be if C was not there.
9	B	A: stakeholders are managed, not controlled. C is false. D is done during planning.
10	A	B: the PM would not have authority to decide. C is false. D could be if A was not there.
11	A	B and C are not appropriate. D is false.
12	D	A, B, and C are true.
13	D	A, B, and C are processes. D is not a process.
14	B	A is false. C could be if B was not there. D is the project definition.
15	C	A could be if C was not there. B is false. D is done after C.

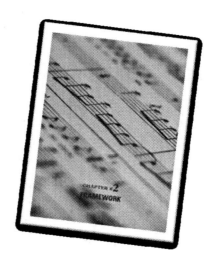

Answers to Exam 3 – Processes

Quest. #	Correct	Explanation
1	A	B and C are false. D is not appropriate.
2	D	A was already done during initiating. B is false: first assumptions, then the risks. C is false: first metrics, then planning.
3	B	A, C, and D: the project team should be VERY involved.
4	C	A, B, and D: inputs to initiating. C is an output of initiating.
5	C	A is not appropriate. B could be if C was not there. D is false: you should not blame people.
6	A	B, C, and D are inputs to the network diagram. A is done afterwards.
7	B	After initiating comes planning. A, C, and D are false.
8	A	A is an input. B, C, and D are outputs of executing.
9	B	After initiating comes planning. A is executing. C and D are monitoring and control.
10	C	C corresponds to executing.
11	B	A, C, and D are false.
12	A	Planning requires much iteration. B and C are false. D is included in A.
13	B	A is false: changes are inevitable, if it said "mitigate" it would be true. C is not appropriate: restrictions could be external to stakeholders. D could be if B was not there.
14	B	A and C are done after B. D is done before the schedule.
15	A	B, C, and D are inputs to Monitoring and Control. A is a process output.

Answers to Exam 4 – Integration

Quest. #	Correct	Explanation
1	D	Both the location and the time and cost limitations are restrictions to the project.
2	A	B: PM's role. C is not appropriate. D: role of the PM and its team.
3	B	Contracts tend to have restrictions on the duration and costs. A, C, and D are not appropriate.
4	B	A Change control: how will project deliverables be controlled, changed, and approved. B Configuration management: how will a product or service's functional and physical characteristics be identified and documented. C Work authorization: procedures to notify the team or contractors when to start the work. D Scope management. DOES NOT APPLY.
5	D	A change in the market affects the strategy, which is more important than other changes.
6	B	A does not exist. B: communication infrastructure is included in the PMIS. C and D are not appropriate.
7	A	The Sponsor is responsible for the project charter.
8	D	A and B are true, but D is the most important. C is false.
9	A	After planning comes executing. A: All are Executing activities. B: Planning, Monitoring and Control. C: EVM is used for Monitoring and Control. D: Planning, Monitoring and Control.
10	D	A is false. B and C are true, but are done after D.
11	B	Lessons learned are part of the closing process.
12	A	Deliverable reviews are part of the contract closure (external closure). B is false; updating the directory of qualified providers is part of the administrative closure (or internal closure).
13	D	D: automatic changes do not exist.
14	A	B and D are false, the work authorization system does not mention Who. C is true, but incomplete compared to A.
15	B	A and C are inputs. B is an output of the process. D is a tool or technique.

Answers to Exam 5 – Scope

Quest. #	Correct	Explanation
1	D	A, B, and C are tools to control the scope.
2	D	1st control accounts, 2nd planning packages, 3rd work packages, and 4th activities.
3	D	A, B, and C are process outputs and are part of the baseline. D is an input to the process.
4	B	A, C, and D are false.
5	C	A is false. B and D are true, but not as important as C.
6	D	1st D, 2nd C, 3rd B, 4th A
7	D	A and B would be true during planning. C is false. D is true during the executing phase.
8	C	A, B, and D are related with the next process of creating the WBS. C: work packages are not sequenced.
9	A	B, C, and D are false.
10	C	Every change must pass through the integrated change control process. A is already done. B and D are not appropriate.
11	B	All stakeholders include the Client. If the client already formally approved the WBS and then wants a change, he should pay for it.
12	B	A is not appropriate. C is already done. D is not appropriate.
13	A	B, C, and D are not examples of verifying the scope.
14	A	1st A, 2nd D, 3rd C. B is not appropriate.
15	C	A: The WBS dictionary's objective is not to define activities. B and D are false.

Answers to Exam 6 – Time

Quest. #	Correct	Explanation
1	D	ACFH = 30 ADFH = 33 ADGH = 35 BDFH = 31 BDGH = 33 BEGH = 36 Critical Path: St-B-E-G-H-End
2	B	The longest path that includes A is ADGH (35 weeks). The slack for that path and activity A, is 1 week (36 – 35).
3	B	Duration for each path if F is extended by 3 additional weeks: ACFH = 33 ADFH = 36 ADGH = 35 BDFH = 34 BDGH = 33 BEGH = 36 Now there are two critical paths and the project is more risky.
4	D	A is false, compression adds costs. B is false, fast tracking adds risks. C is false, compression shortens duration.
5	C	A, B, and D are not appropriate.
6	A	B, C, and D are inputs to this process. A has already been done in the past.
7	B	PERT A (4 days) + PERT B (6 days) + PERT C (6 days) = 16 days VAR A (1,778 d.) + VAR A (1 d.) + VAR A (2,778 d.) = 5,556 Project STANDARD DEVIATION = square root 5.556 = 2.357 days Average +/- 2 Std Dev = 16 +/- 2 x 2.357 = (11.29 ; 20.71)
8	A	B could be a case of sub-contracting. C is not appropriate to manufacture without the matrix. D is false.
9	D	A is false; PDM is not the same as GERT. B is false; PDM allows 4 dependencies and ADM one type of dependency. C is false, PDM is more used than ADM.
10	C	A, B, and D tend to be used. The dependency Start to Finish is rarely used.
11	B	A and C are false. D is not appropriate.
12	B	$[(20 - 9) / 6]\, ^\wedge\, 2 = 3.36$
13	D	A, B, and C are tools for schedule control, as well as tools for schedule development. The three-point estimate is a tool for estimating activity duration.
14	A	B, C, and D are false.
15	D	A, B, and C are false.

Quest. #	Correct	Explanation
1	A	A is false. The baseline includes contingency reserves. Management reserve is included in the budget.
2	C	$4,000 / 5 years = $800
3	D	A, B, and C are not correct. D is true.
4	A	When adding the flow of net funds without discount, you obtain a value of $90. Discounting the flow of funds at a 12% annual rate, the NPV will be lower than $90. The only answer lower than $90 is A.
5	D	If the NPV is positive and the discount rate is 12%, the IRR should be greater than 12%. The only possible answer is D.
6	A	You need 3 years to recuperate the initial $100 investment.
7	C	Any change to the baseline must be previously authorized.
8	B	EAC = BAC / CPI
9	D	If all the pine trees have been planted, EV will be equal to $50. If an activity has been finalized, the SPI is 1.
10	B	A and C are outputs of the Determine Budget process. D is an output of Estimate Costs.
11	C	A could be if C was not there, but the variance does not measure efficiency. B and D are false. C is true because the SPI is a ratio that measures efficiency.
12	A	B, C, and D are false.
13	B	A, C, and D are false.
14	C	If the projects are not repeatable you should select the one with the greater NPV. If the projects are repeatable you should select the one with the greatest equivalent (not seen on this book).

15 | B |

Activity	PV	AC	Progress	EV
A	600	550	80%	480
B	300	350	60%	180
C	200	300	100%	200
Total	1,100	1,200		860

CPI = EV / AC = 860 / 1,200 = 0.7167

Answers to Exam 8 – Quality

Quest. #	Correct	Explanation
1	C	A and B are assurance tools. D is a control tool. C is a control tool, but it can also be used during Planning.
2	C	A refers to the cause and effect diagram, B refers to the control chart, and D refers to the trend diagram.
3	B	A, C, and D are conformance costs. B is a nonconformance cost.
4	D	A, B, and C are false.
5	A	Surely the company is incurring in nonconformance costs such as B, C, and D. A is a conformance cost, a proactive policy which the company is not implementing.
6	D	The project manager is the main responsible for the quality of a project. B could be correct if option D was not there.
7	D	A is the average of the R diagram. B is false. C refers to a control chart.
8	C	A is false. B and D are not correct because requirements definition refers to Planning.
9	A	A is an output of the quality control process.
10	D	A, B, and C are not used to analyze the correlation between two variables.
11	C	A is false because small improvements are not done in all processes, but in a few. B and D refer to Kairyo techniques.
12	D	A, B, and C are false.
13	B	A, C, and D are inputs to the quality assurance process. B is false because is an input to quality control.
14	B	A is not appropriate. C is a disadvantage of JIT. D is false. The main advantage is that it lowers inventory.
15	C	A refers to a standard deviation. B is false. D refers to two standard deviations.

Answers to Exam 9 – Human Resources

Quest. #	Correct	Explanation
1	D	A and C are false. B could be, but it is not good for tracking the assignment of resources across time.
2	C	A could be, but is too generic because each project is unique. B is false because each project could use a different organizational structure. D is incorrect because it is difficult having the same group of people available.
3	D	A and B are false. C is a tool for Monitoring and Control. D is true and means placing team members in the same physical place.
4	C	A and D tend to be one of the least probable causes of conflict. B is false. C is true; the main causes of conflict are schedule, priorities, and resources.
5	B	A, C, and D are false.
6	A	B is theory X. C refers to the Ouchi model. D is theory Y.
7	A	B, C, and D are false.
8	B	A and C are hygiene factors. D is false because the workplace is a hygiene factor, but recognition is indeed a motivational agent.
9	B	A and C are false. D could be if B was not there.
10	B	A, C, and D are outputs to this process. B is false because resource assignment is done after planning.
11	D	D refers to planning, not the executing phase.
12	D	A is false, it refers to conflict resolution. B is false; it is not a tool for conflict resolution. C is false; it does not mean to give in. D is true, compromising is a synonym of conceding, which implies "lose-lose".
13	B	A is false; it refers to levels of personal development. C is false, it refers to organizational models. D is false; consensus is not a leadership style.
14	C	1st Physiological needs, 2nd Safety, 3rd Social needs, 4th Esteem, 5th Self-Actualization.
15	A	A well managed confrontation is the best form of conflict resolution, because it ends in "win-win". Compromising could be the second best option.

Answers to Exam 10 – Communications

Quest. #	Correct	Explanation
1	D	A would not be appropriate if the members are physically separated. B and C are not correct.
2	B	A would be correct after communicating in an informal way. B is the most appropriate to communicate for the first time in order to find the root cause of the problem. C and D are not appropriate.
3	D	A, B, and C are false.
4	C	A and B are not appropriate. D is false, because the noises between the sender and the receiver are inevitable.
5	C	A, B, and D are false.
6	B	A and C could be correct if B was not there. The first thing to do is to analyze the communications management plan. D is false.
7	D	A, B, and C are false. Approximately 55% is non-verbal communication.
8	C	A, B, and D are true. C corresponds to the communication's receiver.
9	D	A, B, and C are examples of performance reports. D is false.
10	B	A and D are included in the communications management plan. C must be done before the communications plan.
11	B	A, B and D are true. However, the tone of the voices and the corporal gestures are more important than what is being said. C is false.
12	A	CPI = EV / AC ; EV = CPI x AC = 0.80 x $100 = $80
13	A	B does not allow for anonymity. C and D are false.
14	D	A, B, and C are true. D includes all of the above.
15	D	The project manager and his 5 team members make 6 persons. Initial channels = (6 x 5) / 2 = 15. Channels with 3 new persons = (9 x 8) / 2 = 36. There are 21 new communication channels: 36 - 15.

Answers to Exam 11 – Risk

Quest. #	Correct	Explanation
1	B	A, C, and D are false. The expected monetary value is the probability of occurrence multiplied by the impact.
2	A	B corresponds to the risk identification process. C is an output of the qualitative risk analysis. D is a tool of the Monitoring and Control process.
3	C	A = 50% x $50,000 – 50% x $10,000 = $20,000 B = 30% x $40,000 + 70% x $10,000 = $19,000 C = 60% x $50,000 – 40% x $15,000 = $24,000
4	A	A is an output of the risk response plan. B, C, and D are tools or strategies for positive risks.
5	C	Prob (E1) + Prob (E2) – Prob (E1 + E2) = 1/6 + 1/6 – (1/6 x 1/6) = 11/36
6	B	A and C have already been done. B is the first thing that should be done. D will be done after the risks are identified and quantified.
7	C	C is first, B is second, and D is third. A is false.
8	C	A is a tool of the qualitative and quantitative risk analysis. B and D are tools of the quantitative risk analysis. C is a tool of the qualitative risk analysis.
9	D	A and C do not correspond. B is part of the project baseline.
10	B	A is an output of the qualitative analysis. C is an output of the quantitative analysis. D is a tool to identify risks. Generally, the risk response plan implies scope changes, so the work packages and the WBS must be changed.
11	D	A, B, and C are false.
12	A	Tractor A = $10,000 + 30% x $4,000 + 70% x $0 = $11,200 Tractor B = $12,000 + 5% x $1,000 + 95% x $0 = $12,050 The cheapest option is tractor A.
13	A	B and D are false. C could be if A was not there. A is the most correct answer because a scope change is a good example of avoiding risk.
14	D	A, B, and C are false because risks are not identified during quantitative or qualitative analysis. The risk register is created during the identification and then updated during Monitoring and Control.
15	B	1st C, 2nd D, 3rd A, and 4th B.

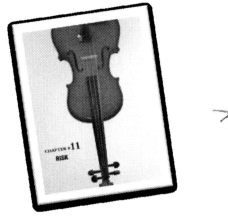

Answers to Exam 12 – Procurement

Quest. #	Correct	Explanation
1	D	A, B, and C generally do not include in detail the activities that will be done, they just include the price.
2	B	A, C, and D are true. B is false, in big projects that is performed by the procurement department.
3	B	($1,200 / days) + $20 = $80 ; days = $1,200 / $60 = 20 days
4	A	$80,000 cost + $20,000 fees + 20% x ($100,000 - $80,000) = $104,000
5	D	A, B, and C are contract closure activities. C is also part of the administrative closure. D is part of the administrative closure.
6	D	A, B, and C are false. The bidder conference is one of the activities of the Conduct Procurements process.
7	C	A, B, and D are false.
8	A	B, C, and D are false.
9	A	When the scope is known and the market prices are transparent, fixed price contracts are the most appropriate. B, C, and D refer to cost-reimbursement contracts.
10	D	A and C are false. B is a bad practice because the contract does not say that. D is the first thing that should be done, and at the same time start an investigation and negotiation of that contract.
11	B	A, C, and D are false. The hourly fees are a good example of time and material contracts.
12	A	In order to be legal, every contract needs to have an offer, object, and parties' agreement. B and D are false. C does not always go in contracts, for example the price could not figure in a cost-reimbursement contract.
13	C	A is not proactive. B is false. C is the first thing you should do. D could be if C was not there.
14	B	A, C, and D are false.
15	C	More cost risk for the seller: 1st fixed-price, 2nd Fixed-price economic price adjustment, 3rd time and materials, 4th cost-plus-incentive.

Answers to Final Exam

#	Answer	#	Answer	#	Answer	#	Answer	#	Answer
1	D	41	A	81	A	121	C	161	D
2	C	42	D	82	B	122	B	162	C
3	B	43	C	83	D	123	B	163	C
4	C	44	C	84	B	124	B	164	C
5	D	45	C	85	C	125	D	165	C
6	A	46	C	86	D	126	D	166	B
7	A	47	C	87	B	127	B	167	B
8	B	48	C	88	D	128	D	168	A
9	A	49	B	89	D	129	B	169	D
10	A	50	B	90	D	130	D	170	A
11	A	51	D	91	D	131	A	171	B
12	D	52	C	92	D	132	D	172	A
13	C	53	D	93	A	133	A	173	A
14	B	54	D	94	D	134	A	174	A
15	C	55	C	95	D	135	B	175	B
16	A	56	B	96	B	136	D	176	B
17	D	57	A	97	B	137	A	177	D
18	A	58	B	98	D	138	D	178	D
19	B	59	A	99	A	139	B	179	A
20	C	60	C	100	B	140	B	180	C
21	C	61	C	101	B	141	C	181	D
22	C	62	C	102	C	142	B	182	C
23	B	63	B	103	C	143	C	183	A
24	A	64	A	104	A	144	C	184	B
25	A	65	A	105	D	145	B	185	C
26	B	66	C	106	C	146	C	186	C
27	B	67	B	107	C	147	C	187	C
28	A	68	B	108	A	148	A	188	A
29	A	69	D	109	A	149	B	189	C
30	C	70	A	110	D	150	D	190	A
31	B	71	A	111	B	151	C	191	A
32	D	72	D	112	C	152	D	192	C
33	B	73	A	113	C	153	D	193	C
34	C	74	B	114	B	154	A	194	A
35	B	75	D	115	A	155	B	195	B
36	C	76	A	116	B	156	A	196	C
37	C	77	B	117	B	157	B	197	C
38	A	78	B	118	D	158	D	198	C
39	D	79	B	119	A	159	C	199	A
40	D	80	A	120	A	160	B	200	A

Explanation for this test's frequently asked questions can be found in the test simulator that you can buy at www.pablolledo.com.

Enjoy the projects that you do...

And do the projects that you most enjoy!

I wish you the best of success with your
PMP® certification

www.pablolledo.com